THE READER'S CORNER

Expanding Perspectives Through Reading

FOURTH EDITION

Carol C. Kanar
Valencia Community College

WADSWORTH
CENGAGE Learning™

Australia • Brazil • Japan • Korea • Mexico • Singapore • Spain • United Kingdom • United States

The Reader's Corner: Expanding Perspectives Through Reading, Fourth Edition
Carol C. Kanar

Publisher/Executive Editor: Lyn Uhl

Acquisition Editor: Annie Todd

Development Editor: Maggie Barbieri

Assistant Editor: Melanie Opacki

Media Editor: Amy Gibbons

Marketing Manager: Kirsten Stoller

Marketing Coordinator: Ryan Ahern

Marketing Communications Manager: Stacey Purviance

Content Project Management: PreMediaGlobal

Art Director: Jill Ort

Manufacturing Buyer: Betsy Donaghey

Rights Acquisition Specialist (Text): Katie Huha

Senior Rights Acquisition Specialist (Image): Jennifer Meyer Dare

Compositor: PreMediaGlobal

Cover Designer: Harold Burch

Cover Image: iSpot.com

For product information and technology assistance, contact us at **Cengage Learning Customer & Sales Support, 1-800-354-9706**

For permission to use material from this text or product, submit all requests online at **www.cengage.com/permissions**
Further permissions questions can be emailed to **permissionrequest@cengage.com**

Library of Congress Control Number: 2010927644

ISBN-13: 978-0-495-80256-3

ISBN-10: 0-495-80256-5

Wadsworth
20 Channel Center Street
Boston, MA 02210
USA

Cengage Learning is a leading provider of customized learning solutions with office locations around the globe, including Singapore, the United Kingdom, Australia, Mexico, Brazil and Japan. Locate your local office at **www.cengage.com/global**

Cengage Learning products are represented in Canada by Nelson Education, Ltd.

For your course and learning solutions, visit **www.cengage.com**

Purchase any of our products at your local college store or at our preferred online store **www.cengagebrain.com**

nted in the United States of America
5 6 7 14 13 12 11

CONTENTS

PART 2
AMERICANS IN TRANSITION   25

PART 4
HARD QUESTIONS FOR ALL   155

PART 5
FOCUS ON WORK AND CAREER   215

PREFACE

The essays and apparatus that make up *The Reader's Corner*, Fourth Edition, are based on the following premises. First, reading is an essential skill that is vital to success in college, work, and life. Reading is the foundation of most courses, a source of ideas, and a springboard to critical thought and action. Being able to read efficiently and critically will help students stay current in their chosen careers or professions, navigate the Internet, and update their knowledge and skills in a world that is exploding with rapidly changing information and new technology. On a personal level, reading is the vehicle that propels students into inner space, challenging their opinions, arousing new interests, and facilitating their intellectual growth. Most importantly, reading gives students ideas to think about, write about, and talk about so that they can assume their rightful places in any discourse community. Guided by these principles, *The Reader's Corner* promotes a holistic approach to reading that encourages both the discovery of the reading process and the development of literal and critical reading skills.

CHANGES IN THE FOURTH EDITION

- Because reading and writing share several essential skills, a new section, *The Reading and Writing Connection*, has been added to Part 1. As students become aware of the connection between reading and writing, they will be able to put themselves in the author's place to more fully engage with the ideas presented.
- Eleven reading selections are completely new; in addition, textbook selections have been updated.
- Two new poetry selections have been added. "The Road Not Taken" by Robert Frost appears in Part 2, and Part 5 contains "I Hear America Singing" by Walt Whitman.

- The *Thinking Deeper* feature has been reworked so that all four open-ended questions require students to make inferences either from facts stated in the readings or from their own experience. The fifth item now contains two writing prompts to help students make the reading and writing connection.

In addition, *The Reader's Corner* helps students build and sustain their reading skills in several ways:

- The reading selections in *The Reader's Corner*, thematically organized into five parts (Parts 2–6), promote critical thinking and self-examination. The selections are written by a culturally diverse group of writers on a wide variety of thought-provoking topics that entertain, inform, and challenge students.
- One or more textbook excerpts in each part (after Part 1) provide students with an academic perspective on a wide range of disciplines: business, psychology, history, physical science, social science, and communication. Each textbook selection is clearly marked in the table of contents with a "book" icon.
- Carefully constructed apparatus before and after each selection leads students through the stages of the reading process, from pre-reading, through careful reading, to post-reading review, and interpretation.
- A combination of both objective and open-ended questions encourages students to both read and think analytically and critically.
- Questions for discussion and writing invite students to examine their ideas and share what they have learned, making their own the knowledge gained from reading.

SPECIAL FEATURES OF THE TEXT

Each reading selection is framed by pre-reading and post-reading activities that are designed to lead students logically through the processes of analytical reading and critical thinking. The following features form the apparatus of *The Reader's Corner*:

- *First Thoughts* consists of three questions that help students preview the selection and access their prior knowledge about the author's topic.
- *Word Alert* is a vocabulary feature that lists, defines, and cites by paragraph number words that may be unfamiliar to students or that may have special meanings that are essential to understanding the reading selection. Within each reading selection, Word Alert words appear in boldface for easy reference.
- The *headnote* preceding each selection contains information about the author or the selection and is designed to generate interest in and provide context for the reading.
- *Comprehension Check* consists of ten questions—including multiple-choice, true/false, and open-ended questions—that help students build and practice skill in finding the author's topic, purpose, and main idea; in identifying stated details; and in making inferences. These thought-provoking questions focus students' attention on both what is stated and implied, promoting analytical and critical-thinking skills.

- *Working with Words* is an exercise in deriving meaning from context. Students are given a group of sentences to complete, using words from the Word Alert feature. This activity tests students' understanding of each word's meaning and their ability to recognize it in a different context. In addition, students are asked to create two of their own original sentences using any two Word Alert words.
- *Thinking Deeper* consists of four open-ended questions that encourage students to think critically about the reading selection. The fifth and sixth questions are writing prompts; however, any one of the questions could be used either for writing or for discussion.

Taken together, these features encourage students to build background before reading, to engage actively in the process during reading, and to reflect after reading on what they have learned.

ANCILLARIES

An Instructor's Edition (ISBN: 111134602X) containing answers to the post-reading questions is available. An instructor's manual with additional exercises and teaching materials is offered on *The Reader's Corner* instructor's website which can be accessed through login.cengage.com. Also available to adopters of the book is ReadingSpace, a web-based reading assessment program that features sixty-five readings selected from textbooks, periodicals, and literary texts. The readings vary in length and are accompanied by Pre-, Practice, or Mastery Tests that assess ten essential reading skills. These interactive tests provide instant feedback and enable students to identify their weaknesses and focus on improving reading comprehension. All results can be emailed to instructors. A *User's Guide* is available to adopters of ReadingSpace. To order *The Reader's Corner*, Fourth Edition with ReadingSpace for your class, request ISBN 978-0-495-80256-3 when submitting your textbook order to the bookstore.

ACKNOWLEDGMENTS

A textbook is a combined effort among author, editors, and others who played a role in its conception, execution, and production. I am grateful to all those at Wadsworth Cengage Learning who played a part in bringing this book into being, especially Annie Todd, who made it possible; Maggie Barbieri, for her help in developing the manuscript; Dewanshu Ranjan, who guided me through the book's production; and Melanie Opacki, for attending to the details that are part of this process. Thanks also to Kirsten Stoller for her enthusiastic support of my work. I am grateful to the many others at Cengage Learning with whom I have not worked directly but whose efforts behind the scenes made this book possible. As always, I thank my husband, Steve Kanar, for the way he encourages me and champions all my efforts; my friends and colleagues who shared their ideas; and the students whose needs, interests, and aspirations shaped my writing of the apparatus and my choice of the reading selections.

Finally, I am grateful for the many excellent suggestions I received from colleagues who helped me develop this new edition of *The Reader's Corner:*

Geri Gutwein, *Harrisburg Area Community College*

Pam Lau, *Parkland College*

Michael G. Spinks, *Piedmont Community College*

Chae Sweet, *Hudson County Community College*

Marie G. Eckstrom, *Rio Honda College*

Nancy S. Hoefer, *Central Carolina Technical College*

Cynthia Ross, *Manatee Community College*

Raymond Watkins, *Central Carolina Technical College*

Carol C. Kanar

STARTING POINTS

Reading is many things. It is a process, a skill set, a journey into an author's mind, an exploration of inner space. From your daily newspaper, to the college classroom, to work, and to the Internet, reading is one of the primary means by which you acquire knowledge and information. Reading opens your mind to new ideas, expanding your perspective. Reading is often the basis for writing both in college and in the workplace. Through reading, you gather information that will help you think about and compose answers to questions, write essays and research papers, and compile written reports. In fact, the reading and writing processes have much in common as you will see.

Part 1 explains the process of reading, the reading and writing connection, and eight essential skills that you can develop to become an active, engaged reader:

- *Find the topic and main idea.*
- *Identify the supporting details.*
- *Determine an author's purpose.*
- *Look for an organizational pattern.*
- *Make inferences from stated details.*
- *Use context clues to define unfamiliar words.*
- *Read graphics with understanding.*
- *Evaluate what you read.*

Practice these skills. Discover and develop your own reading process and, above all, enjoy the reading selections in this book.

Wouldn't it be wonderful if you could open a book or turn to the first page of an article with the confidence that not only would you understand what you read, but you would be able to remember the essential information? Wouldn't it be great if you could prepare yourself for the reading so that you could dive right in, without procrastinating?

You can.

Two facts about reading will serve as starting points. First of all, reading requires at least two people: you and the author. Think of reading as a conversation with another person. When you have a conversation, you listen to someone else's ideas, you think about them, and you offer your own opinion. Sometimes you agree; sometimes you disagree. When you do not understand some part of the conversation, you ask questions. Throughout the conversation, in the back of your mind, you may be relating what you are hearing to what you already know about the topic. Reading is like that. Although you cannot see or hear the author, you have his or her words on the page in front of you. The conversation takes place in your mind, as you read. For example, you may find yourself thinking, "What does this word mean?" or "Why does the author have this opinion?" In the back of your mind, you may also be thinking about experiences of your own that are similar to those you are reading about.

Second, reading is a process. When you read, your brain takes in information and either discards it or stores it for later use. What you may not realize is that *you can control this process*. You can improve your understanding and your memory by taking certain actions before, during, and after reading.

Remember that reading is a conversation between you and the author. To control the reading process, you need to become actively involved in the conversation. We call this *active reading*, and it can make all the difference in your ability to understand, remember, and enjoy reading.

The next four sections tell you more about the readings in this book and how to read and write about them actively.

THE READINGS IN THIS BOOK

This book takes you on a journey through the contemporary human mind. The authors are from different cultural, national, and ethnic backgrounds, and they offer many perspectives on a variety of topics and issues that are of general interest. The readings come from books, magazines, newspapers, and other sources. They range in length from short pieces to longer selections. Following Part 1, the readings are arranged in five thematic units: *Part 2: Americans in Transition; Part 3: Personal Challenges; Part 4: Hard Questions for All; Part 5: Focus on Work and Career;* and *Part 6: More Perspectives*. Each unit opens with an explanation of the theme that is addressed in the ten readings that follow. The *Thinking Deeper* exercises following each selection encourage you to think critically, discuss, and write about the author's ideas and the unit theme.

The purpose of this collection is to provide you with a varied reading experience and a chance to develop your own reading process. Reading, like any other skill, takes time and practice. The readings in this collection and the exercises that accompany the readings will help you hone your existing skills and perhaps develop some new ones as well.

READING AS A PROCESS

Reading is the process of taking in, sorting, and storing information. If you are reading passively—not paying attention, allowing yourself to become distracted, letting your mind wander—you are not in control of the process. As a result, you will not remember what you read. If you are reading actively—concentrating, ignoring distractions, thinking about the author's ideas—you are in control. As a result, you are more likely to understand and remember what you read. This section explains how the reading process works and what actions you can take before, during, and after reading that will put you in control.

BEFORE READING

At any given time, you are bombarded with all kinds of information: *It's hot. I'm tired. The phone is ringing. I have to be at work at 3:00 P.M. What was I supposed to study for the test?* These thoughts and others like them are going through your mind when you sit down to read. Therefore, unless you focus your attention on the reading, your other thoughts will dominate and will have a negative effect on your comprehension.

To focus your attention, find out what you can about the topic and the author. Then preview the selection by doing the following: First, read the title to determine the author's topic, and take a few minutes to explore what you may already know about it. Your prior knowledge may serve as a context for the author's ideas and expand your understanding. If you have no prior knowledge of the topic, then ask questions such as these to help you build context:

- What can I find out about the topic?
- How does the topic relate to what we are studying in class?
- Have I read or heard anything related to the topic?

Next, read the first and last paragraphs. One of these may contain a stated purpose, a main idea, or a strong clue to one or the other. Finally, read any other information that may be available, such as questions before or after the reading, or a list of vocabulary words and definitions. If the selection is divided into sections with headings, read them. Headings tell you the major divisions of the author's topic and may provide a strong clue to the author's main idea or purpose.

As you can see, the reading process actually begins *before* you read. Take an active step to clear your mind and set the stage for reading.

DURING READING

Reading rarely proceeds smoothly from first word to last. College reading especially introduces new ideas, unfamiliar words or terms, and different styles of writing and organizational methods. Therefore, you may get off to a good start, then find yourself backtracking, stopping to look up the meaning of a word, or taking a few moments to think about what you have read. This is as it should be.

What happens during the reading process is that your brain is sorting the incoming information—separating the important from the nonessential, relating what is new to what you already know, and searching for the meanings of difficult words and sentences. If you are not paying attention, not actively engaging yourself in a conversation with the author, you are interrupting this natural process.

Active reading strategies to use during reading include the following:

- Read one paragraph at a time.
- Jot down in the margin or in a notebook thoughts or questions that occur to you as you read.
- Pay attention to the author's choice of words. What do they tell you about the author's attitude or feeling toward the topic?
- If you did not identify a purpose or main idea before reading, try to identify it during reading.
- Pay attention to how the ideas are organized. Is the author making comparisons, explaining steps in a process, narrating a series of events, describing a place or a person?
- If you are able to identify a main idea, find and mark the details that support or expand it. Ask yourself which of these details are the most significant.
- Think about the ideas and how they relate to what you already know or need to find out about the author's topic.

As you can see, the key to reading actively is to read for *ideas* and to discover which ideas are more important than others. When all else fails, keep going back to the title and the first paragraph. Often these are your strongest clues to the author's overall topic or main idea.

AFTER READING

As soon as you finish reading, you begin to forget. The more time passes, the less you remember—unless you take active steps to prevent forgetting. Like a computer, your brain can store only what you tell it to save. This is why review is so important.

Review is the key to remembering. Review immediately after reading, while the ideas are still fresh in your mind. If you know you will be tested on the information, review frequently thereafter to refresh your memory. This will prevent you from cramming on the night before a test, or from drawing a blank during class discussions.

A good way to review is to try this three-step strategy: **Think, Write, Discuss.** First, *think* deeply about what you have learned and how you can use the information or apply it in your everyday life. Second, *write* a summary of the information. (A summary is a few sentences, in your own words, that express an author's main idea and significant details.)

Third, *discuss* the reading with a study partner or group. By sharing your thoughts with others, you may get new insights or fill in gaps in your understanding. In addition, writing and discussing create new sensory pathways into your memory.

Table 1 on page 5 summarizes the reading process and active reading strategies explained in this section.

TABLE 1	THE READING PROCESS AND STRATEGIES FOR ACTIVE READING

Stages of the Process	Active-Reading Strategies to Use Anytime
BEFORE READING	Read the title and first and last paragraphs. Determine the topic, main idea, purpose, and pattern. Access any prior knowledge about the topic. Read any headings for clues. Ask questions to guide your thinking.
DURING READING	Read one paragraph at a time. Jot notes in the margins. Ask questions to guide your reading. Affirm or rethink the author's topic, main idea, purpose, and pattern. Mark significant details. Think about the author's ideas and relate them to what you know.
AFTER READING	Review immediately after reading, then frequently thereafter. Think about what you have learned and how you can use the information. Summarize what you have read in writing, and talk about it with a study partner or group.

THE READING AND WRITING CONNECTION

Like reading, writing is an active process that you can control by doing certain things before, during, and after writing. For example, before you write, take some time to think about the topic you have been assigned or the question you must answer. Brainstorm to discover what you already know about the topic versus what the author says about it. How has your knowledge expanded or your viewpoint changed as a result of your reading? Take notes or make an outline of what you want to write. During writing, concentrate on jotting your ideas down on paper or typing them online. This will result in a rough draft. Writing your rough draft is just the beginning; you will then rewrite or refine it to improve its content, organization, and choice of words. As a final step after writing, proofread to correct errors.

Some of the same skills that you use to read actively can also be used to write actively. Table 2 on page 6 shows how reading and writing connect through several shared skills. Asking the right questions and practicing these skills not only will help you get more out of your reading but will also help you write good responses to any assignment.

The *Thinking Deeper* exercises at the end of each selection in this book can also be used for writing. When planning your written response to an exercise, follow the suggestions in Table 2. Whether you write a short paragraph or a longer answer, be sure to state your topic, main idea, and purpose. Support the main

TABLE 2 | HOW TO READ AND WRITE WITH CONFIDENCE

Questions to Ask	What to Look for When Reading	What to Include in Your Writing
What is the topic?	Look for clues in the title and first sentence or paragraph.	Choose a topic that interests you, or write about one interesting aspect of an assigned topic.
What is the main idea?	Find a sentence or identify details that tell you what the author thinks about the topic.	Write a sentence that states your main idea.
What details support the topic?	Look for facts, reasons, or examples that explain the author's main idea.	Support your main idea with specific details.
What is the purpose?	Determine what the author wants you to learn or understand.	Clearly explain what you want readers to learn or understand.
How are the details organized?	Look for a pattern: For example, does the author make comparisons, define a term, explain a process?	Organize your details in a meaningful way.
What do the ideas mean?	Make inferences from your reading: For example, relate the author's ideas to your experience.	Conclude your writing by explaining the usefulness or significance of your ideas.
Are there any new or unfamiliar terms?	Read for clues in the context that will help you define unfamiliar terms.	Define any terms you want to use that you think readers may not understand.

idea with enough specific details to help readers understand. Organize your details so that readers can follow them easily. Then end your writing with a conclusion that gives readers information to think about or use in their own lives.

PRACTICAL STRATEGIES FOR THE READINGS

The exercises and information that accompany each reading are designed to help you apply active-reading strategies before, during, and after reading. Through consistent use of these strategies, you will develop a reading process that will lead to successful outcomes in all your reading.

For a brief overview, Table 3 on page 7 breaks down the reading process as it applies to the readings in this book and lists the exercises to do or information to read at each stage.

BEFORE YOU READ

First Thoughts is an exercise that helps you build a context for the reading. By answering the questions, you will find out what you already know about the author's

TABLE 3	How to Read Each Reading Selection
Stages of Reading	**What to Do at Each Stage of the Process**
BEFORE READING	Do *First Thoughts* to build background and preview the reading. Read *Word Alert* so that you will know what words to watch for.
DURING READING	Read the selection. Refer to *Word Alert* as needed for definitions of boldfaced words. Use margin for note taking. Think about the author's ideas and ask questions as you read. Then look for answers.
AFTER READING	Do *Comprehension Check* to test yourself and practice your reading skills. Do *Working with Words* to add new words to your vocabulary. Do *Thinking Deeper* as part of your review.

topic. Your first thoughts should raise questions in your mind that enable you to enter into a mental conversation with the author.

The headnote at the beginning of each reading may provide information about the author, the reading, or both. This information, along with the definitions in *Word Alert,* a vocabulary feature, provides additional ideas for you to think about before reading.

One more thing you can do before reading is to look up the reading selection in the Table of Contents and read the brief summary following the title. The summary may arouse your interest and provide additional clues to the author's purpose or main idea.

These prereading activities focus your attention on the reading, create a context for the author's ideas, and put you in a receptive frame of mind. Do the activities on your own or with a partner or group.

During Reading

As you think about the author's ideas during the process of reading, you can decide whether they expand or challenge your existing knowledge of the topic. Important details may stand out, or questions may occur to you. If so, make notes in the margin or in a notebook. Pay attention to vocabulary and the way ideas are organized. These activities help you read actively, keep your attention focused, and encourage a mental conversation with the author.

After You Read

Reading occurs on two levels: **the literal level** (what an author says) and **the critical level** (what an author means). The questions in **Comprehension Check** are carefully structured to help you apply several essential reading skills to unlock the author's meaning on both these levels. **Working with Words** helps you apply another essential skill: using context clues to determine the meaning of an unfamiliar word. The next section provides a brief review of these essential skills.

Thinking Deeper, a feature following each reading selection, includes exercises for discussion and writing that address the selection's theme and content. This exercise helps you make inferences from your reading and and also helps you review what you have learned. Through this process, you can integrate new ideas within your existing framework of knowledge and access them, if needed, at a later time.

ESSENTIAL READING SKILLS

To comprehend what you read, look ahead. Anticipate what comes next and predict a discussion's outcome. Effective anticipation and prediction depend on your being able to follow an author's ideas, separating essential from nonessential information. Fortunately, anyone can improve comprehension. Understanding the reading process so that you read more actively is one way. Developing your reading skills is another.

Reading involves a number of skills applied simultaneously. To understand these skills, it helps to consider them separately. This section explains eight reading skills that will not only help you answer the comprehension check questions successfully, but also help you analyze, or think through, *any* reading selection for its literal and critical meaning:

- Find the author's topic and main idea.
- Identify the details that support the main idea.
- Determine the author's purpose.
- Look for an organizational pattern.
- Make inferences from stated details.
- Use context clues to define unfamiliar words.
- Read graphics with understanding.
- Evaluate what you read.

FIND THE TOPIC AND MAIN IDEA

Reading is not just about words; it is about ideas. Some ideas are more important than others. The **main idea** is the most important idea in a selection. Everything else in the selection—every example, every other detail—supports the main idea. In a longer selection, the main idea is sometimes called the **central idea** to distinguish it from the main idea of a paragraph.

The main idea of a paragraph is often stated in a **topic sentence.** The topic sentence can appear anywhere in a paragraph, but it is usually the first sentence. To find the topic sentence, ask yourself these two questions:

- What is the author's topic?
- What does the author say about the topic?

The **topic** is what the whole paragraph is about. After reading a paragraph, you should be able to state the topic in one word or a short phrase. For example, "This paragraph is about *memory*" or "This paragraph is about *how the memory works.*" When you have identified the topic, ask questions like these to determine the author's comment: "What does the author say about memory?" "What stages of memory does the author explain?" Finally, look for a sentence that expresses both topic and comment. This is the topic sentence. In the following example, the topic sentence is underlined:

> <u>Your memory operates through three stages to take in, sort, and store information for later use.</u> **Encoding** is the first stage, during which ideas are processed through your five senses. During the **storage** stage, information is either discarded or sorted and then retained briefly in short-term memory or transferred into long-term memory, where it may become permanent. **Retrieval**, the third stage of memory, allows you to recall stored ideas and images.

In this paragraph, the topic sentence comes first. The author's topic is memory, and the author's comment is that memory operates through three stages. What are the stages? How do they work? Each of the remaining sentences in the paragraph contains a detail that answers these questions.

Notice too that the topic sentence is a broad, **general** statement. It summarizes what the whole paragraph is about. Each of the other sentences is a narrow, or **specific**, idea that supports or explains the main idea. A good rule to keep in mind is that main ideas are general ideas, and details are specific ideas. Now read the next example, in which the topic sentence is underlined:

> When you listen to a lecture, your senses are assaulted by the room's temperature, the lighting, the comfort or discomfort of your chair, and various sounds that compete with the lecturer's voice for your attention. Feelings of hunger or tiredness also affect concentration. <u>Internal and external distractions like these interfere with the encoding stage of memory.</u>

In this paragraph, the topic sentence comes last. Notice that the topic sentence is a general statement that distractions interfere with encoding. Also notice that each of the preceding sentences lists specific types of distractions as details.

Now read the following example, in which the topic sentence is underlined:

> Suppose a friend introduces you to someone at a party. You talk for a while and move on. A few minutes later, you forget the name. Does this scenario sound familiar? <u>By following a few simple steps, you can improve your memory.</u> Next time you meet someone, say the name in conversation; write it down. Associate the name with something distinctive about the person. These steps enhance encoding by opening aural, tactile, and visual pathways into your memory.

In this paragraph, the topic sentence is the fifth sentence. The first four sentences introduce the topic. The sixth through eighth sentences provide the details that support the main idea.

Every paragraph has a main idea, but some paragraphs do not have a topic sentence. When there is no topic sentence, you must **infer**, or guess, the main idea. When you cannot find a main idea, try these tips for inferring the main idea: First, read the whole paragraph. Look for key words or repeated terms that help you determine the author's topic. Try to state the topic in one word or a short phrase. Next, read each sentence. Try to determine what all the ideas expressed in each sentence add up to. What one idea do they all seem to support? Once you have identified the topic, ask yourself, "What is the author's comment about the topic?" Look for details in the paragraph that answer your question. These steps should enable you to form in your own mind a sentence that expresses the author's main idea. Now read the following paragraph, which does not have a topic sentence. What is the main idea?

Motivation can be *extrinsic* or *intrinsic*. Students who are extrinsically motivated expect their instructors to keep them interested and provide reasons for learning. These students do not see a connection between effort and grades. They make excuses for poor performance or blame the instructor. Students who are intrinsically motivated are self-motivated. They believe that their grades reflect their effort. Instead of making excuses for failure, they try to identify their mistakes and learn from them. What is your source of motivation, and does it help or hinder your performance in college?

First of all, *motivation* is repeated twice and echoed in the terms *motivated* and *self-motivated*. Students are described as being either *intrinsically* or *extrinsicallyl* motivated. Therefore, the topic must be *sources of motivation*. What does the author say about this topic? The details in the paragraph compare the actions and beliefs of two types of students, those who are extrinsically motivated and those who are intrinsically motivated. The concluding sentence asks you to determine your own source of motivation and how it affects you. From these facts, you can infer this main idea: *Motivation comes from two main sources, extrinsic and intrinsic sources.* This is only one possible topic sentence for the paragraph. Though the wording may vary, the meaning should be the same.

To find the central idea of a longer selection, such as the readings in this book, first ask yourself these questions:

- What is the topic of the entire selection?
- What is the author's comment about the topic?

To find the topic, read the title, which may provide a strong clue. Then read the first paragraph or two. Look for a sentence in the opening paragraphs that states the author's topic and comment. This sentence is the central idea. If you do not find such a sentence, then read the last paragraph, which may be a summary paragraph that states the central idea. Of course, the central idea of a selection can appear anywhere in the selection. Or it may be unstated. If reading the title and the first and last paragraphs does not help, look for clues in the details. Look for repeated words that may suggest the author's topic or comment. Look for examples or reasons and ask yourself, "What do these details mean?" "What central idea do they all seem to support?"

Now read the following introductory paragraphs to a longer selection, in which the central idea is underlined.

Good Kids Are Not Hard to Find

Although teen pregnancy is on the decline, it still interrupts the lives of far too many young girls. Although smoking in the United States is declining overall, more teenage girls and young women are taking up the habit. We hear reports of widespread drug and alcohol abuse among high school students and binge drinking among college students. But most alarming are the reports of violence and death among teenagers. School shootings, fights, bullying resulting in suicide, and staged acts of violence filmed for YouTube have caused parents, educators—everyone—to ask "Why?"

These dire reports paint a frightening picture of American youth, but they do not tell the whole story. Far more young people do not drink, take drugs, get pregnant, beat up or kill their peers. <u>Most of the kids in every school, college, and community are busy studying, working, and preparing for a future filled with hope and pride.</u> Who are these young people, and what can we learn from them?

The topic, *Good Kids*, is stated in the title. The clues are *teen, young girls, teenage girls, young women, high school students, college students, kids, American youth,* and *young people.* The author's comment is that good kids are working to achieve worthwhile goals. Topic and comment are expressed in slightly different words in the third sentence, second paragraph. The last sentence states the author's purpose: to find out who the good kids are and what we can learn from them. As a reader, you can expect the author's details to answer the question posed in the last sentence.

IDENTIFY THE SUPPORTING DETAILS

A **detail** is a fact, reason, or example that supports a main idea. Remember that the main idea is a **general** statement. The details that support it are **specific** ideas. Following is a topic sentence (main idea) and a list of details that support it.

Edson Arantes do Nascimento, generally known as Pélé, dominated soccer for two decades.

1. In 1956, Pélé joined the Santos Football Club.
2. In 1958, he played in the World Cup for the first time, leading Brazil to victory.
3. In 1970, in another victory for Brazil, Pélé played his final World Cup.
4. In 1974, Pélé retired, then came out of retirement to play for the New York Cosmos in 1975.
5. In 1977, Pélé retired from the Cosmos.
6. In 1994, he was appointed Brazil's Minister of Sports.

The topic sentence tells you that *Pélé* (topic) *dominated soccer for two decades* (author's comment). Each detail lists one of Pélé's achievements. These details are facts that support the main idea. Notice that each sentence in the list begins with a date. These dates serve two purposes: They let you know that important facts follow, and they help you follow a sequence of events.

Facts include dates, names of people and places, historical events, information that is part of the public record—anything that can be verified either by direct observation or by consulting an authoritative source. For example, President John F. Kennedy was assassinated in 1963—this is a fact that no one disputes. However, opinions differ as to whether there was one shot or two and whether Lee Harvey Oswald, the killer, was working alone.

As a reader, you should be able to distinguish facts from opinions. When in doubt about a detail, ask yourself, "Where could I go to find out whether this information is factual?" Pélé's achievements in the list above can be verified from a number of sources. For example, a biographical index would have this information. You could also find these facts in books, magazines, newspaper articles, or Internet sources that contain information about Pélé.

Some authors support their main ideas with reasons. A **reason** is an explanation that answers the question *why?* or *how?* Following is a topic sentence and a list of reasons that support it.

Jackie Robinson is an athlete I admire.

1. For one reason, he broke the color barrier in baseball.
2. Also, when faced with prejudice and discrimination, he refused to let these disappointments affect his game.

3. Another reason I admire Robinson is that he tried to convince others to hire blacks as coaches and managers.
4. One more reason I admire Robinson is that he was a gentleman who treated his fans with respect.

The topic sentence tells you that the author admires Robinson. Why? The details that follow provide the reasons. Each reason in the list above is introduced with a transition: *for one reason, also, another reason,* and *one more reason.* A **transition** is a word or phrase that connects ideas. Watch for transitions that help you find and follow an author's important details.

Examples are another type of detail that authors use to support main ideas. An **example** is an illustration or explanation that appeals to your senses or makes a comparison. Following is a topic sentence and a list of examples that support it.

Female athletes in most major sports have proved that they can compete successfully with male athletes.

1. For example, in the seventies, Billie Jean King defeated Bobby Riggs in the "Battle of the Sexes" tennis tournament at the Houston Astrodome.
2. Also, Manon Rheaume made history as the first woman to play in an NHL preseason game.
3. Katie Hnida, the first woman to play in a Division 1-A football game, showed that women can compete with men in this tough sport.
4. In 2003, Annika Sorenstam, the first female golfer since 1945 to be invited to play in a PGA tour event, didn't make the cut but played admirably.

The topic sentence tells you that *female athletes* (topic) *have proved that they can compete with male athletes* (comment). What are the signs of this ability? The details that follow provide several examples. Transitions in each detail sentence signal that an example follows: *for example, also, showed,* and *most recently.*

Now read the following short passage and identify the author's overall main, or central, idea and the significant details that support it.

How the Civil Rights Movement Began

1 It started with a seamstress from Montgomery, Alabama, who refused to give up her seat on a city bus. Her name was Rosa Parks. Every morning, she got on the bus and sat in the back, as black people were required to do. But December 1, 1955, was different. On that day, Parks got on the bus as usual and took her seat in the back. When a white passenger was unable to find a seat in the front of the bus, the driver told Parks to give up her seat. She refused.

2   Parks was arrested for breaking the law; she was tried on December 5 and found guilty. Supporters of equal rights for black people, led by Martin Luther King, Jr., rallied around Parks and staged a boycott of the city bus system that lasted a little more than a year. The Supreme Court's decision to end segregation on public transportation ended the boycott.

3   The boycott was only the first in a series of nonviolent demonstrations that reached a high point in 1963, when King led the march on Washington, D.C., where he told those assembled, "I have a dream." King's dream was of an America where all people could live in peace and racial harmony. The movement's persistence led to the enactment of the Civil Rights Act in 1964, which outlawed segregation in public

facilities and in hiring practices. Two other important pieces of legislation followed: the Voting Rights Act of 1965 and the Fair Housing Act of 1968.

4   From one woman's stand against the Montgomery city bus system in 1955 to the enactment of anti-discriminatory laws in the 1960s had been a long ride. Following these legislative victories, the movement and its supporters turned their attention to improving education and eradicating racial prejudice.

The central idea of the entire passage is stated in the first sentence, first paragraph. The movement started with one woman who refused to give up her seat. The details in the rest of the selection tell you not only what happened to Rosa Parks, but also what the far-reaching consequences of her actions were. Following is a list of the significant details that support the central idea.

1.   On December 1, 1955, Parks refused to give up her seat in the back of the bus to a white passenger (paragraph 1).
2.   Parks was arrested for breaking the law (paragraph 2).
3.   She was tried on December 5 and found guilty (paragraph 2).
4.   A boycott of the city bus system led by Martin Luther King, Jr., lasted for over a year (paragraph 2).
5.   In 1963, King led the march on Washington, the high point of the civil rights movement (paragraph 3).
6.   The Civil Rights Act of 1964 outlawed segregation (paragraph 3).
7.   Other important legislation, the Voting Rights Act of 1965 and the Fair Housing Act of 1968, was passed (paragraph 3).
8.   After 1968, the movement focused on improving education and ending racial prejudice (paragraph 4).

These details are historical facts. They include the significant dates and key events of the civil rights movement that began with Rosa Parks's protest.

As you can see, identifying important details is an essential part of your reading process. Details support or explain an author's main idea. Details provide the facts, reasons, and examples that help you follow the development of an idea from an author's first sentence to the last.

DETERMINE AN AUTHOR'S PURPOSE

An author's **purpose** is his or her reason for writing. Sometimes the purpose is stated, sometimes not. More often, you must determine the purpose by learning what you can from the topic, main idea, and details. The language (choice of words) and overall mood or feeling (tone) may also provide clues.

Three types of purposes motivate most writing: to **inform**, to **persuade**, or to **entertain**. The informing purpose is a teaching purpose. The author wants you to know, understand, or be able to do something. The following paragraph is written to inform.

Dr. Beatrice Hahn of the University of Alabama at Birmingham is credited with the discovery of the origins of HIV-1, the virus responsible for AIDS. Her findings were published in the journal *Nature* in February 1999. Hahn traced the virus to an African primate, a subspecies of the chimpanzee. Hahn and her colleagues were able to trace the chimps to the same region where humans were first known to have been infected with AIDS. How did humans get the virus? Hahn speculates that since the chimps were hunted for food, blood from the animals may have entered the human body through a wound.

The topic is *the discovery of HIV-1*, and the main idea is stated in the first sentence. The author's purpose is to inform readers about the discovery, who was responsible, and how it was done.

The goal of persuasive writing is to influence the way you think or feel about an issue. The author who wants to persuade has a strong opinion and may hope that you either already agree or are willing to change your mind. The following paragraph is written to persuade.

Opinion is divided on who should teach kids about sex. Some say it is the parents' responsibility. Others believe that the schools should take the lead. They're both wrong. Sex education is everyone's responsibility. If even one girl gets pregnant, if even one boy dies from AIDS, we have fallen down on the job. As parents, we need to talk to our children. As educators, we must find better ways to reach more kids. As citizens, we must demand that the media—songwriters and filmmakers—take responsibility for the unwholesome images they project to young people.

In this paragraph, the main idea is stated in the fifth sentence, and the purpose is to persuade readers that sex education is each person's responsibility. The phrases *we need* and *we must* suggest that this author's purpose is to influence our opinions about sex education.

Writing that entertains may provoke an emotional response, such as laughter or sadness, or it may express an idea, using images that appeal to your senses. The following paragraph is written to entertain readers.

For a couple of weeks my husband and I had been watching the nest that a bird had made on top of our back porch light. We were certain that she had laid her eggs, and we were eager for them to hatch. The nest was right under our bedroom window, and each day we would listen for the baby birds. Days passed and we heard nothing. We had decided that the mother bird had abandoned her nest, probably because of so much activity around our house. One day we decided to take a peek at the nest. We got within about ten feet of it, and five heads shot up. Then with a flurry of wings, five small chickadees flew out of the nest and went in separate directions. Was this their first flight? I guess we'll never know.

In this paragraph, the main idea is implied: Two people watch a bird's nest, hoping to see the baby birds. The author's purpose is to entertain readers with a story about the birds. Descriptive details help you visualize the scene.

The key to determining an author's purpose is to ask yourself, "What does this author expect of me, the reader?" Read the title and the first and last paragraphs. If you still cannot determine the purpose, keep reading. Find the central idea, which may contain a clue to the author's purpose. For example, the title "How the Civil Rights Movement Began" is a clue that the author's purpose is to *inform* readers about who or what started the movement. The central idea of the short passage about Rosa Parks on page 12 is stated in the first paragraph: *It started with a seamstress from Montgomery, Alabama, who refused to give up her seat on a city bus.* Based on this central idea, what does the author expect you to know? The author

TABLE 4 | UNDERSTANDING AN AUTHOR'S PURPOSE

Author's Purpose	Supporting Details	Expected Readers' Response
INFORM (to teach or explain)	Facts, examples, and other kinds of information	To understand or be able to apply information gained from reading
PERSUADE (to influence or convince)	Facts or other details chosen for their persuasive value or effect	To be convinced or moved to take action
ENTERTAIN (to express, arouse feeling, excite imagination)	Descriptive details and facts chosen for their entertainment value	To experience pleasure, both emotionally and intellectually

wants you to know what happened. The purpose is to inform you about the event that started the civil rights movement.

Suppose that after reading the title and the first and last paragraph and finding the central idea, you still cannot tell what the purpose is. Then let your response be a guide. Read the entire passage. Then ask questions to determine how you have responded to the reading. Your answers may lead you to the author's purpose. Questions to ask are these: "Did the author teach me something?" (inform); "Did the author try to influence me or change my point of view?" (persuade); "Did the author make me laugh or arouse another feeling, or create images in my mind?" (entertain).

Table 4 lists purposes, details that may help you identify them, and responses that authors expect from readers. Please note that Table 4 makes a general comparison only. As you become a more experienced reader, you will find that purposes overlap. For example, an author may first need to inform readers by citing facts about an issue before trying to persuade them to form an opinion. But even when more than one purpose is apparent, only one purpose will dominate.

LOOK FOR AN ORGANIZATIONAL PATTERN

Ideas expressed in English follow certain patterns. For example, it is common to say *the clock chimes at ten,* or *at ten the clock chimes,* but not *chimes clock ten at the.* Why? Because in English, as in any language, certain established sentence patterns dictate the placement of subjects, verbs, articles, and modifying phrases and clauses. Paragraphs, too, as well as longer selections, follow certain organizational patterns. By recognizing an author's chosen pattern, you can more easily anticipate what is to come. What are these patterns, and what are the signs by which you can recognize them?

Organizational patterns represent ways in which people think. For example, it is natural in conversation to make comparisons, define terms, explain how something works, list steps or stages in a process, or trace a sequence of events. Authors use patterns as handy ways to organize their ideas. The choice of a pattern is directly influenced by an author's purpose. For example, after the September 11, 2001, attack on the World Trade Center, authors whose purpose was to re-create the event used the **sequence** pattern to describe what happened from the moment the first tower was hit until both towers imploded from the impact. The following list briefly explains six common organizational patterns.

Generalization, then Example. A general statement or idea is supported by one or more examples that explain and clarify the idea.

Sequence/Process. Sequences explain *when* and *in what order* events occur. Sequences are traced through dates, times, or numbers. Processes explain *how* things happen and the steps or stages that are involved. Sequence and process often occur together.

Comparison/Contrast. Objects or ideas are analyzed either according to their similarities (comparison) or according to their differences (contrast). Usually both similarities *and* differences are considered.

Division/Classification. Division explains how parts relate to a whole. For example, to understand how an automobile engine works, you need to know how each part functions in relation to the whole engine. **Classification** establishes categories into which items can be sorted according to shared characteristics. For example, the cards in a deck can be sorted into clubs, spades, hearts, and diamonds. Division and classification sometimes occur together.

Cause/Effect. This pattern explains *why* things happen (the reasons or causes) and their consequences (results or effects). Causes and effects usually occur together.

Definition. This pattern provides either a brief explanation or an in-depth analysis of the meaning of a word, term, or idea.

Authors often mix patterns. For example, in a long essay that defines a term like *success* or *character,* an author may use examples or make comparisons even though the overall pattern is definition.

Questioning can help you discover an author's organizational pattern. For example, suppose you open the morning paper and read this headline: *Roof Collapses, Damages Sought.* Questions you could ask are: Why did the roof collapse? Whose fault was it? Did anyone get hurt? How much were the damages? Who will pay? Answers to the first two questions will tell you the *reasons* the accident happened. Answers to the last three questions will tell you the *results* or *consequences* of the accident. These questions and answers should help you determine that the author's pattern is *cause and effect.* Now you can anticipate what comes next: a detailed explanation of what caused the roof to collapse and what happened as a result.

Here is another example. You have been assigned to read an article titled *What Is Self-Esteem?* You might ask yourself the same question. The answer you come up with would be based on your prior knowledge. But without reading the article, do you know what the author means by self-esteem? Can you guess what organizational pattern the author follows? Since the answer to the question posed by the title would be a definition of self-esteem, you can guess that the pattern is *definition.* Now you have something to anticipate: What *is* the author's *definition,* and does it add to or contradict yours?

Another way to identify an author's pattern is to look for *transitions*: signal words and phrases that reveal the relationship of one idea to another. For example, the words *first, next,* and *then* can signal either a sequence of events or the steps of a process. Table 5 on page 17 lists organizational patterns and the transitions that help you identify them.

TABLE 5	ORGANIZATIONAL PATTERNS AND TRANSITIONS THAT SIGNAL THEM

Patterns	Transitions
GENERALIZATION, THEN EXAMPLE	for example, for instance, such as, to illustrate, specifically, also, in addition, another, moreover, furthermore, to clarify
SEQUENCE/ PROCESS	first, next, then, now, before, after, later, following, step, stage, method, procedure, how to, trace, numbers: 1, 2, 3, etc.
COMPARISON/ CONTRAST	like, unlike, similar, different, as, as if, however, but, yet, although, on the other hand, on the contrary, to compare, to contrast, conversely
DIVISION/ CLASSIFICATION	part, member, branch, section, segment, group, kind, type, class, category, division, to classify
CAUSE/EFFECT	reason, result, cause, effect, because, thus, since, therefore, consequently, due to
DEFINITION	for example, to illustrate, such as, means, to define, stands for

The following example passages illustrate six common organizational patterns. In each passage, the transitions that signal the author's pattern are underlined.

1. **Generalization, then Example**
   The days of the week were named after the gods and goddesses of ancient times. For example, Sunday, then as now, was the first day of the week and was "the day of the sun." Monday was "the day of the moon." Ancient people of many cultures worshiped the sun and moon, believing that these celestial bodies were gods. Tuesday gets its name from *Tiw,* later called Mars, the god of war. Wednesday was named for *Woden,* "the furious one," a Germanic god. Thursday takes its name from *Thor,* the old Norse god of thunder. *Frig,* a goddess and the wife of Woden, gave her name to Friday, Saturday comes from *Saturn,* the Roman god of agriculture.

   In this paragraph, the days of the week and the origins of their names are the examples that explain the generalization made in the first sentence.

2. **Sequence/Process**
   What happens during the nine months of pregnancy? During the first three months, cells divide to become an embryo. The embryo becomes a fetus. At this stage, there is little increase in size but much differentiation of tissue. The next three months show more activity. The fetus becomes larger; it has a heartbeat, and its first movements occur. In the last three months of pregnancy, the fetus continues to grow. Its movements increase as it prepares for birth.

   This paragraph traces the events that occur during the three stages of pregnancy. It describes both a sequence and a process.

3. **Comparison/Contrast**
   When recent high school graduates arrive on college campuses, they soon learn that college differs from high school in several ways. First of all, high school teachers have close relationships with students and are likely to interact with them outside the classroom in sports and club activities. In college, however, the relationships are less close. Although some professors do get involved in extracurricular activities, many do not.

Second, the workload in college differs from that in high school. College students have more reading to do, the reading is more difficult, and most professors assign homework every time class meets. But in high school, most of the work is done in class, with students having homework only one or two nights a week on the average. A third <u>difference</u> is that students have more freedom in college. What students do between classes is their business. When they do not have a class scheduled, they neither have to be on campus nor have to account for their whereabouts. <u>On the contrary,</u> high school students, with few exceptions, must remain on campus during school hours.

This paragraph explains three ways in which college differs from high school: relationships with teachers, workload, and the amount of freedom students have.

4. Division/Classification

The student body of Fairview Community College is <u>composed of</u> 35 percent recent high school graduates, 55 percent adult learners, and 10 percent seniors.

Students in these categories have the following <u>characteristics.</u> Recent high school graduates are seventeen to nineteen years old and are attending college for the first time. Most of them plan to transfer to a four-year college when they graduate. Adult learners, the largest <u>category,</u> are in their twenties and thirties. Some are attending college for the first time, while others are returning students who dropped out of college earlier in life to work, to raise families, or for some other reason. Most of them are in college to improve their skills and thus their job prospects. The senior learners are in their forties or older. Students in this <u>category</u> have come to retrain, to make career changes, or to find self-fulfillment.

The first paragraph *divides* Fairview's student body into three groups based on what percentage of the whole student population they represent. The second paragraph *classifies* the students in each category on the basis of their ages and reasons for coming to college.

5. Cause/Effect

Yesterday my instructor returned my algebra test, and I was disappointed with my grade. I barely passed the test. Fortunately, I know the <u>reasons</u>. To begin with, I went into the test unprepared. I had put off my review until the night before the test. Then I spent only an hour studying, which was not enough time to review all the concepts and rules that were covered. The <u>second reason</u> is that I got nervous as a result of knowing that I was not prepared. My anxiety caused my mind to go blank, and I was unable to recall what I *had* studied. The <u>most important reason</u> is that I made some careless errors. Had I taken the time to proofread my paper before handing it in, I might have corrected my errors and earned a better grade. All things considered, I'm not surprised that I did so poorly.

This paragraph explains the causes and effects of being unprepared for a test.

6. Definition

Recent scandals involving government officials at every level have left voters wondering whether any candidate's character can stand up to public scrutiny. Some have forgotten the <u>definition</u> of the term itself. *Character,* now as always, <u>describes</u> a set of personal qualities that we used to call virtues. These virtues include honesty, dependability, trustworthiness, fairness, and temperance. If we demanded these qualities of those who run for public office, how many would be eligible? Perhaps, like the marines, voters should insist on "a few good men" and women of character to serve the public.

This paragraph defines *character* as the possession of certain personal qualities.

MAKE INFERENCES FROM STATED DETAILS

An **inference** is an educated guess about something you do not know based on what you *do* know. Inferences can be valid or invalid. A **valid** inference has sufficient knowledge and experience to back it up. An **invalid** inference does not.

Everyone makes inferences. For example, your decision to attend college was influenced by the inferences you made about your financial status (Can I afford the tuition?), your record of achievement (Will I be successful?), and your self-knowledge (Can I handle the workload?). Physicians make inferences about your health based on your symptoms and examination results. Using information gained from a résumé or interview, an employer makes inferences about an applicant's job qualifications. Buying an affordable home requires you to make valid inferences about your potential income and your ability to make mortgage payments. In each case, the inferences you make are based on the facts at hand. So it is with reading. To understand what an author *means,* consider what he or she *says.* In addition, your knowledge about the author's topic and your experience will also help you make valid inferences.

Read the following short paragraph followed by four inferences. Decide which inference is valid.

> A woman gets out of her car carrying a poodle. She enters a building. The sign on the building says Hawthorne Veterinary Clinic.

> 1. The woman owns the clinic.
> 2. The dog was injured in a car accident.
> 3. The woman is probably taking her dog to see the vet.
> 4. The woman wants to use the telephone.

First of all, consider the facts that are given: A woman carrying a dog into a building and the sign on the building that identifies it as a veterinary clinic. Second, what do you know from experience? People take their dogs to a veterinarian either because the dog needs care or because they need to board the dog. Taking facts and experience into account, the first inference is invalid because there are no facts in the paragraph to suggest that the woman owns the clinic. The second inference is invalid for the same reason: Nothing in the paragraph indicates that the dog is injured or that there was an accident. Facts and experience make the fourth inference invalid also. First of all, people usually do not go to veterinary clinics to use the telephone. Second, most people would probably leave the dog in the car while they made a phone call. Third, the facts in the paragraph do not indicate that the woman even wants to make a call. The third inference is a valid inference because the facts support it. The word *probably* also helps to make this inference valid. Even though experience suggests that the woman is taking the dog to the vet, you cannot say for certain what her purpose is without more information.

The most important thing to remember about inferences is that they are *guesses* about what is reasonable or probable based on whatever information is available. Therefore, get in the habit of questioning what you read and asking of the author, "How do you know?" and "Who says so?"

The following question is based on "How the Civil Rights Movement Began" on page 12. Read the question and the list of inferences that follows it. Which inference is valid?

Why was the Supreme Court's decision to end all segregation on public transportation important to Rosa Parks and the demonstrators?

1. It meant that Parks could not be arrested again.
2. It put an end to racial discrimination.
3. It guaranteed that blacks would be treated fairly in court.
4. It showed that blacks could achieve their goals through nonviolent protest.

The first inference is invalid because the court decision was based solely on Parks's refusal to give up her seat, not on any other alleged crime. The second inference is invalid because racial discrimination has continued, as history and experience have shown. The third inference is invalid because some blacks have continued to receive unfair treatment in court—in the selection of juries, for example. Only the fourth inference is valid. The boycott had worked. African Americans could therefore assume that additional goals might be achieved through nonviolent forms of protest, such as boycotting businesses.

Two or more comprehension questions following each reading selection in *The Reader's Corner* ask you to make inferences as do the *Thinking Deeper* exercises at the end of each selection. When completing these activities, rely on your experience and the author's stated details to form your opinions.

USE CONTEXT CLUES TO DEFINE UNFAMILIAR WORDS

Often in your reading you may encounter an unfamiliar word. Of course you can use your dictionary to determine the word's meaning, but before you do that, look for clues in the context that may help you define the word. Then use your dictionary to verify the meaning if you are still uncertain. By identifying and using four types of clues, you can improve your ability to define words in context.

Context refers to the sentence in which an unfamiliar word appears. If the sentence contains no clues, enlarge the context by looking for clues in the sentences just before and just after the one that contains the word you are trying to define. The four types of clues are *definition, example, contrast,* and *experience.*

The **definition clue** consists of either punctuation marks that set off a synonym or longer definition or key words that signal the reader to look for a definition. In the following examples, words to be defined are in bold type.

Jane **commiserated**, or sympathized, with a friend whose dog was lost. (A synonym is set off by commas.)

Cognition (the study of how people think and learn) attracts many psychology majors as a field of specialization. (The definition is set off by parentheses.)

To **harass** someone means to annoy him or her repeatedly. (The word *means* signals that a definition follows.)

The **example clue** is an illustration or explanation that defines an unfamiliar word either by creating familiar images in your mind or by recalling familiar objects, ideas, or situations. The following sentences contain example clues and a boldfaced word to be defined.

Headaches, minor coughs and colds, and muscular aches and pains illustrate a few of the common **ailments** that are usually not serious unless they persist. (The examples of headaches, minor coughs and colds, and muscular aches and pains are clues that some ailments are minor illnesses.)

Humans have **physiological needs** such as those for safety, food, and sex. (The examples of safety, food, and sex are clues that physiological needs are those required to sustain life.)

The **contrast clue** is an antonym, or a word having an opposite meaning to that of the word you are trying to define. The following sentences contain antonyms to help you define the boldfaced words.

Although we first thought that the painting was a **forgery**, it turned out to be genuine. (*Genuine* is an antonym of *forgery. Genuine* means real or authentic, so *forgery* means fake.)

Drinking water should be clear, but the water coming out of my faucet looks **murky**. (*Clear* is an antonym of *murky*. Therefore, *murky* means unclear or clouded.)

The **experience clue** is one that you bring to the reading along with your skill of making an inference. By using the information an author has provided in a sentence and by using what you have learned from experience in similar situations, you may be able to determine the meaning of an unfamiliar word. What clues can you find in the following sentences to help you define the boldfaced words?

Some carry a rabbit's foot, but my **talisman** is a four-leaf clover. (If you know that a rabbit's foot and a four-leaf clover are good luck charms, then you can guess that a talisman is also a good luck charm.)

The bookstore manager was **irate** when the student demanded a refund for a book that was dirty and filled with marginal notes. (How would you feel if someone to whom you had loaned a book returned it dirty and marked? You probably would be very angry, or irate, as was the bookstore manager.)

When you encounter an unfamiliar word in your general reading, try to define it in context by using the clues of *definition, example, contrast,* and *experience.* If you need additional help, consult your dictionary. When reading textbook chapters, remember that terms of the discipline are essential to your understanding. These terms often appear in bold type, italics, or another color and may be defined in context, in the margins, or listed in a glossary.

READ GRAPHICS WITH UNDERSTANDING

Textbooks and periodicals often contain **graphics** such as charts, tables, and diagrams. Graphics condense and summarize complex information in ways that make it more accessible. Some students will skip over graphics as they are reading. Do not make this mistake. The information presented in a graphic clarifies concepts in ways that broaden your understanding of the chapter or article in which the graphic appears.

To read a graphic with understanding, determine its **purpose**, discover the **relationship** among the ideas that the graphic illustrates, and read the **text** that accompanies the graphic. To help you recall these three steps, remember the acronym **PRT**.

1. To determine a graphic's purpose, read the title and the caption. Taken together, the title and the caption will help you answer the question: What am I expected to know?

2. To discover the relationship among ideas, determine the graphic's type. For example, if the graphic is a **diagram**, look for steps or stages in a process or identify parts and their functions. To read a **pie chart**, determine how the percent or amount represented by each slice of the pie compares to the amount represented by the pie as a whole. On a **bar graph** or **line graph**, the lines or bars can represent times, amounts, or increases or decreases in certain **variables** or quantities. To read a bar or line graph, identify the variables and follow the trends. **Tables** compare or classify large amounts of information or statistical data. To read a table, determine what is being compared or classified and look for similarities and differences among the items or amounts listed on the table.
3. Read the text that accompanies a graphic The text places the graphic in context and may suggest ways to read it or may explain why the information it contains is significant.

To try out the PRT strategy, examine the pie chart below and answer the questions. To test your understanding, read the explanation that follows the list of questions.

1. What is the graphic's purpose?
2. What is the relationship of each slice to the whole pie?
3. What is Rick's greatest monthly expense?
4. On what does Rick spend the least amount each month?
5. How much has Rick budgeted for household expenses?
6. According to the text from which this graphic is taken, Rick's monthly income is $1,295. Assuming that Rick sticks to his budget next month, how much will he have left over after expenses?

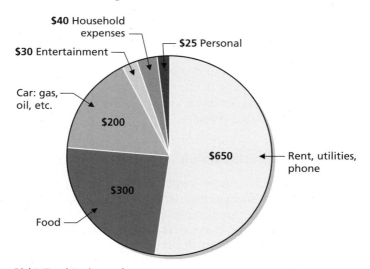

Rick's Total Budget = $1,245

FIGURE 14.6 | RICK'S BUDGET FOR OCTOBER

Source: Carol C. Kanar, *The Confident Student*, Seventh Edition, © 2011 by Wadsworth, Cengage Learning. Reprinted with permission.

The purpose of the graphic is to illustrate how Rick spent the money he had budgeted for October. The pie as a whole represents Rick's total budget of $1,245. Each slice of the pie represents one of Rick's expenses and the amount of money he has allotted to that expense. Rent, utilities, and phone are Rick's greatest expense. He has allotted the least amount for personal items. To find how much Rick will have left over after expenses, subtract $1,245 from his monthly income of $1,295 to get $50. What inferences can you make from these figures? For one thing, Rick has a safety net of $50. If his expenses in any one area increase, or if he has a new expense, he is covered, or he can add whatever is left to his savings.

EVALUATE WHAT YOU READ

To evaluate what you read means to determine its worth or value. Three standards will help you make this judgment: *reliability, objectivity,* and *usefulness.* To evaluate for **reliability**, find out what you can about the author's credentials or expertise in the subject. How current is the information? Currency is another test

TABLE 6	STANDARDS FOR EVALUATING ONLINE SOURCES
Apply These Standards	**Ask These Questions**
AUTHORITY	What is the source (author, editor, host, or Web master)? What are the source's *credentials* (degrees, publications, areas of expertise)? What are the source's *affiliations* (known groups/companies to which the source belongs and which may reveal bias)?
COVERAGE	Is the coverage thorough but specific? Is the coverage balanced, presenting more than one side of an issue?
DOMAINS	What is the address (URL)? Is the domain *affiliated* (.edu, .gov), *unaffiliated* (.net), or *restricted* (.info)? Caution: Affiliated sites tend toward trustworthiness; others may be questionable.
CURRENCY	What is the posting date? Is the site updated regularly?
LINKS	Is the site linked to other sites (an indication of usefulness)? Are the links of the same quality?
DOCUMENTATION	Is the information attributed to a source? How much information is from primary sources (an author's own words)? How much information is from secondary sources (interpretations of an author's words)? Caution: Primary sources are more reliable.
STYLE	Is the style appropriate for the material? Is there an absence of slang, jargon, and grammatical errors?

Source: Carol C. Kanar, *The Confident Student,* Seventh Edition. © 2011 by Wadsworth, Cengage Learning. Used with permission.

for reliability. To evaluate for **objectivity**, become a bias detector. Are all sides represented fairly, or is one side clearly favored over the other? Is the language slanted or inflammatory? Unfairly represented viewpoints, emotional language, and insufficient factual support for opinions all indicate bias. **Usefulness** is a subjective standard. In other words, is the information accessible to *you*? Does it fulfill your need to know or answer your questions? To evaluate for usefulness, ask these questions: "What have I learned, and how can I apply the knowledge in my everyday life?"

Because anyone can develop a Web page and because most Web searches will generate a long list of sites, you have to be very careful that the information you are getting is reliable, objective, and useful. Table 6 on page 23 lists some additional standards for evaluating online sources. Some of these standards apply to print sources as well.

Self-questioning is a strategy that keeps your mind active and focused on your reading. As a review, Table 7 below lists the essential reading skills covered in Part 1 and questions to ask that will guide your reading. Remember that in reading, two people are involved: you and the author. As you become actively involved in a mental conversation with an author, your understanding will grow, and your enjoyment of reading will increase.

TABLE 7 | QUESTIONS FOR ACTIVE READERS

Strategy	Questions to Ask
FIND THE MAIN IDEA	What is the author's topic? What is the author's comment?
IDENTIFY THE DETAILS	What are the stated facts, reasons, or examples? What do the facts, reasons, or examples explain? What transitions can I find?
DETERMINE THE PURPOSE	Why did the author write this? What does the author expect of me? What do the title and the main idea tell me?
LOOK FOR PATTERNS	What are the author's main idea and purpose? How are the details related? What do the transitions tell me?
MAKE INFERENCES	What do I already know? What are the stated details? What do the details mean?
DEFINE WORDS IN CONTEXT	What are the author's clues? What signal words can I find? What does my experience tell me?
READ GRAPHICS WITH UNDERSTANDING	What is the graphic's *purpose?* What is the *relationship* among ideas or variables? What does the *text* say about the graphic?
EVALUATE WHAT YOU READ	Is it *reliable:* credible and trustworthy? Is it *objective:* fair and free from bias? Is it *useful:* applicable to everyday life or needs?

AMERICANS IN TRANSITION

The United States has seen a lot of changes in its more than 200 years. Your grandparents, and some of your parents, grew up without computers, cell phones, MTV, and McDonald's. They played records instead of CDs, listened to Frank Sinatra and Elvis instead of Rihanna and Beyonce, and dressed up to go downtown.

The 1960s ushered in some of the most sweeping social and cultural changes in our history. More recently, we have seen a new wave of immigrants, mainly from Spanish-speaking cultures, who will soon outnumber African Americans as our largest minority population. The twenty-first century promises medical and technological advances that will change lives and challenge our ethics. In 2008, we elected our first African American president. Worldwide, we are regarded as an experiment in democracy—at times loved, hated, or feared. However you look at us, we remain optimistic as a people and always evolving as a nation.

The selections in Part 2 are about Americans in transition, meeting the challenges of a changing nation and world. As you read each selection, reflect on what it means to be an American now.

FIRST THOUGHTS

To build background for the reading selection, answer the following questions, either on your own or in a group discussion.

1. Who was Jackie Robinson, and what do you know about him?
2. What do you know about the game of baseball, the National League, or the sport's most famous players?
3. Preview the title, headnote, and first one or two paragraphs. What do you think will follow?

WORD ALERT

Each word below is followed by its paragraph number. Preview the words and definitions before reading. Then review them as necessary during reading. Use context clues and your dictionary to define any additional unfamiliar words.

barnstorming (1) traveling around the country, making speeches or performing

gawk (1) to stare stupidly

mocked (3) ridiculed, scorned, made fun of

vile (4) unpleasant or objectionable

forbearance (4) patience, restraint

suppress (5) to check or inhibit the expression of an impulse, to deliberately hold back

rattling (7) unnerving, upsetting

reverence (8) a feeling of awe and respect and often love

mission (9) a special assignment given to a person or group

appalled (12) upset, dismayed

◆ Jackie Robinson

HENRY AARON

Henry ("Hank") Aaron holds the major league home run record (755) and works for the Atlanta Braves organization. In this article, he explains how baseball great Jackie Robinson influenced his career and what Robinson's life has meant to the sport of baseball and to the nation.

I WAS 14 YEARS old when I first saw Jackie Robinson. It was the spring of 1948, the 1
year after Jackie changed my life by breaking baseball's color line. His team, the Brooklyn Dodgers, made a stop in my hometown of Mobile, Alabama, while **barnstorming** its way north to start the season, and while he was there, Jackie spoke to a big crowd of black folks over on Davis Avenue. I think he talked about segregation, but I didn't hear a word that came out of his mouth. Jackie Robinson was such a hero to me that I couldn't do anything but **gawk** at him.

They say certain people are bigger than life, but Jackie Robinson is the only 2
man I've known who truly was. In 1947 life in America—at least my America, and Jackie's—was segregation. It was two worlds that were afraid of each other. There were separate schools for blacks and whites, separate restaurants, separate hotels, separate drinking fountains and separate baseball leagues. Life was unkind to black people who tried to bring those worlds together. It could be hateful. But Jackie Robinson, God bless him, was bigger than all of that.

Jackie Robinson had to be bigger than life. He had to be bigger than the Brook- 3
lyn teammates who got up a petition to keep him off the ball club, bigger than the pitchers who threw at him or the base runners who dug their spikes into his shin, bigger than the bench jockeys who hollered for him to carry their bags and shine their shoes, bigger than the so-called fans who **mocked** him with mops on their heads and wrote him death threats.

When Branch Rickey first met with Jackie about joining the Dodgers, he told 4
him that for three years he would have to turn the other cheek and silently suffer all the **vile** things that would come his way. Believe me, it wasn't Jackie's nature to do that. He was a fighter, the proudest and most competitive person I've ever seen. This was a man who, as a lieutenant in the Army, risked a court-martial by refusing to sit in the back of a military bus. But when Rickey read to him from *The Life of Christ,* Jackie understood the wisdom and the necessity of **forbearance**.

To this day, I don't know how he withstood the things he did without lashing 5
back. I've been through a lot in my time, and I consider myself to be a patient man, but I know I couldn't have done what Jackie did. I don't think anybody else could have done it. Somehow, though, Jackie had the strength to **suppress** his instincts, to sacrifice his pride for his people's. It was an incredible act of selflessness that brought the races closer together than ever before and shaped the dreams of an entire generation.

Before Jackie Robinson broke the color line, I wasn't permitted even to think 6
about being a professional baseball player. I once mentioned something to my

father about it, and he said, "Ain't no colored ballplayers." There were the Negro Leagues of course, where the Dodgers discovered Jackie, but my mother, like most, would rather her son be a schoolteacher than a Negro Leaguer. All that changed when Jackie put on No. 42 and started stealing bases in a Brooklyn uniform.

7   Jackie's character was much more important than his batting average, but it certainly helped that he was a great ball player, a .311 career hitter whose trademark was **rattling** pitchers and fielders with his daring base running. He wasn't the best Negro League talent at the time he was chosen, and baseball wasn't really his best sport—he had been a football and track star at UCLA—but he played the game with a ferocious creativity that gave the country a good idea of what it had been missing all those years. With Jackie in the infield, the Dodgers won six National League pennants.

8   I believe every black person in America had a piece of those pennants. There's never been another ball player who touched people as Jackie did. The only comparable athlete, in my experience, was Joe Louis.[1] The difference was that Louis competed against white men: Jackie competed with them as well. He was taking us over segregation's threshold into a new land whose scenery made every black person stop and stare in **reverence**. We were all with Jackie. We slid into every base that he swiped, ducked at every fastball that hurtled toward his head. The circulation of the Pittsburgh *Courier*, the leading black newspaper, increased by 100,000 when it began reporting on him regularly. All over the country, black preachers would call together their congregations just to pray for Jackie and urge them to demonstrate the same forbearance that he did.

9   Later in his career, when the "Great Experiment" had proved to be successful and other black players had joined him, Jackie allowed his instincts to take over in issues of race. He began striking back and speaking out. And when Jackie Robinson spoke, every black player got the message. He made it clear to us that we weren't playing just for ourselves or for our teams; we were playing for our people. I don't think it's a coincidence that the black players of the late '50s and '60s—me, Roy Campanella, Monte Irvin, Willie Mays, Ernie Banks, Frank Robinson, Bob Gibson and others—dominated the National League. If we played as if we were on a **mission**, it was because Jackie Robinson had sent us out on one.

10   Even after he retired in 1956 and was elected to the Hall of Fame in 1962, Jackie continued to chop along the path that was still a long way from being cleared. He campaigned for baseball to hire a black third-base coach, then a black manager. In 1969 he refused an invitation to play in an old-timers' game at Yankee Stadium to protest the lack of progress along those lines.

11   One of the great players from my generation, Frank Robinson (who was related to Jackie only in spirit), finally became the first black manager, in 1975. Jackie was gone by then. His last public appearance was at the 1972 World Series, where he showed up with white hair, carrying a cane and going blind from diabetes. He died nine days later.

12   Most of the black players from Jackie's day were at the funeral, but I was **appalled** by how few of the younger players showed up to pay him tribute. At the time, I was 41 home runs short of Babe Ruth's career record, and when

---

[1] Born in 1914, Joe Louis was an American prizefighter. He held the world heavyweight title from 1937 to 1949. He successfully defended this title 25 times. He died in 1981.

Jackie died, I really felt that it was up to me to keep his dream alive. I was inspired to dedicate my home-run record to the same great cause to which Jackie dedicated his life. I'm still inspired by Jackie Robinson. Hardly a day goes by that I don't think of him.

Comprehension Check

Purpose and Main Idea

1. What is the author's topic?
   a. sports
   b. baseball
   c. Jackie Robinson
   d. African American athletes
2. What is the author's central idea?
   a. African Americans have made significant contributions to the field of sports.
   b. Baseball is one of America's best-loved sports.
   c. Many African Americans have achieved fame in baseball.
   d. Jackie Robinson broke the color line and changed baseball forever.
3. The author's primary purpose is to
   a. express his ideas about Robinson's influence on his own life and our national life.
   b. inform readers about what life was like for minorities in 1947.
   c. persuade readers to take more of an interest in team sports.
   d. entertain us with amusing stories about the life of Jackie Robinson.

Details

4. In the author's opinion, the only athlete comparable to Jackie Robinson was Joe Louis.
   a. True
   b. False
5. According to the author, in what other sports did Jackie Robinson excel?
   a. golf and tennis
   b. basketball and hockey
   c. football and track
   d. soccer and swimming
6. According to the author, Jackie's race was more important than his batting average.
   a. True
   b. False
7. Jackie Robinson accomplished all of the following *except* which one?
   a. He became a .311 career hitter.
   b. He was elected to the Hall of Fame.
   c. He played in an old-timers' game at Yankee Stadium in 1969.
   d. He helped his team win six National League pennants.

8. What is the author's dominant organizational pattern?
    a. Sequence: The author traces the development of Robinson's career.
    b. Comparison/contrast: The author compares baseball players to other athletes.
    c. Cause/effect: The author explains the reasons behind Robinson's success.
    d. Definition: The author defines sportsmanship in baseball.

Inferences

9. In the first sentence of paragraph 9, what does the author mean by "Great Experiment"?
10. According to the author, Robinson "understood the wisdom and the necessity of forbearance." Therefore, who would Robinson probably have admired more: Malcolm X or Dr. Martin Luther King, Jr., and why?

Working with Words

Complete sentences 1–10 with these words from Word Alert:

barnstorming	rattling	reverence	mission	gawk
forbearance	suppress	appalled	mocked	vile

1. When the algebra instructor accidently punched a hole in his pocket with his pen, the students could not _____ their laughter.
2. Athletes who have become celebrities can expect people to _____ at them whenever they appear in public.
3. Raymond took a big gulp of his soda and immediately spit it out because it tasted _____.
4. The instructor said to the students, "I am _____ that you would think I do not treat everyone fairly."
5. When someone shouts at you in anger, do you have the _____ not to shout back?
6. Michael Jordan's fans treat him with a respect that amounts to _____.
7. "It is my _____," said the instructor, "to make sure that everyone develops the skills needed to pass this course."
8. Because the other students were _____ her by talking about the test and all the information she had not studied, Ramona became increasingly anxious.
9. The rock group Anorexia performed to sold-out audiences while _____ their way from Anchorage, Alaska, to Key West, Florida.
10. The fifth graders _____ their teacher by making faces and drawing unflattering pictures.

Write your own sentences, using any two of the words from Word Alert.

11. _____

12. _____

Thinking Deeper

Ideas for reflection, discussion, and writing

Make Inferences from Your Reading

1. The author says that Jackie Robinson is the only man he knew who truly was bigger than life. Explain what you think the author means by "bigger than life." Discuss athletes or others who also fit this description.
2. The author says that Jackie Robinson's sacrifice and selflessness "brought the races closer together than ever before and shaped the dreams of an entire generation." Discuss someone from the past or recent times whose efforts or accomplishments have brought people closer together.
3. How had Americans' attitudes about African American athletes changed between the time Robinson first played for the Dodgers in 1947 and his retirement in 1956? Do race issues trouble national or college athletic teams today? If so, how are athletes and their fans dealing with these issues?

4. Do a Web search on Jackie Robinson to see what inferences you can make about his life and career. Type his name to generate a list of sites. Then select two or more sites to research, take notes, and share your findings in a class discussion. What have you learned about Robinson from your search that you can apply in your own life?

Write About It

5. In this selection, the author writes about a man who both influenced his career and served as a role model. Write about a person you admire and respect, someone who has had a positive influence on your life.
6. Write about someone in the public eye who is or is not someone worthy of our respect.

FIRST THOUGHTS

To build background for the reading selection, answer the following questions, either on your own or in a group discussion.

1. What fast-food restaurants are available in your area?
2. What are the restaurants' similarities and differences?
3. Preview the title, headnote, and first one or two paragraphs. What do you think will follow?

WORD ALERT

Each word below is followed by its paragraph number. Preview the words and definitions before reading. Then review them as necessary during reading. Use context clues and your dictionary to define any additional unfamiliar words.

precursor (1) predecessor, forerunner; an indicator of something that is to come
conglomerate (1) a group of businesses or companies under one central management
rubric (3) a rule or direction
reiterated (3) said or done again, repeated
cater (4) to provide food service, to attend to someone's needs
demeanour (5) behavior (American spelling, demeanor)
proprietor (5) owner
adheres (6) remains attached, follows devotedly
ramifications (6) developments, consequences

◈ The Ritual of Fast Food

MARGARET VISSER

In this selection from *The Rituals of Dinner*, the author explains the appeal of fast-food restaurants: why we like them and how they serve our needs.

AN EARLY PRECURSOR of the restaurant meal was dinner served to the public at fixed 1
times and prices at an eating house or tavern. Such a meal was called, because of its predetermined aspects, an "ordinary," and the place where it was eaten came to be called an "ordinary," too. When a huge modern business **conglomerate** offers fast food to travellers on the highway, it knows that its customers are likely to desire No Surprises. They are hungry, tired, and not in a celebratory mood; they are happy to pay—provided that the price looks easily manageable—for the safely predictable, the convenient, the fast and ordinary.

Ornamental formalities are pruned away (tables and chairs are bolted to the 2
floor, for instance, and "cutlery" is either nonexistent or not worth stealing); but rituals, in the sense of behaviour and expectations that conform to preordained rules, still inform the proceedings. People who stop for a hamburger—at a Wendy's, a Hardee's, a McDonald's, or a Burger King—know exactly what the building that houses the establishment should look like; architectural variations merely ring changes on rigidly imposed themes. People want, perhaps even need, to *recognize* their chain store, to feel that they know it and its food in advance. Such an outlet is designed to be a "home away from home," on the highway, or anywhere in the city, or for Americans abroad.

Words and actions are officially laid down, learned by the staff from hand- 3
books and teaching sessions, and then picked up by customers in the course of regular visits. Things have to be called by their correct names ("Big Mac," "large fries"); the McDonald's **rubric** in 1978 required servers to ask "Will that be with cheese, sir?" "Will there be any fries today, sir?" and to close the transaction with "Have a nice day." The staff wear distinctive garments; menus are always the same, and even placed in the same spot in every outlet in the chain; prices are low and predictable; and the theme of cleanliness is proclaimed and tirelessly **reiterated**. The company attempts also to play the role of a lovable host, kind and concerned, even parental: it knows that blunt and direct confrontation with a huge faceless corporation makes us suspicious, and even badly behaved. So it stresses its love of children, its nostalgia for cosy warmth and for the past (cottage roofs, warm earth tones), or its clean, brisk modernity (glass walls, smooth surfaces, red trim). It responds to social concerns—when they are insistent enough, sufficiently widely held, and therefore "correct." McDonald's, for example, is at present busy showing how much it cares about the environment.

Fast-food chains know that they are ordinary. They *want* to be ordinary, and 4
for people to think of them as almost inseparable from the idea of everyday food consumed outside the home. They are happy to allow their customers time off for feasts—on Thanksgiving, Christmas, and so on—to which they do not **cater**. Even those comparatively rare holiday times, however, are turned to a profit, because the

companies know that their favourite customers—law-abiding families—are at home together then, watching television, where carefully placed commercials will spread the word concerning new fast-food products, and re-imprint the image of the various chain stores for later, when the long stretches of ordinary times return.

5   Families are the customers the fast-food chains want: solid citizens in groups of several at a time, the adults hovering over their children, teaching them the goodness of hamburgers, anxious to bring them up to behave typically and correctly. Customers usually maintain a clean, restrained, considerate, and competent **demeanour** as they swiftly, gratefully, and informally eat. Fast-food operators have recently faced the alarming realization that crack addicts, craving salt and fat, have spread the word among their number that French fries deliver these substances easily, ubiquitously, cheaply, and at all hours. Dope addicts at family "ordinaries"! The unacceptability of such a thought was neatly captured by a news story in *The Economist* (1990) that spelled out the words a fast-foods **proprietor** can least afford to hear from his faithful customers, the participants in his polite and practiced rituals: the title of the story was "Come on Mabel, let's leave." The plan to counter this threat included increasing the intensity of the lighting in fast-food establishments—drug addicts, apparently, prefer to eat in the dark.

6   The formality of eating at a restaurant belonging to a fast-food chain depends upon the fierce regularity of its product, its simple but carefully observed rituals, and its environment. Supplying a hamburger that **adheres** to perfect standards of shape, weight, temperature, and consistency, together with selections from a pre-set list of trimmings, to a customer with fiendishly precise expectations is an enormously complex feat. The technology involved in performing it has been learned through the expenditure of huge sums on research, and after decades of experience—not to mention the vast political and economic **ramifications** involved in maintaining the supplies of cheap beef and cheap buns. But these costs and complexities are, with tremendous care, hidden from view. We know of course that, say, a Big Mac is a cultural construct: the careful control expended upon it is one of the things we are buying. But McDonald's manages—it must do so if it is to succeed in being ordinary—to provide a "casual" eating experience. Convenient, innocent simplicity is what the technology, the ruthless politics, and the elaborate organization serve to the customer.

Comprehension Check

Purpose and Main Idea

1. What is the author's topic?
    a.   family meals
    b.   food service
    c.   restaurant management
    d.   fast-food restaurants
2. What is the central idea of this selection?
    a.   Wendy's, McDonald's, and Burger King are three examples of the typical fast-food restaurant.
    b.   Consumers expect convenience, simplicity, and cleanliness from a fast-food restaurant.

c. Fast-food chains meet consumers' expectations through an elaborate system of preordained rules and behaviors.

d. No longer a purely American phenomenon, the fast-food restaurant has spread to other nations around the world.

3. The author's primary purpose is to
   a. express her viewpoint that fast-food restaurants need improvement.
   b. persuade readers that one fast-food restaurant is better than all the others.
   c. inform us about what we expect from fast-food chains and what they do to meet our expectations.
   d. entertain us with the variety of fast-food restaurants and menus that are available.

Details

4. In the author's opinion, consumers expect all but which one of the following from their favorite fast-food restaurant?
   a. simplicity
   b. convenience
   c. cleanliness
   d. variety

5. A conglomerate that offers fast food knows that travelers want no surprises.
   a. True
   b. False

6. According to the author, all but which one of the following are characteristic of the fast-food chains?
   a. They do not respond to social concerns.
   b. Menus and uniforms do not change.
   c. They want to be ordinary.
   d. They cater to families.

7. According to the author, fast-food operators responded to the threat of drug addicts as customers by changing the restaurants' atmosphere.
   a. True
   b. False

8. What is the author's dominant organizational pattern?
   a. Sequence: She traces the development of the fast-food restaurant in the United States.
   b. Comparison: She compares two fast-food restaurants.
   c. Cause and effect: She explains the reasons we like to eat in fast-food restaurants.
   d. Definition: She defines the term *fast-food restaurant*.

Inferences

9. According to the author's definition of *ordinary*, Burger King and Wendy's fall into this category. Describe a restaurant with which you are familiar that does not fit the author's definition of *ordinary* and explain why.

10. Apart from any concerns about crime, why did fast-food restaurants not want drug addicts as customers?

Working with Words

Complete sentences 1–9 with these words from Word Alert:

ramifications	precursor	demeanor
conglomerate	proprietor	rubric
reiterated	adheres	cater

1. Finding a husband or wife may be difficult for a person who expects someone to _____ to his or her every need.
2. Before you make a decision, think ahead to its possible _____ and whether you can live with them.
3. "No, I won't accept your paper tomorrow," said the instructor. "How many times have I _____ today's deadline?"
4. Today's race car could be the _____ of tomorrow's sports sedan.
5. As the _____ of this store, I am the one who establishes business hours and the rules of operation.
6. "I don't like your _____ today," said the instructor to the children, who were talking and not paying attention.
7. Under the _____ of faculty responsibilities, instructors must meet all classes at their scheduled times or make prior arrangements.
8. Students appreciate an instructor who _____ to posted office hours and is, therefore, available to answer questions.
9. Ours is only one of many companies that have become a huge _____ of businesses, offering diverse services to consumers.

Write your own sentences, using any two of the words from Word Alert.

10. _____
11. _____

Thinking Deeper

Ideas for reflection, discussion, and writing

Make Inferences from Your Reading

1. In paragraph 2, the author defines *rituals* in context as "behavior and expectations that conform to preordained rules." According to this definition, what does the author mean by the "ritual" of fast food?
2. What do you expect from a fast-food restaurant? In what way do the interior and exterior design, the words and actions of employees, the restaurant's image, and the food offered meet your needs? Do your experiences reflect the author's analysis of what customers want and how the fast-food chains serve them? What inferences can you make about fast-food restaurants and their customers based on your own experience?

3. In the past, the morning or evening meal at home was for most American families a ritual that encouraged feelings of closeness. But many of today's families eat fewer meals together and eat more meals out. Is this a positive or a negative cultural development, and why?

4. Go to your favorite fast-food restaurant online. Type in the name of the restaurant with no spaces between words and then add *.com*. Explore the site to find out what inferences you can make about its customers based on its menu, prices, policies, employment opportunities, and so on. In a class discussion, be prepared to explain how the information you found online either does or does not support what the author says about the ritual of fast food.

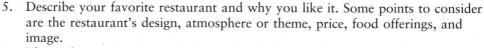

Write About It

5. Describe your favorite restaurant and why you like it. Some points to consider are the restaurant's design, atmosphere or theme, price, food offerings, and image.

6. The author writes about the "ritual" of fast food. Write about one or more of your own food or mealtime rituals, either from the past or more recently.

FIRST THOUGHTS

To build background for the reading selection, answer the following questions, either on your own or in a group discussion.

1. What do you know about the history of oral contraceptives?
2. What impact do you think the pill has had on American women's lives?
3. Preview the title, headnote, and first one or two paragraphs. What do you think will follow?

WORD ALERT

Each word below is followed by its paragraph number. Preview the words and definitions before reading. Then review them as necessary during reading. Use context clues and your dictionary to define any additional unfamiliar words.

aspirations (5) desires for achievement or advancement

depleted (8) used up, emptied out

incarnation (9) embodiment or form

circumvented (12) avoided, overcame

constraining (12) confining, restraining

cohorts (16) people within a group

resurgence (19) renewal or revival

complementary (19) supplying mutual needs, completing

◈ The Power of the Pill

CLAUDIA GOLDIN AND LAWRENCE F. KATZ

Claudia Goldin is the Henry Lee Professor of Economics at Harvard University, and Lawrence F. Katz is a professor of economics at Harvard University. Both are research associates at the National Bureau of Economic Research in Cambridge, Massachusetts.

THE PILL—THE female oral contraceptive—is almost 50 years old and, in its lifetime, has changed not only the sexual lives of American women, but their economic ones, as well.   1

It is a middle-age medical miracle. Slimmed down in its progestin and estrogen content from the original Enovid pill, it remains the contraceptive of choice of American women.   2

Almost 80 percent of women now between 53 and 63 took the pill at some time.   3

The pill was an overnight success. The fraction of married women (under 35 years) who were "on the pill" came close to its historic maximum just five years after its release in 1960. But the pill did not immediately become as common among young unmarried women, and that is a large part of our story concerning the social impact of the pill.   4

We have sought to understand how the pill affected the **aspirations** and career choices of young women in the late 1960s and how it enabled women to be accepted as equals in the most prestigious, highly paid and demanding occupations.   5

Up until 1970, less than 10 percent of medical students were women, while the comparable figures for law (4 percent), dentistry (1 percent) and business (3 percent) were even lower. But just a decade later the share was about one-third in medicine and business, more than one-third in law, one-fifth in dentistry. By the early 1990s, women were more than 40 percent of all first-year medical and law students, and more than 35 percent of all first-year MBA and dentistry students.   6

Did the pill play a role in these changes? We think the answer is "yes." A safe, reliable, easy-to-use, female-controlled contraceptive enabled young women to enter careers that involved extensive and up-front time commitments in education. But how?   7

A young woman beginning a degree program had to evaluate—in addition to the financial costs of her education—the social consequences of a career track. If she did not marry before her professional education began and lacked an almost foolproof contraceptive such as the pill, she would have to pay the penalty of abstinence or cope with considerable uncertainty regarding pregnancy. If she delayed marriage (as many did), she would have to consider the social consequences of a **depleted** marriage market.   8

In its early high-dose **incarnation** the pill was monumentally more reliable than other contraceptive methods. (Its other pluses are that it is female-controlled, non-messy and can be taken well in advance of sex.)   9

10   The pill allowed a woman to "have it all." She could have sex and plan for a future career. In addition, the pill encouraged an increase in the age at first marriage. A career woman who decided to delay marriage would encounter a depleted marriage market if the typical age at first marriage were low. But if the marriage age for college graduates rose, as it did throughout the 1970s, the delay would involve far less of a penalty.

11   But what accounts for the lag of almost 10 years from the pill's introduction in 1960 to the start of the career response for young women?

12   The explanation is simple. Single women in the 1960s were thwarted from obtaining the pill by archaic state laws. As late as 1960, 30 states prohibited advertisements regarding birth control, and 22 had some prohibition on the sale of contraceptives. Married persons easily **circumvented** these laws, but the laws had **constraining** effects on young, single women. As the laws were relaxed, they were able to obtain the pill and, subsequently, the marriage age rose and career aspirations changed.

13   By the late 1960s and early 1970s almost all states had lowered the age of legal majority to 18 and granted to youth the rights of adults through "mature minor" decisions. These legal changes, by the way, were not driven by a desire to extend family-planning services nor by feminist action.

14   Rather, they were motivated by the same factors that led to the 26th Amendment (1971) lowering the voting age to 18. The Vietnam War had awakened Americans to the inconsistency between the rights and responsibilities of young people.

15   With sufficient ingenuity, a determined unmarried woman could have obtained the pill without benefit of the law. But our cross-state statistical analysis for 1971 shows that pill use among young women was considerably higher in states having more lenient laws regarding the rights of minors. The laws mattered. Until 1969 few, if any, college health clinics made family planning services available to students without regard to age or marital status. By the mid-1970s, most on large campuses did.

16   To measure trends in pill usage for young, unmarried women we have used two retrospective surveys from the 1980s. Taken together, our data show that the widespread use of the pill among young unmarried women began more than five years after it did for married women. More important, the data also show that pill use among single, college-graduate women began to greatly increase with **cohorts** born at about 1948. These were precisely the cohorts that first began to enter professional schools around the 1970s.

17   The timing of the changes in the fraction of females among first-year professional students and the use of the pill could, of course, have been a coincidence. But we have additional, and more convincing, evidence that the relationship was causal.

18   Young unmarried women in states that lowered the age of majority or had passed legislation extending the mature minor decision (or had judicial rulings that did so) were considerably more likely to use the pill. Also, the age at first marriage increased for college-graduate women who turned 18 years old at about the time that the state laws changed. That is, the availability of the pill to young college women appears to have led to an increase in the age of first marriage. The increased age at first marriage among college-graduate women is striking. Among women born from the early 1930s to the end of the 1940s, about 50 percent married before age 23. But among women born in 1957, only 30 percent married before age 23.

The case for the pill as the primary factor driving women's career decisions is 19 strong. But it was not the only factor. The **resurgence** of feminism, anti-discrimination legislation and legalized abortion (nationwide in 1973 by Roe vs. Wade and earlier in several states) are some others. We have found that abortion legalization was not as potent as the pill in encouraging later marriage for college women, although its impact on careers was **complementary**.

Young American women in the late 1960s had hoped to follow in their mother's 20 footsteps, but in just a few years their aspirations had changed radically. Our work shows that the pill had a large effect on career and marriage. Without the pill these changes would, presumably, have come later. How much later, though, we do not know.

Comprehension Check

Purpose and Main Idea

1. What is the authors' topic?
   - a. motherhood versus career
   - b. birth control methods
   - c. effects of the pill
   - d. contraceptive devices
2. The central idea of the entire selection is best stated in which one of the following sentences?
   - a. Invented decades ago, the pill was an overnight success.
   - b. The pill is a safe, reliable, easy-to-use form of birth control.
   - c. The oral contraceptive, best known as "the pill," is a powerful form of birth control.
   - d. The pill has changed the lives of American women both sexually and economically.
3. In this selection, the authors' purpose is to
   - a. persuade readers that the pill is still the most effective form of birth control.
   - b. explain how the pill affected young women's career choices in the later 1960s.
   - c. entertain readers with anecdotes about women's reproductive choices in earlier times.
   - d. inform readers about the wide variety of contraceptive devices on the market today.

Details

4. Until 1970, less than 4 percent of women were medical students.
   - a. True
   - b. False
5. For young women in the 1960s, all but which one of the following were possible social consequences of a career track?
   - a. a depleted marriage market
   - b. abstinence in the absence of marriage or reliable birth control
   - c. the financial costs of an education
   - d. uncertainty regarding pregnancy

6. According to the authors, when did the widespread use of the pill among young, unmarried women begin?
    a. before it did for married women
    b. about the same time as it did for married women
    c. soon after it did for married women
     d. more that five years after it did for married women
7. According to the authors, lowering the age of legal majority to eighteen resulted from the Vietnam War.
     a. True
    b. False
8. According to the authors, which one of the following, along with the pill, had a complementary effect on careers?
    a. the resurgence of feminism
    b. abortion legalization
    c. antidiscrimination laws
    d. lowering the voting age

Inferences

9. Based on the context, define *thwarted* in paragraph 12, second sentence.
10. Based on the authors' details in this selection, would they most likely agree or disagree with the following statement, and why? "Young women today are as likely as men to pursue professional careers."

Working with Words

Complete sentences 1–8 with these words from Word Alert:

complementary	constraining	aspirations	depleted
circumvented	resurgence	incarnation	cohorts

1. From time to time, fashions of the past have seen a _____ in popularity.
2. Jan's parents wanted her to follow in their footsteps and become an attorney, but her _____ were to pursue a career in architecture.
3. Age and skill are two _____ factors that may keep a young person from getting a driver's license.
4. Environmentalists fear that our high energy consumption will leave us with _____ oil reserves.
5. When the family resemblance is great, a child may seem to be the _____ of a parent.
6. Police can point to many instances where people have _____ laws, to their own regret.
7. Baby Boomers and the Millennials are two _____ that researchers have studied.

8. The blue tablecloth was _____ to the china's blue and white pattern.

Write your own sentences, using any two of the words from Word Alert.

9. _____

10. _____

Thinking Deeper

Ideas for reflection, discussion, and writing

Make Inferences from Your Reading

1. The authors conclude that "the pill had a large effect on career and marriage." Where in the article is the evidence to support this conclusion? Do you agree or disagree with the authors' conclusion? What inferences can you make about other factors that might account for the pill's effect on career and marriage?
2. The authors say that the changes brought about by the pill "would, presumably, have come later" without the pill. Is this a valid inference? Why or why not?
3. The authors attribute several changes in marriage and career patterns to the widespread use of the pill during the late 1960s. How have these changes affected women's and men's lives for better or worse?
4. Research the history of the pill. Find out when it was developed, and who some of the big names involved in its development and promotion were. Begin your search by typing "contraceptives" and "history." Then be prepared to discuss the conclusions that you draw from this information.

Write About It

5. What are your life and career goals? Do you feel any constraints that would prevent you from achieving your goals? Write about your aspirations and how you plan to achieve them.
6. Explain one or more ways in which your life is or will be similar to that of one of your parents.

FIRST THOUGHTS

To build background for the reading selection, answer the following questions, either on your own or in a group discussion.

1. Do you think that kids today grow up too soon?
2. What age or experience marked the end of your adolescence and the beginning of your adulthood, or are you still somewhere in between?
3. Preview the title, headnote, and first one or two paragraphs. What do you think will follow?

WORD ALERT

Each word below is followed by its paragraph number. Preview the words and definitions before reading. Then review them as necessary during reading. Use context clues and your dictionary to define any additional unfamiliar words.

deferment (2) the act of delaying, putting off
postmodern (3 and 15) refers to social and political changes since the 1960s
cynical (4) believing that all people are motivated by selfishness
intimacy (11) familiarity, close association
tarnished (13) tainted, morally defiled
ellipsis (17) an omission of some part
obliged (20) indebted to service
disillusioned (21) freed from false notions of reality
notorious (27) known widely and usually unfavorably, infamous
relinquish (28) give up, abandon

◆ Growing Up Old in Los Angeles

RICHARD RODRIGUEZ

Richard Rodriguez, son of Mexican immigrants, was born in San Francisco in 1944 and educated at Stanford, Columbia, and the University of California at Berkeley. He is the author of several books and articles, notably his autobiography *Hunger of Memory: The Education of Richard Rodriguez* (1982).

AMERICA'S GREATEST CONTRIBUTION to the world of ideas is adolescence. European no- 1
vels often begin with a first indelible memory—a golden poplar, or Mama standing in the kitchen. American novels begin at the moment of rebellion, the moment of appetite for distance, the moonless night Tom Sawyer pries open the back-bedroom window, shinnies down the drainpipe, drops to the ground, and runs.

America invented a space—a **deferment**, a patch of asphalt between childhood 2
and adulthood, between the child's ties to family and the adult's re-creation of family. Within this space, within this boredom, American teenagers are supposed to innovate, to improvise, to rebel, to turn around three times before they harden into adults.

If you want to see the broadcasting center, the trademark capital of adoles- 3
cence, come to Los Angeles. The great postwar, **postmodern**, suburban city in Dolby sound was built by restless people who intended to give their kids an unend-ing spring.

There are times in Los Angeles—our most American of American cities—when 4
teenagers seem the oldest people around. Many seem barely children at all—they are tough and **cynical** as ancients, beyond laughter in a city that idolizes them. Their glance, when it meets ours, is unblinking.

At a wedding in Brentwood, I watch the 17-year-old daughter of my thrice- 5
divorced friend give her mother away. The mother is dewey with liquid blush. The dry-eyed daughter has seen it all before.

I know children in Los Angeles who carry knives and guns because the walk to 6
and from school is more dangerous than their teachers or parents realize. One teen-ager stays home to watch her younger sister, who is being pursued by a teenage stalker. The girls have not told their parents because they say they do not know how their parents would react.

Have adults become the innocents? 7

Adults live in fear of the young. It's a movie script, a boffo science-fiction thriller 8
that has never been filmed but that might well star Jean-Claude Van Damme or Sylvester Stallone.

A friend of mine, a heavyweight amateur wrestler, wonders if it's safe for us 9
to have dinner at a Venice Beach restaurant. (There are, he says, 12-year-old gang-sters who prowl the neighborhood with guns.)

Some of the richest people in town have figured out how to sell the idea of 10
American adolescence to the world. The children with the most interesting dilemma

are the children of 90210. What does adolescence mean when your father is a record producer who drives to work in a Jeep to audition rap groups? What do you do when your father—who has a drug habit and is nowhere around in the years when you are growing up—is an internationally recognizable 50-foot face on the movie screen?

11   On the other hand: What can it feel like to grow up a teenager in South Central when your mama is on crack and you are responsible for her five kids? Teenagers who never had reliable parents or knew **intimacy** are having babies. There are teenagers in East L.A. who (literally) spend their young lives searching for family—"blood"—in some gang that promises what they never had.

12   It is every teenager's dream to "get big." In L.A. you can be very big, indeed. Fame is a billboard along Sunset Boulevard. Mexican-American gangstas pass the Southern California night by writing crypto-nonsense on sides of buildings, because the biggest lesson they have taken from the city is that advertisement is existence. Los Angeles is a horizontal city of separate freeway exits, separate malls, suburb fleeing suburb. Parents keep moving their children away from what they suppose is the diseased inner city. But there is no possibility of a healthy suburb radiant from a corrupt center. *No man is an island entire of itself.* Didn't we learn that in high school?

13   The children of East L.A. live in the same city as Madonna and Harvard-educated screenwriters who use cocaine for inspiration, selling a believably **tarnished** vision of the world to children of the crack mothers in Compton.

14   And look: There's always a TV in the houses of Watts. And it is always on. In the suburbs, white kids watch black rappers on MTV. Suburbanites use TV to watch the mayhem of the inner city. But on the TV in the inner city, they watch the rest of us. The bejeweled pimp in his gold BMW parodies the Beverly Hills matron on Rodeo Drive.

15   Elsewhere in America, we like to tell ourselves that Los Angeles is the exception. The truth is that, for all its eccentricity, Los Angeles tells us a great deal about adolescence in rural Kansas. And postmodern L.A. is linked to colonial Boston. Today's gangsta with a tattooed tear on his face is kin to young men fighting Old Man Europe's wars in the trenches of 1914 or 1941, to the young rebels who overthrew Old Man Englande rather than submit to another curfew, and to Judy Garland, who will always be a stagestruck teenager.

16   The earliest Americans imagined that they had fled the past—motherland, fatherland—and had come upon land that was without history or meaning. By implication, the earliest Americans imagined themselves adolescent, orphans. Their task was self-creation, without benefit or burden of family. The myth that we must each create our own meaning has passed down through American generations.

17   Young Meriwether Lewis heads out for the territory. He writes to his widowed mother, "I ... hope therefore you will not suffer yourself to indulge any anxiety for my safety...." The **ellipsis** is adolescence: estrangement, embarrassment, self-absorption, determination. The adolescent body plumps and furs, bleeds and craves to be known for itself. In some parts of the world, puberty is a secret, a shameful biological event, proof that you have inevitably joined the community of your gender. In America, puberty is the signal to rebel.

American teenagers invent their own tongue, meant to be indecipherable to 18
adult hearing. Every generation of adolescents does it. Adults are left wondering
what they mean: *Scrilla. Juking. Woop, woop, woop.*

"Children grow up too quickly," American parents sigh. And yet nothing trou- 19
bles an American parent so much as the teenager who won't leave home.

Several times in this century, American teenagers have been **obliged** to leave 20
home to fight overseas. Nineteen-year-old fathers vowed to their unborn children that
never again would the youth of the world be wasted by the Potentates of Winter.

My generation, the baby boom generation, was the refoliation of the world. We 21
were the children of mothers who learned how to drive, dyed their hair, used May-
belline, and decorated their houses for Christmas against the knowledge that winter
holds sway in the world. Fathers, having returned from blackened theaters of war,
used FHA loans to move into tract houses that had no genealogy. In such suburbs,
our **disillusioned** parents intended to ensure their children's optimism.

Prolonged adolescence became the point of us—so much the point of me that I 22
couldn't give it up. One night, in the 1950s, I watched Mary Martin, a middle-aged
actress, play an enchanted boy so persuasively that her rendition of "I Won't Grow
Up" nurtured my adolescent suspicions of anyone over the age of 30.

My generation became the first in human history (only hyperbole can suggest 23
our prophetic sense of ourselves) that imagined we might never grow old.

Jill, a friend of mine whose fame was an orange bikini, whose face has fallen, 24
whose breasts have fallen, whose hair is gray, is telling me about her son who has
just gone to New York and has found there the most wonderful possibilities. My
friend's eyes fill with tears. She fumbles in her handbag for the pack of cigarettes
she had just sworn off.

What's wrong? 25

"Dammit," she says, "I'm a geezer." 26

From my generation arose a culture for which America has become **notorious**. 27
We transformed youth into a lifestyle, a political manifesto, an aesthetic, a religion.
My generation turned adolescence into a commodity that could be sold worldwide by
45-year-old executives at Nike or Warner Bros. To that extent, we control youth.

But is it unreasonable for a child to expect that Mick Jagger or Michael 28
Jackson will grow up, thicken, settle, and slow—**relinquish** adolescence to a new
generation?

At the Senior Ball, teenagers in the ballroom of the Beverly Hills Hotel, beauti- 29
ful teenagers in black tie and gowns, try very hard not to look like teenagers. But
on the other hand, it is very important not to look like one's parents.

The balancing trick of American adolescence is to stand in-between—neither to 30
be a child nor an adult.

Where are you going to college? 31

The question intrudes on the ball like a gong from some great clock. It is mid- 32
night, Cinderella. Adolescence must come to an end. Life is governed by inevitabilities and consequences—a thought never communicated in America's rock-and-roll
lyrics.

American storytellers do better with the beginning of the story than the conclu- 33
sion. We do not know how to mark the end of adolescence. Mark Twain brings
Huck Finn back to Missouri, to Hannibal, and forces his young hero to bend

toward inevitability. But Huck yearns, forever, "to light out for the territory ... because Aunt Sally she's going to adopt me and sivilize me, and I can't stand it."

34   And then comes the least convincing conclusion ever written in all of American literature: THE END, YOURS TRULY, HUCK FINN.

Comprehension Check

Purpose and Main Idea

1. What is the author's topic?
    a.   Los Angeles as a cultural center
    b.   adolescence in Los Angeles
    c.   coming of age in America
    d.   the passage from childhood to adulthood
2. In which one of the following sentences is the author's central idea stated?
    a.   The idea of adolescence is one of America's great contributions.
    b.   Teenagers are growing up old today.
    c.   California is a cultural center that draws young people.
    d.   Los Angeles is the center of what it means to be an adolescent today.
3. The author's *primary* purpose is to
    a.   explain how growing up is harder for teenagers than it was for their parents
    b.   persuade readers that Los Angeles is the most American of cities
    c.   define the idea of adolescence through the lens of California
    d.   entertain readers with a glimpse of life on the West Coast

Details

4. According to the author, America invented adolescence as a space between childhood and adulthood.
    a.   True
    b.   False
5. The author uses all but which one of the following examples to describe adolescent life in Los Angeles?
    a.   Teenagers are tough and cynical.
    b.   Today's adolescents have a host of responsibilities.
    c.   Children carry knives and guns on the way home from school.
    d.   At a wedding, the bride is given away by her teenaged daughter.
6. According to the author, his generation, the Baby Boomers, were characterized by which one of the following?
    a.   being an object of worship
    b.   following in their parents' footsteps
    c.   growing old before their time
    d.   having a prolonged adolescence
7. Paragraphs 10 and 11 are related by which organizational pattern?
    a.   definition
    b.   classification

    c.   contrast

    d.   process

8. The question "Where are you going to college?" is intrusive, according to the author, because it suggests that adolescence must end.

    a.   True

    b.   False

Inferences

9. In paragraph 15, the author says "Los Angeles tells us a great deal about adolescence in rural Kansas." What do you think he means? In what way is life for the American teenager in any city like life in Los Angeles?

10. In paragraph 33, the author says "Life is governed by inevitabilities and consequences." What are some of the "inevitabilities and consequences" that govern your life?

Working with Words

Complete sentences 1–10 with these words from Word Alert:

disillusioned	deferment	cynical
relinquish	tarnished	ellipsis
postmodern	notorious	obliged
intimacy		

1. When students sign up for a course, they are _____ to attend class and do the work.

2. Voters are tired of _____ representatives who are willing to sell their votes to the highest bidder.

3. Are you willing to _____ your seat on a bus to someone who is standing uncomfortably?

4. Some people prefer the _____ of a small college over the anonymity of a large university

5. Unfortunately, too many celebrities have _____ images because of bad public behavior.

6. A _____ of your student loan is just a postponement; eventually, it will have to be paid.

7. After a short _____ between junior and senior year, the student returned to campus.

8. Children who become _____ when they learn that there is no Santa Claus get over their disappointment as they grow older.

9. An entertainer may become _____ for pushing the envelop in performance.

10. Some actors are the _____ counterparts of beloved stars from the past.

    Write your own sentences, using any two of the words from Word Alert.

11. _____

12. _____

Thinking Deeper

Ideas for reflection, discussion, and writing

Make Inferences from Your Reading

1. Have you ever been to Los Angeles? Based on the author's details, what impression do you get of this city? Do the author's details match your own experience? If you had to describe Los Angeles in one word, what word would you choose?

2. What do you think is the author's tone or attitude toward his subject? For example, does he look favorably or unfavorably on Los Angeles as a place to grow up? Does he think growing up old is a good thing or a bad thing? What specific words or examples help you to infer the author's tone?

3. In Paragraph 27, the author says that his generation "transformed youth into a lifestyle, a political manifesto, an aesthetic, a religion ... a commodity that could be bought and sold." Do you agree or disagree? How do people in your generation regard the idea of youth?

4. Reflect on one person in the media—a writer, singer, actor, politician, or other public figure who has shaped your views and behavior. Research his or her life on the Internet. Type the person's name for a list of possible sites to visit. Your instructor may have more suggestions. Take notes for sharing in a class discussion.

Write About It

5. No other generation has been as influenced by the media as today's children. Everything from the clothes they wear to their attitudes and values are shaped by advertising and other media. Write about one positive or negative effect of a movie, TV show, or piece of music. How has this media offering affected young people's values or behavior?

6. Rodriguez writes about what it means to be an adolescent. What does it mean to be an adult? Write your own definition of adulthood.

FIRST THOUGHTS

To build background for the reading selection, answer the following questions, either on your own or in a group discussion.

1. How many languages do you speak?
2. What is the value of knowing more than one language?
3. Preview the title, headnote, and first one or two paragraphs. What do you think will follow?

WORD ALERT

Each word below is followed by its paragraph number. Preview the words and definitions before reading. Then review them as necessary during reading. Use context clues and your dictionary to define any additional unfamiliar words.

extolled (1) praised highly

parochial (2) supported by a church parish

immersed (5) deeply involved, absorbed

ironic (5) contrary to what is expected

enclaves (8) distinctly bounded areas enclosed within a larger unit; ethnic
  neighborhoods within a city

reproach (10) disapproval, criticism

facility (11) ease in doing

◈ My Spanish Standoff

GABRIELLA KUNTZ

The author, a retired elementary-school teacher, lives in Cape Girardeau, Missouri.
In this selection, she explains her reasons for insisting that her children learn English.

1 ONCE AGAIN MY 17-year-old daughter comes home from a foreign-language fair at her high school and accusingly tells me about the pluses of being able to speak two languages. Speaker after speaker has **extolled** the virtues of becoming fluent in another language. My daughter is frustrated by the fact that I'm bilingual and have purposely declined to teach her to speak Spanish, my native tongue. She is not the only one who has wondered why my children don't speak Spanish. Over the years friends, acquaintances and family have asked me the same question. Teachers have asked my children. My family, of course, has been more judgmental.

2 I was born in Lima, Peru, and came to the United States for the first time in the early '50s, when I was 6 years old. At the **parochial** school my sister and I attended in Hollywood, California, there were only three Hispanic families at the time. I don't know when or how I learned English. I guess it was a matter of survival. My teacher spoke no Spanish. Neither did my classmates. All I can say is that at some point I no longer needed to translate. When I spoke in English I thought in English, and when I spoke in Spanish I thought in Spanish. I also learned about peanut-butter-and-jelly sandwiches, Halloween and Girl Scouts.

3 We went to a high school in Burbank. Again, there were few Hispanic students at the time. My sister and I spoke English without an "accent." This pleased my father to no end. He would beam with pleasure when teachers, meeting him and my mother for the first time and hearing their labored English, would comment that they had no idea English was not our native tongue.

4 My brother was born in Los Angeles in 1959, and we would speak both English and Spanish to him. When he began to talk, he would point to an object and say its name in both languages. He was, in effect, a walking, talking English-Spanish dictionary. I have often wondered how his English would have turned out, but circumstances beyond our control prevented it.

5 Because of political changes in Peru in the early '60s (my father being a diplomat), we had to return to Peru. Although we had no formal schooling in Spanish, we were able to communicate in the language. I was thankful my parents had insisted that we speak Spanish at home. At first our relatives said that we spoke Spanish with a slight accent. But over time the accent disappeared, and we became **immersed** in the culture, our culture. My brother began his schooling in Peru, and even though he attended a school in which English was taught, he speaks the language with an accent. I find that **ironic** because he was the one born in the United States, and my sister and I are the naturalized citizens.

6 In 1972 I fell in love and married an American who had been living in Peru for a number of years. Our first son was born there, but when he was 6 months old, we came back to the States. My husband was going to get his doctorate at a university in Texas.

7 It was in Texas that, for the first time, I lived in a community with many Hispanics in the United States. I encountered them at the grocery store, the laundry, the

mall, church. I also began to see how the Anglos in the community treated them. Of course, I don't mean all, but enough to make me feel uncomfortable. Because I'm dark and have dark eyes and hair, I personally experienced that look, that unspoken and spoken word expressing prejudice. If I entered a department store, one of two things was likely to happen. Either I was ignored, or I was followed closely by the salesperson. The garments I took into the changing room were carefully counted. My check at the grocery store took more scrutiny than an Anglo's. My children were complimented on how "clean" they were instead of how cute. Somehow, all Hispanics seemed to be lumped into the category of illegal immigrants, notwithstanding that many Hispanic families have lived for generations in Texas and other Southwestern states.

To be fair, I also noticed that the Latinos lived in their own **enclaves**, attended 8 their own churches, and many of them spoke English with an accent. And with their roots firmly established in the United States, their Spanish was not perfect either.

It was the fact that they spoke neither language well and the prejudice I experi- 9 enced that prompted my husband and me to decide that English, and English only, would be spoken in our house. By this time my second dark-haired, dark-eyed son had been born, and we did not want to take a chance that if I spoke Spanish to them, somehow their English would be compromised. In other words, they would have an accent. I had learned to speak English without one, but I wasn't sure they would.

When our eldest daughter was born in 1980, we were living in southeast 10 Missouri. Again, we decided on an English-only policy. If our children were going to live in the United States, then their English should be beyond **reproach**. Of course, by eliminating Spanish we have also eliminated part of their heritage. Am I sorry? About the culture, yes; about the language, no. In the Missouri Legislature, there are bills pending for some sort of English-only law. I recently read an article in a national magazine about the Ozarks where some of the townspeople are concerned about the numbers of Hispanics who have come to work in poultry plants there. It seemed to me that their "concerns" were actually prejudice. There is a definite creeping in of anti-Hispanic sentiment in this country. Even my daughter, yes, the one who is upset over not being bilingual, admits to hearing "Hispanic jokes" said in front of her at school. You see, many don't realize despite her looks, that she's a minority. I want to believe that her flawless English is a contributing factor.

Last summer I took my 10-year-old daughter to visit my brother, who is work- 11 ing in Mexico City. She picked up a few phrases and words with the **facility** that only the very young can. I just might teach her Spanish. You see, she is fair with light brown hair and blue eyes.

Comprehension Check

Purpose and Main Idea

1. What is the author's topic?
   a. the difficulty of learning languages
   b. why her children don't speak Spanish
   c. her reasons in favor of bilingual education
   d. the benefits of speaking two languages

2. Which sentence from the selection states the author's central idea?
   a. "Speaker after speaker...." paragraph 1, second sentence
   b. "My daughter is...." paragraph 1, third sentence
   c. "It was the fact that...." paragraph 9, first sentence
   d. "If our children...." paragraph 10, third sentence
3. The author's primary purpose is to
   a. express her opinion about teaching only English to her children.
   b. persuade Hispanic parents to teach their children Spanish.
   c. entertain readers with stories about her life in a South American country.
   d. inform readers about the status of bilingual education in the United States.

Details

4. The author was born in California.
   a. True
   b. False
5. In Texas, the author noticed all but which one of the following about Latinos?
   a. They spoke both English and Spanish well.
   b. They lived in their own enclaves.
   c. They all seemed to be regarded as legal immigrants.
   d. They attended their own churches.
6. The author cites all but which one of the following as examples of unspoken prejudice?
   a. Garments she took into the changing room were counted.
   b. Her checks received extra scrutiny from clerks.
   c. She was ignored in department stores.
   d. Being fluent in two languages is seen as a virtue.
7. According to the author, one drawback of not teaching her children to speak Spanish is that part of their heritage is lost.
   a. True
   b. False
8. What is the author's dominant organizational pattern?
   a. Sequence: She traces her development from childhood to the present.
   b. Process: She explains a method for teaching students to be bilingual.
   c. Comparison/contrast: She compares living in Peru with living in the United States.
   d. Cause and effect: She explains why she has chosen not to teach her children to speak Spanish.

Inferences

9. Explain the author's meaning in this sentence from paragraph 10, "There is a definite creeping in of anti-Hispanic sentiment in this country."
10. Based on your understanding of the author's viewpoint, do you think the author would support legislation requiring schools to provide bilingual instruction for Hispanic students?

Working with Words

Complete sentences 1–7 with these words from Word Alert:

immersed	parochial	extolled	ironic
reproach	facility	enclaves	

1. Everyone was amazed by the _____ with which Yvonne picked up a few Spanish phrases on the trip to Mexico sponsored by the Humanities Department.
2. Many instructors have _____ the educational benefits of international travel, such as experiencing a culture firsthand and practicing the use of new language skills.
3. In addition to religious training, _____ schools are known for their emphasis on a traditional education in the liberal arts.
4. San Francisco's Chinatown is one of the largest _____ of Asian Americans in the United States.
5. When Rochelle visited Milan, she _____ herself in that city's culture, language, and history.
6. It seems _____ that some American tourists refuse to "go native" when they are abroad, preferring to stay in American hotels and eat American food.
7. When Jane was planning to spend her junior year abroad, her parents helped her find an apartment in a neighborhood that was beyond _____ in terms of safety.

Write your own sentences, using any two of the words from Word Alert.

8. _____
9. _____

Thinking Deeper

Ideas for reflection, discussion, and writing

Make Inferences from Your Reading

1. Is English a requirement for success in the United States? Does being bilingual have advantages? Discuss your views on language as they relate to this selection. What inference can you make about the value of English worldwide?
2. The author expresses concern that by eliminating Spanish at home, she has eliminated part of her children's heritage. Does not learning a second language necessarily rob children of their culture? Discuss whether it is possible for children to learn a different language and still maintain their heritage. What could parents do to reach this goal?
3. What *is* American culture? Who are today's Americans, and how are they different from Americans of the past?
4. Do you know how many languages are spoken in the United States, or what percentage of people speak those languages? Do you know how many languages are spoken worldwide? What is the oldest language? Begin your search

by typing "English language and history" and see where it leads you. Based on your research, what conclusions can you draw about languages in the United States? Share the results of your search in a class discussion.

Write About It

5. What aspect of your culture or history would you like to pass on to your children? What would you tell them about their family background and traditions? Write about one important thing that you would like them to know and remember.
6. Write about a place you have visited that is very different from your home. Describe the place and what you learned from your experiences there.

FIRST THOUGHTS

To build background for the reading selection, answer the following questions, either on your own or in a group discussion.

1. What do you seek in a marriage partner, a career, or a place to live and make your home?
2. Are your expectations in these areas the same as or different from those of your parents?
3. Preview the title, headnote, and first one or two paragraphs. What do you think will follow?

WORD ALERT

Each word below is followed by its paragraph number. Preview the words and definitions before reading. Then review them as necessary during reading. Use context clues and your dictionary to define any additional unfamiliar words.

obeisance (2) respectful gesture or attitude

queries (5) questions

ransacked (6) searched thoroughly

mirthless (6) without cheer, unhappy

flippant (9) disrespectfully humorous or casual

rhapsodizing (12) expressing oneself in an overly enthusiastic way

compromise (14) a settlement of differences in which each side gives up something

indentured (15) bound into the service of another

vague (17) unclear

paradoxes (18) unexplainable or contradictory aspects

◈ The Good Daughter

CAROLINE HWANG

Caroline Hwang is the author of a novel, *In Full Bloom*, published in 2003. In this selection she discusses how her dreams and plans for the future differ from those of her parents.

1 THE MOMENT I WALKED into the dry-cleaning store, I knew the woman behind the counter was from Korea, like my parents. To show her that we shared a heritage, and possibly get a fellow countryman's discount, I tilted my head forward, in shy imitation of a traditional bow.

2   "Name?" she asked, not noticing my attempted **obeisance**.

3   "Hwang," I answered.

4   "Hwang? Are you Chinese?"

5   Her question caught me off-guard. I was used to hearing such **queries** from non-Asians who think all Asians all look alike, but never from one of my own people. Of course, the only Koreans I knew were my parents and their friends, people who've never asked me where I came from, since they knew better than I.

6   I **ransacked** my mind for the Korean words that would tell her who I was. It's always struck me as funny (in a **mirthless** sort of way) that I can more readily say "I am Korean" in Spanish, German and even Latin than I can in the language of my ancestry. In the end, I told her in English.

7   The dry-cleaning woman squinted as though trying to see past the glare of my strangeness, repeating my surname under her breath. "Oh, *Fxuang*," she said, doubling over with laughter. "You don't know how to speak your name."

8   I flinched. Perhaps I was particularly sensitive at the time, having just dropped out of graduate school. I had torn up my map for the future, the one that said not only where I was going but who I was. My sense of identity was already disintegrating.

9   When I got home, I called my parents to ask why they had never bothered to correct me. "Big deal," my mother said, sounding more **flippant** than I knew she intended. (Like many people who learn English in a classroom, she uses idioms that don't always fit the occasion.) "So what if you can't pronounce your name? You are American," she said.

10   Though I didn't challenge her explanation, it left me unsatisfied. The fact is, my cultural identity is hardly that clear-cut.

11   My parents immigrated to this country 30 years ago, two years before I was born. They told me often, while I was growing up, that, if I wanted to, I could be president someday, that here my grasp would be as long as my reach.

12   To ensure that I reaped all the advantages of this country, my parents saw to it that I became fully assimilated. So, like any American of my generation, I whiled away my youth strolling malls and talking on the phone, **rhapsodizing** over Andrew McCarthy's blue eyes or analyzing the meaning of a certain upper-classman's offer of a ride to the Homecoming football game.

To my parents, I am all American, and the sacrifices they made in leaving 13
Korea—including my mispronounced name—pale in comparison to the opportunities
those sacrifices gave me. They do not see that I straddle two cultures, nor that I feel
displaced in the only country I know. I identify with Americans, but Americans do
not identify with me. I've never known what it's like to belong to a community—
neither one at large, nor of an extended family. I know more about Europe than the
continent my ancestors unmistakably come from. I sometimes wonder, as I did that
day in the dry cleaner's, if I would be a happier person had my parents stayed in
Korea.

I first began to consider this thought around the time I decided to go to gradu- 14
ate school. It had been a **compromise**: my parents wanted me to go to law school;
I wanted to skip the starched-collar track and be a writer—the hungrier the better.
But after 20-some years of following their wishes and meeting all of their expectations, I couldn't bring myself to disobey or disappoint. A writing career is riskier
than the law, I remember thinking. If I'm a failure and my life is a washout, then
what does that make my parents' lives?

I know that many of my friends had to choose between pleasing their parents 15
and being true to themselves. But for the children of immigrants, the choice seems
more complicated, a happy outcome impossible. By making the biggest move of
their lives for me, my parents **indentured** me to the largest debt imaginable—I owe
them the fulfillment of their hopes for me.

It tore me up inside to suppress my dream, but I went to school for a Ph.D. in 16
English literature, thinking I had found the perfect compromise. I would be able to
write at least about books while pursuing a graduate degree. Predictably, it didn't
work out. How could I labor for five years in a program I had no passion for?
When I finally left school, my parents were disappointed, but since it wasn't what
they wanted me to do, they weren't devastated. I, on the other hand, felt I was star-
ing at the bottom of the abyss. I had seen the flaw in my life of halfwayness, in my
planned life of compromises.

I hadn't thought about my love life, but I had a **vague** plan to make concessions 17
there, too. Though they raised me as an American, my parents expect me to marry
someone Korean and give them grandchildren who look like them. This didn't seem
like such a huge request when I was 14, but now I don't know what I'm going to
do. I've never been in love with someone I dated, or dated someone I loved. (Since
I can't bring myself even to entertain the thought of marrying the non-Korean men
I'm attracted to, I've been dating only those I know I can stay clearheaded about.)
And as I near that age when the question of marriage stalks every relationship,
I can't help but wonder if my parents' expectations are responsible for the lack of
passion in my life.

My parents didn't want their daughter to be Korean, but they don't want her 18
fully American, either. Children of immigrants are living **paradoxes**. We are the first
generation and the last. We are in this country for its opportunities, yet filial duty
binds us. When my parents boarded the plane, they knew they were embarking on
a rough trip. I don't think they imagined the rocks in the path of their daughter
who can't even pronounce her own name.

Comprehension Check

Purpose and Main Idea

1. What is the author's topic?
    a. the difficulty of being a good daughter
    b. Koreans' and Americans' cultural differences
    c. problems of adjustment for immigrants
    d. family values in the Korean community
2. What is the author's central idea?
    a. Children are happiest when they choose a career that their parents approve.
    b. Having to choose between your parents' dreams and your own makes being a good daughter difficult.
    c. Children of immigrants feel displaced because they have roots in two cultures.
    d. To reap the advantages of living in the United States, immigrant children must become fully assimilated.
3. The author's primary purpose is to
    a. entertain readers with a story about a Korean family.
    b. inform readers about aspects of Korean culture.
    c. persuade readers to follow the wishes of their parents.
    d. explain why it is hard to be a good daughter.

Details

4. Among Koreans, the traditional gesture of respect is to shake hands.
    a. True
    b. False
5. The author says that she speaks all but which one of the following languages?
    a. German
    b. Spanish
    c. Chinese
    d. English
6. It was the author's dream to become a writer.
    a. True
    b. False
7. The author says that her cultural identity is not clear-cut for all but which one of the following reasons?
    a. She knows more about Europe than about the country her ancestors came from.
    b. Her parents saw to it that she became fully assimilated.
    c. She has been able to maintain her Korean culture and language.
    d. She was born in the United States, but her parents were born in Korea.
8. The author's dominant pattern in this selection is
    a. definition.
    b. contrast.
    c. process.
    d. sequence.

Inferences

9. In what way has the author been "the good daughter," as the title suggests?
10. What do you think this statement from paragraph 16 means? "I had seen the flaw in my life of halfwayness, in my planned life of compromises."

Working with Words

Complete sentences 1–10 with these words from Word Alert:

rhapsodizing	obeisance	ransacked	flippant
compromise	mirthless	queries	
indentured	paradoxes	vague	

1. Although the moon is clear and bright at night, in daylight it is only a _____ shadow of itself.
2. To bow or curtsy before the Queen of England is an act of _____.
3. Robbers _____ the house, looking for jewels or any items of value.
4. Although our guest speaker cannot stay to answer questions, the committee members will remain as long as necessary to field your _____.
5. After all your _____ about this restaurant, I certainly hope the food is as good as you say.
6. Since we each want to go to a different movie, let's _____ by seeing one of them tonight and the other next week.
7. Why some parents drink and smoke in the home yet insist that their children abstain from these habits is one of life's _____.
8. Having to fire employees because their jobs have been eliminated is a _____ task.
9. My boss's many acts of kindness made me feel _____ to him.
10. When the student's comment provoked disrespectful laughter from the class, the instructor scolded him for his _____ remark.

   Write your own sentences, using any two of the words from Word Alert.

11. _____
12. _____

Thinking Deeper

Ideas for reflection, discussion, and writing

Make Inferences from Your Reading

1. The author says that she is torn between her parents' dreams and her own. Do you think that most people would identify with this dilemma? How do sons and daughters compromise between their parents' wishes and their own?
2. In paragraph 13, the author says, "I identify with Americans, but Americans do not identify with me." What inference can you make from this statement? What do you think the author means?

3. One of our long-standing American values is that children should be free to choose their own mates, careers, and lifestyles. But immigrant parents from some cultures do not embrace this value, believing instead that parents should make these choices for their children. Conflicts result when the children of these immigrants demand more freedom of choice as an American right. What resolution to these differences do you see? In the future, do you see parents becoming more or less involved in their adult children's lives and choices?

4. To learn about the author, visit her website, carolinehwang.com. What books has she written? Where is she from? Where was she educated, and what is her working experience? What else have you learned from the website that broadens your understanding of the views expressed in the reading selection?

Write About It

5. This selection begins with an anecdote (brief story) that illustrates how the author learned something important about herself: She did not know how to pronounce her name. Relate an incident from your past that taught you something important or broadened your perspective.

6. Write about your own struggle to be a good daughter or good son.

FIRST THOUGHTS

To build background for the reading selection, answer the following questions, either on your own or in a group discussion.

1. What ideas or people come to mind when you hear the term "feminist"?
2. Do you consider yourself a feminist? Why or why not?
3. Preview the title, headnote, and first one or two paragraphs. What do you think will follow?

WORD ALERT

Each word below is followed by its paragraph number. Preview the words and definitions before reading. Then review them as necessary during reading. Use context clues and your dictionary to define any additional unfamiliar words.

feminist (2) one who believes in the social, political, and economic equality of the sexes

pondering (4) thinking, reflecting on, weighing carefully in the mind

halting (5) hesitant, reluctant, slow to speak, act, or decide

disdain (7) to reject, to treat or regard with contempt

endorse (7) approve, support

aspiration (11) a desire for achievement

sup (12) to dine, to have supper

◈ Rejecting Feminism Makes No Sense

LEONARD PITTS

Leonard Pitts is a syndicated columnist who writes about race issues and current affairs. Author of the book *Becoming Dad: Black Men and the Journey to Fatherhood*, Pitts is also the winner of the 2004 Pulitzer Prize for commentary.

1   BRACE YOURSELF. I'M going to use a word that offends folks. I'm talking the "F" word.

2   **Feminist.**

3   This woman sent me an e-mail Monday and it got me thinking. See, in describing herself, she assured me she was not "a 'women's libber'"—the late 1960s equivalent of feminist. She also said she was retired from the U.S. Navy. There was, it seemed to me, a disconnect there: She doesn't believe in women's liberation, yet she is retired from a position that liberation made possible.

4   Intrigued, I asked my 17-year-old daughter if she considers herself a feminist. She responded with a mildly horrified no. This, by the way, is the daughter with the 3.75 GPA who is presently **pondering** possible college majors including political science, psychology and ... women's studies. I asked her to define "feminist."

5   There began a **halting** explanation that seemed to suggest shrillness wrapped around obnoxiousness. Abruptly, she stopped. It's hard to explain," she said.

6   Actually, it's not. Jessica Valenti, author of *Full Frontal Feminism: A Young Woman's Guide to Why Feminism Matters,* calls it the I'm-Not-A-Feminist-But syndrome. As in the woman who says, "I'm not a feminist, but ..." and then "goes on to espouse completely feminist values. I think most women believe in access to birth control, they want equal pay for equal work, they want to fight against rape and violence against women."

7   "Feminist," it seems, has ended up in the same syntactical purgatory as another once-useful, now-reviled term: liberal. Most people **endorse** what that word has historically stood for—integration, child labor laws, product safety—yet they treat the word itself like anthrax. Similarly, while it's hard to imagine any young woman really wants to return to the days of barefoot, pregnant and making meatloaf, many now **disdain** the banner under which their gender fought for freedom. They scorn feminism even as they feast at a table feminism prepared.

8   Says Valenti, "The word has been so effectively misused and so effectively mischaracterized by conservatives for so long that women are afraid to identify with it. They'll say everything under the sun that's feminist, but they won't identify with it because they've been taught feminists are anti-men, feminists are ugly."

9   Dr. Deborah Tannen agrees. She is a professor of linguistics at Georgetown University and author of a number of books on gender and communication, including: *You're Wearing That?: Understanding Mothers and Daughters in Conversation.* "The reason, I believe, is that meanings of words come from how they're used. And since the word 'feminist' is used as a negative term rather than a positive one, people don't want to be associated with it."

With apologies to Malcolm X, they've been had, they've been hoodwinked, 10 they've been bamboozled. And it's sad. I've lost track of how many times, visiting high schools or teaching college classes, I have met bright girls juggling options and freedoms that would've been unthinkable a generation ago, smart young women preparing for lives and careers their foremothers could not have dreamt, yet if you use the "F" word, they recoil.

We have, I think, lost collective memory of how things were before the F-word. 11 Of the casual beatings. Of casual rape. Of words like "old maid" and "spinster." Of abortion by coat hanger. Of going to school to find a man. Of getting an allowance and needing a husband's permission. Of taking all your spirit, all your dreams, all your ambition, **aspiration**, creativity, and pounding them down until they fit a space no larger than a casserole dish.

"I'm not a feminist, but…?" That's a fraud. It's intellectually dishonest. And it's 12 a slap to the feminists who prepared the table at which today's young women **sup**.

So for the record, I am a feminist. My daughter is, too. 13

She doesn't know it yet. 14

Comprehension Check

Purpose and Main Idea

1. What is the author's topic?
   a. women's rights
   b. liberalism versus conservatism
   c. feminism
   d. gender
2. Which sentence best states the author's central idea?
   a. A person can be a feminist and not know it.
   b. "Feminist" is a word that offends people..
   c. Conservatives have defined feminism.
   d. It makes no sense to reject feminism.
3. What is the author's *primary* purpose?
   a. to express dismay at those who reject feminism
   b. to inform readers about what feminists have accomplished
   c. to define what it means to be a feminist
   d. to entertain us by raising questions about feminism

Details

4. According to the author, some women who believe in the things feminists fought for are hesitant to call themselves feminists/
   a. True
   b. False
5. Deborah Tannen describes the "I'm-not-a-feminist-but syndrome."
   a. True
   b. False

6. According to the author, the use of terms like "old maid" and "spinster" is which one of the following?
   a. an effect of feminism
   b. an example of feminist jargon
   c. a political statement
   d. a reflection of pre-feminist times
7. Dr. Tannen calls "feminist" a _____ term.
   a. negative
   b. positive
   c. neutral
   d. meaningless
8. What is the organizational pattern in paragraph 7?
   a. cause and effect
   b. comparison and contrast
   c. generalization then example
   d. division and classification

Inferences

9. Why does the author think that it is intellectually dishonest to reject feminism?
10. Reflect on your answers to questions 1 and 2 in First Thoughts. Have your views stayed the same? Has reading Pitt's article changed your views or expanded your knowledge? Whatever your answer, explain your reasoning.

Working with Words

Complete sentences 1–7 with these words from Word Alert:

aspiration   feminist   endorse   sup
pondering   halting   disdain

1. At Thanksgiving, we _____ on traditional foods that are homemade.
2. Why would a young woman be offended when called a _____?
3. People of opposing political viewpoints are likely to _____ each other's arguments.
4. Raymond spent the whole afternoon _____ a topic for his research paper.
5. Politically active students are quick to _____ their candidates' policies.
6. In a _____ voice, the nervous student gave a speech to the class.
7. Cynthia's greatest _____ was to be a physical therapist.

Write your own sentences, using any two of the words from Word Alert.

8. _____
9. _____

Thinking Deeper

Ideas for reflection, discussion, and writing

Make Inferences from Your Reading

1. One of the experts quoted in this selection says that the meanings of words come from how they are used. For example, a word might take on a new meaning or develop positive or negative connotations, or associations, that are different from its dictionary definition. What word can you think of that follows this pattern? What is its dictionary meaning versus its connotation?

2. The author uses several food images to make his point. See paragraph 7, sentences 3 and 4; paragraph 11, last sentence; and paragraph 12, last sentence. What purpose can you infer from these images, and do you think the images are effective?

3. Women's rights and roles have changed with the times and so has our understanding of what it means to be a feminist. Share with the class the story of a woman in your family who defied traditional roles to work outside the home or pursue a career in what was regarded as a "male" profession. What inference can you make about the quality of women's and men's lives in the future as a result of feminism?

4. Leonard Pitts is a frequent commentator on culture and society. Find another of his essays on a theme of social change, feminism, or gender roles, read it, and prepare to discuss in class what you have learned. Begin your search at http://www.who2.com, where you can link to a biography of Pitt and an archive of his columns. Remember that sites and their content change frequently, so ask your librarian for a URL or other source if you have trouble finding the essay.

Write About It

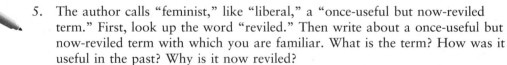

5. The author calls "feminist," like "liberal," a "once-useful but now-reviled term." First, look up the word "reviled." Then write about a once-useful but now-reviled term with which you are familiar. What is the term? How was it useful in the past? Why is it now reviled?

6. Write about one of your dreams or aspirations and what you are doing to achieve it.

FIRST THOUGHTS

To build background for the reading selection, answer the following questions, either on your own or in a group discussion.

1.   Speaking from your own experience, are boys and girls treated differently in school?
2.   When you were growing up, did you ever think that your gender kept you from doing or accomplishing something you wanted?
3.   Preview the title, headnote, and first one or two paragraphs. What do you think will follow?

WORD ALERT

Each word below is followed by its paragraph number. Preview the words and definitions before reading. Then review them as necessary during reading. Use context clues and your dictionary to define any additional unfamiliar words.

plummet (1) to decline suddenly or steeply, plunge
rambunctious (2) boisterous and disorderly; noisy and undisciplined
mired (4) stuck, entangled, trapped
spate (6) a sudden flood, rush, or outpouring
rash (8) outbreak of events within a brief time
rhetoric (10) pretentious, insincere, intellectually vacant language
scoffs (10) ridicules, mocks
inclusiveness (11) the state of taking in all or everything in its scope
advocates (13) supporters of a cause

◈ Beyond the Gender Myths

MARGOT HORNBLOWER

In this selection from *Time*, the author questions whether boys and girls have special needs and suggests a different focus for today's parents and educators.

GIRLS TODAY ARE in trouble. They lose confidence in early adolescence. Their grades 1 **plummet,** and, following sexual stereotypes, their interest in math and science flags. They are plagued by eating disorders, suffer depression, get pregnant, attempt suicide. And it all makes headlines, spawns research projects and prompts calls for single-sex education.

Boys today are in trouble too. They are locked into rigid classroom routines 2 before they are ready; their **rambunctious** behavior, once thought normal, is now labeled pathological, with such diagnoses as attention-deficit disorder and hyperactivity. They lose self-esteem and lag behind girls in reading and writing—erupting in violent behavior, killing themselves more often than girls. It all makes headlines, spawns research projects and prompts calls for remedial measures.

What's a parent to think? 3

Mired in the sociology, education theory and hype surrounding "gender eq- 4 uity," we sometimes overlook the common humanity of children: what they share and how they differ, regardless of gender. "The focus on girls has translated into the notion that somehow if you help girls, you hurt boys," says Susan Bailey, executive director of the Wellesley Centers for Women. "People want a quick fix, but there is no one-size-fits-all solution for either girls or boys."

It was Bailey's 1992 report, *How Schools Shortchange Girls*, that sparked a na- 5 tional hand-wringing epidemic over the plight of adolescent girls—especially their loss of interest in math and science. Financed by the American Association of University Women, the report surveyed a decade of research and concluded that teachers paid less attention to girls than boys, that textbooks reinforced sexual stereotypes and that college-entrance tests favored boys. A year later, another study documented widespread sexual harassment in schools.

A **spate** of books such as Peggy Orenstein's *Schoolgirls: Young Women, Self-* 6 *Esteem and the Confidence Gap* and Mary Pipher's *Reviving Ophelia*, which spent nearly three years on best-seller lists, triggered a surge of creative solutions. A corporate-sponsored program, Take Our Daughters to Work Day, spread across the U.S. in an effort to encourage girls to examine varied careers. In Lincoln, Nebraska, teacher Jane Edwards partners with a local architectural firm to challenge high school girls to use technology, math and science to solve design problems. In Aurora, Colorado, middle school teacher Pam Schmidt has created Eocene Park, a paleontology field school that encourages girls to explore this traditionally male-dominated science.

More controversial has been a renewed interest in segregation. Enrollment in 7 private and religious schools for girls rose more than 15% between 1991 and

1997. New girls' schools were founded, including the public Young Women's Leadership Academy in New York City's Harlem, which is currently under challenge as unconstitutional in a complaint lodged with the U.S. Department of Education. In California, Massachusetts, Virginia, Nebraska and Oklahoma, local school districts began experimenting with single-sex classrooms.

8   Predictably, the renewed attention to girls has sparked a backlash. Parents are demanding that their sons be included in Take Our Daughters to Work Day. A surge of new books, such as Michael Gurian's *A Fine Young Man* and William Pollack's *Real Boys*, focuses on boys' emotional crises and academic problems in reading and writing. Researchers are exploring not just sexual harassment of girls but bullying and teasing of boys. A **rash** of school shootings by boys has brought calls to cut back on violent video games and provide more in-school counseling. And parents are objecting to certain excesses: "Is it really fair," wrote Kathleen Parker, a columnist for the *Orlando Sentinel*, "that one of [my son's] feminist teachers refuses even to use male pronouns, referring to all students as 'shes' and all work as 'hers'?"

9   Pollack, a clinical psychologist who teaches at Harvard Medical School, says most schools are failing boys by forcing them into an "educational straitjacket." Elementary schools lack male teachers, "sending a message to boys that learning is primarily for girls." Young boys, he claims, learn at different tempos, and perhaps the cutoff birth month for starting school should be later for boys than for girls. Once there, boys should be allowed to move around more, taking short recesses when they are restless. They should be able to use computers rather than be forced to write by hand before their small-motor skills are developed. Noting that boys constitute 71% of school suspensions and are less likely to go to college than girls (58% vs. 67%), he says, "Boys' self-esteem as learners is more at risk than that of girls."

10   Are things as bad as some say? Or has the emotionally charged **rhetoric** used by gender-equity theorists overstated the problem? A report last March found no evidence that girls improve their academic performance or their emotional health in single-sex settings. What helps girls is what helps boys: smaller classes, a demanding curriculum and encouragement regardless of gender. In the past decade, the gender gap for math and science, such as it was, has narrowed to the point of statistical irrelevance. Overall, males have somewhat higher standardized math and science test scores, while females have slightly higher school grades. Girls and boys are taking about the same math and science courses in high school, but boys are more likely to take advanced-placement courses in chemistry and physics. Girls are slightly more likely to take AP biology. Patricia Campbell, an education researcher in Groton, Massachusetts, **scoffs** at the notion of "opposite" sexes with different learning styles. "When you just know somebody's gender, you don't know anything about their academic skills or interests," she says. "The stereotypes of girls being collaborative and boys competitive, of girls being into relationships and boys into numbers—that's laughable."

11   Campbell researched the techniques of math and science teachers in three states and found that those who were successful with both boys and girls shared common traits:

- They allowed no disrespect: teachers did not put down students, and students did not make fun of one another.

- They used more than one instruction method—lectures, small-group work, diagrams, peer tutoring—so that kids who learn better with one strategy rather than another were not left behind.
- They divided their attention equally among students, refusing to let a small group monopolize discussion. "Research shows that unless specific action is taken, four to seven people tend to dominate any group," she says. "In a coed class, more of the attention getters may be boys, but a lot of boys, as well as girls, are left out. A single-sex class does not change the pattern—only deliberate **inclusiveness** works for everyone."

Gurian, a Spokane, Wash., therapist who has written two books on boys, notes 12 that four adolescent males drop out of school for every one adolescent female. Among his prescriptions for helping our sons: provide them with mentors; provide twice as much emotional nurturing—spending time with them, developing family rituals, giving them new freedoms and responsibilities; restrict TV, video games and movies. Strikingly, these recommendations are precisely what our daughters need too.

Where boys' and girls' **advocates** generally agree is on the destructive nature 13 of gender stereotyping. If girls are urged to catch up in math and join ice-hockey teams, boys should be encouraged to write poetry and take dance classes without being labeled sissies. Parents can enhance gender-neutral self-esteem by suggesting that a daughter help fix a leaky pipe—or a son whip up an omelet. "A little girl who says she wants to be a doctor gets a lot of support," says Bailey, whose Wellesley Centers are devoting their next gender-equity conference to boys. "But if a boy talks about wanting to be a nurse, the reaction is that it doesn't fit a masculine image. Parents and teachers need to foster an environment where sexual stereotypes don't shape education."

If that ever happens, headline writers and social scientists can stop arguing 14 about which sex is least favored, and teachers can concentrate on paying more nuanced attention to our children as individuals, for that is what they are.

Comprehension Check

Purpose and Main Idea

1. What is the author's topic?
   a. education
   b. equal rights
   c. gender myths
   d. raising children
2. Which of the following statements best expresses the author's central idea?
   a. Boys and girls today are in trouble because of gender stereotyping.
   b. Educators have shown a renewed interest in segregation of boys and girls.
   c. Sociologists and others overlook the common humanity of children.
   d. A backlash has resulted from a renewed attention to girls.
3. The author's *primary* purpose is to
   a. inform readers of the various gender myths.
   b. entertain readers by exposing some of the mistakes researchers have made.
   c. explain how educators meet the needs of children.
   d. persuade readers that children should be treated as individuals.

Details

4. During early adolescence, girls are in trouble because they are prone to violence and hyperactivity.
   a. True
   b. False
5. Boys are in trouble for all but which one of the following reasons, according to the author?
   a. They lag behind girls in reading and writing.
   b. Their rambunctious behavior is labeled pathological.
   c. They are locked into rigid classroom routines before they are ready.
   d. They are plagued by eating disorders and suffer from depression.
6. Boys' and girls' advocates agree on which one of the following?
   a. Parents cannot enhance self-esteem.
   b. Gender stereotyping is destructive.
   c. Stereotypes should shape education.
   d. Nursing does not fit a masculine image.
7. According to the author, both boys and girls benefit from a demanding curriculum.
   a. True
   b. False
8. What is the author's *dominant* pattern in this selection?
   a. The author explains a *process* for eliminating gender stereotyping.
   b. The term *gender myth* is *defined*.
   c. Theories about boys' and girls' characteristics and behaviors are *compared*.
   d. Students are *classified* by gender.

Inferences

9. What kind of classroom environment do you think Patricia Campbell would be most likely to support?
10. Do you think that the author would agree or disagree with the feminist saying "a woman needs a man like a fish needs a bicycle," and why?

Working with Words

Complete sentences 1–9 with these words from Word Alert:

inclusiveness	rhetoric	scoffs	mired	rash
rambunctious	advocates	plummet	spate	

1. I'd like to go to the party tonight, but I'm _____ so deep in assignments that I have to get some studying done.
2. Medora liked the _____ of the student government organization, which encouraged all students to participate.
3. After watching his grades _____, Al decided to buckle down and crack the books.
4. Voters are tired of politicians' _____ and wish candidates would speak honestly and directly.
5. We've had a _____ of rain this week that has caused flooding in some areas.

6. _____ of free speech resist all attempts at censorship, whether of books, movies, or the Internet.
7. My friend, who does not believe I am serious about losing weight, _____ at my attempts to diet and exercise.
8. Police in my neighborhood have cracked down on speeders, following a _____ of accidents during the last two weeks.
9. Some children who are normally _____ may be mistakenly labeled hyperactive.

Write your own sentences, using any two of the words from Word Alert.

10. _____
11. _____

Thinking Deeper

Ideas for reflection, discussion, and writing

Make Inferences from Reading

1. Identify and discuss the gender myths that this author thinks we should get beyond. What are these myths, and what evidence of them have you seen, either in your early school years or in the present?
2. In paragraph 11, the author lists the traits that Campbell found successful teachers share. Discuss these traits. Do they seem characteristic of the good teachers you have known? What examples or instances can you cite that illustrate the opposite behaviors? What additional traits or techniques can you think of that would help teachers encourage the best in every student, regardless of gender?
3. What inference can you make about the future influence of gender myths on the way boys and girls are treated in school? Do you expect sexual stereotyping to continue, or do you think we are more likely to treat children as individuals as the twenty-first century develops? As a parent, or future parent, do you believe that your children's opportunities will be much affected by the way they are treated in school?
4. Do more men or women enroll in college today? Do more men or women graduate from college? What percentage of women versus men enter the professions of law and medicine? To find out, do an Internet search. Your instructor or librarian can suggest sites to try or ways to begin your search. Based on your answers to these questions, what inference can you make about the effects of gender myths or gender stereotyping in higher education?

Write About It

5. Reflect on Selections 7 and 8, which both deal with feminist themes. What similarities or differences do you see in the authors' topics, purposes, and viewpoints? Write a paragraph or short essay in which you compare the two reading selections.
6. Were you always treated fairly in school? Write about an early school experience that has had a positive or negative effect on your life.

FIRST THOUGHTS

To build background for the reading selection, answer the following questions, either on your own or in a group discussion.

1. Do you live near a forest, or have you ever gone for a walk in the woods?
2. Have you ever been in a situation where you had to make a choice, not knowing what the consequences would be?
3. Preview the title, headnote, and first one or two paragraphs. What do you think will follow?

WORD ALERT

Each word below is followed by its line number. Preview the words and definitions before reading. Then review them as necessary during reading. Use context clues and your dictionary to define any additional unfamiliar words.

diverged (1) extended in different directions from the same point
undergrowth (5) low-growing plants and shrubs
claim (7) a right to
trodden (12) past participle of tread, meaning trampled or walked on
hence (17) from this time, from now

◈ The Road Not Taken

ROBERT FROST

Robert Frost (1874–1963) is a celebrated American poet and the only poet who has ever won four Pulitzer Prizes for his work. The author of hundreds of poems, Frost served as Consultant in Poetry at the Library of Congress. Some of his most famous poems include "Birches," "Stopping by Woods on a Snowy Evening," and "The Road Not Taken."

Two Roads diverged in a yellow wood,	1
And sorry I could not travel both	2
And be one traveler, long I stood	3
And looked down one as far as I could	4
To where it bent in the undergrowth;	5
Then took the other, as just as fair,	6
And having perhaps the better claim,	7
Because it was grassy and wanted wear;	8
Though as for that, the passing there	9
Had worn them really about the same,	10
And both that morning equally lay	11
In leaves no step had trodden black.	12
Oh, I kept the first for another day!	13
Yet knowing how way leads on to way,	14
I doubted if I should ever come back.	15
I shall be telling this with a sigh	16
Somewhere ages and ages hence:	17
Two roads diverged in a wood, and I—	18
I took the one less traveled by,	19
And that has made all the difference.	20

Comprehension Check

Purpose and Main Idea

1. What is the author's topic?
   a. the benefits of walking
   b. two roads
   c. the forest as a pleasant place
   d. a destination
2. From which line(s) can the author's central idea best be inferred?
   a. line 1
   b. line 13
   c. lines 14 and 15
   d. lines 18 through 20
3. The author's *primary* purpose is to
   a. *express* a viewpoint
   b. *describe* a scene

c. *inform* or teach
d. *persuade* readers

Details

4. Both roads are beaten down by the feet of many travelers
    a. True
    b. False
5. In this poem, what season of the year is it?
    a. summer
    b. fall
    c. winter
    d. spring
6. According to the speaker both roads
    a. wanted wear.
    b. were thick with undergrowth.
    c. were covered in leaves.
    d. went untraveled.
7. The poem's speaker took the grassy road.
    a. True
    b. False
8. The details in this poem are organized by which one of the following?
    a. process
    b. cause and effect
    c. generalization and example
    d. comparison and contrast

Inferences

9. What meaning do you infer for the word "fair" in line 6? First look up "fair" in your dictionary; then choose the meaning that best fits the context in line 6.
10. What is the poem's central idea? Write a main idea statement to share with the class.

Working with Words

Complete sentences 1–5 with these words from Word Alert:

undergrowth	trodden	claim
diverged	hence	

1. Between the student center and the parking lot, there is a well- _____ pathway through the grass.
2. The hiker's legs were scratched by thorns in the _____ that covered the forest floor.
3. Do you find it difficult to keep your mind on studying when a friend makes a _____ on your attention.

4. Two friends whose political views _____ were always getting into heated arguments.

5. Your grandparents would never have dreamed of the advances in technology to come in the years _____ .

Write your own sentences, using any two of the words from Word Alert.

6. _____

7. _____

Thinking Deeper

Ideas for reflection, discussion, and writing

Make Inferences from Your Reading

1. On a literal level, Frost's poem is about the consequences of choosing one of two roads leading into the woods. What deeper meaning can you infer from the poem? What other choices in life might this poem address?

2. Read again the last three lines. What meaning do you infer from these lines? Does the speaker regret not taking the other road? What is the "difference" that choosing one road over another has made, do you think?

3. What is your reaction to Frost's poem. On an emotional level, how does the poem make you feel? What specific words arouse your feelings? On an intellectual level, what ideas or images in the poem can you relate to your own experience?

4. Based on your reading of "The Road Not Taken" and any other Frost poems that you may have read, what can you infer about this poet's topics or themes? If you need to see more examples, search the Internet for sites that will let you access some of Frost's poems. Begin your search by typing the poet's name, or ask your instructor or librarian to suggest appropriate websites and URLs. Two sites to try are agonia.net and poetryhunter.com.

Write About It

5. Do you have a favorite place in nature such as the woods, the mountains, or a beach? Describe your favorite place and what it means to you.

6. Write about your own "road not taken" or a choice you had to make and its consequences.

altogether: 20 million people identified themselves simply as "American," up more than 50 percent since 1990.

4   During the 1990s, the population of people of color grew twelve times as fast as the white population, fueled by immigration and birth rates. The Latino population alone more than doubled. By 2003, Latinos moved past African Americans to become the second largest ethnic or racial group in the nation (after non-Hispanic whites), making the United States the fifth largest "Latino" country in the world (see Figure 33.3). Immigration from Asia also remained high, and in 2000 people of Asian ancestry made up 3.6 percent of the U.S. population.

5   These rapid demographic changes have altered the face of America. At a Dairy Queen in the far southern suburbs of Atlanta, six miles from the "Gone with the Wind Historical District," teenage children of immigrants from India and Pakistan serve Blizzards and Mister Mistys. In the small town of Ligonier, Indiana, the formerly empty main street now boasts three Mexican restaurants and a Mexican western-wear shop; Mexican immigrants drawn by plentiful industrial jobs in the 1990s cross paths with the newest immigrants, Yemenis, some in traditional dress, and with Amish families riding horse-drawn buggies. Even so, more than half of American counties were still at least 85 percent white in 2000—and more than half of all Latinos lived in just eight metropolitan areas.

A MORE DIVERSE CULTURE

6   American popular culture embraced the influences of this new multiethnic population. Economics were important: the buying power of the growing Latino population exceeded $561 billion in 2000, and average income for Asian American

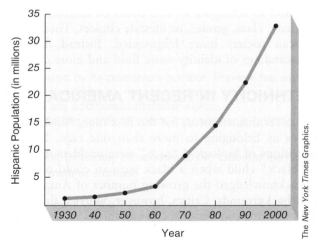

FIGURE 33.3 | THE GROWTH OF THE UNITED STATES HISPANIC POPULATION

"Hispanic" combines people from a wide variety of national origins or ancestries—including all the nations of Central and South America, Mexico, Cuba, Puerto Rico, the Dominican Republic, Spain—as well as those who identify as Californio, Tejano, Nuevo Mexicano, and Mestizo.

households topped all other groups. But American audiences also crossed racial and ethnic lines. Superstar Jennifer Lopez (of Puerto Rican descent) was the most "bankable" musician/actress in the nation; black basketball great Michael Jordan had more commercial endorsements than any other celebrity in America's history. Latin dancing styles swept the club scene; white teens in the nation's suburbs took up urban rap and hip-hop culture. Golfer Tiger Woods became a symbol of this new, hybrid, multiethnic nation: of African, European, Native American, Thai, and Chinese descent, he calls himself "Cablinasian" (CAucasian-BLack-INdian-ASIAN).

THE CHANGING AMERICAN FAMILY

Americans were divided over the meaning of other changes, as well—especially the   7
changing shape of American families (see Figure 33.4). The number of people living together without marriage jumped 72 percent during the 1990s, to 5.5 million. Of those, at least 600,000 were same-sex couples—perhaps 1 percent of households nationwide. A third of female-partner households and one-fifth of male-partner households had children, and in 2002 the American Academy of Pediatrics. endorsed adoption by gay couples. A vocal antigay movement coexisted with rising support for the legal equality of gay, lesbian, transgendered, and bisexual Americans. While many states and private corporations extended domestic-partner benefits to gay couples, the federal Defense of Marriage Act, passed by Congress in 1996, defined marriage as "only" a union between one man and one woman.

More children were born outside marriage than ever before—almost a third of   8
all children, and more than two-thirds of those born to African American women. Mothers of small children commonly worked outside the home, and in the majority of married-couple families with children under eighteen, both parents held jobs. The divorce rate stayed high; statistically, a couple that married in the late 1990s had about a 50–50 chance of divorce. While almost a third of families with children had only one parent present—usually the mother—children also lived in blended families created by second marriages, or moved back and forth between households of parents who had joint custody.

NEW TECHNOLOGIES AND NEW CHALLENGES

Increasingly, new reproductive technologies allowed infertile women or couples   9
to conceive and bear children. In 2000, more than 100,000 attempted in vitro fertilizations—in which sperm and egg combine in a sterile dish or test tube and the fertilized egg or eggs are then transferred to the uterus—resulted in the birth of more than 35,000 babies. From the beginning, such techniques have raised legal and ethical questions. What are the comparable rights and responsibilities of sperm and egg donors, the woman who carries the fetus, and male and female prospective parents? At the same time, the children these new technologies made possible have brought joy to many families.

This rapidly developing field of biogenetics offers even more possibilities for   10
good, and also even knottier philosophical and ethical conundrums. The five- or six-cell blastocytes formed by the initial division of fertilized eggs during in vitro

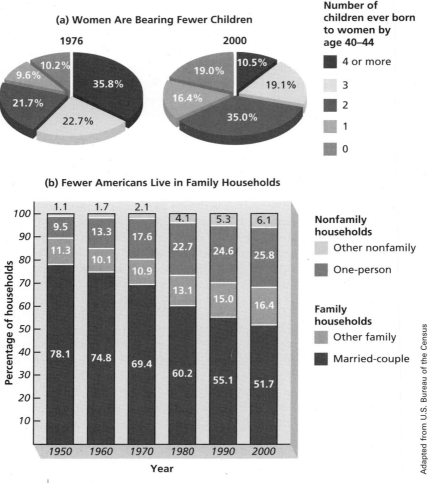

(a) Women Are Bearing Fewer Children

1976

1976: 10.2%, 9.6%, 35.8%, 21.7%, 22.7%

2000

2000: 10.5%, 19.0%, 19.1%, 16.4%, 35.0%

Number of children ever born to women by age 40–44

- 4 or more
- 3
- 2
- 1
- 0

(b) Fewer Americans Live in Family Households

Nonfamily households
- Other nonfamily
- One-person

Family households
- Other family
- Married-couple

Adapted from U.S. Bureau of the Census

Percentage of households

Year	Married-couple	Other family	One-person	Other nonfamily
1950	78.1	11.3	9.5	1.1
1960	74.8	10.1	13.3	1.7
1970	69.4	10.9	17.6	2.1
1980	60.2	13.1	22.7	4.1
1990	55.1	15.0	24.6	5.3
2000	51.7	16.4	25.8	6.1

FIGURE 33.4 | THE CHANGING AMERICAN FAMILY

American households became smaller in the latter part of the twentieth century, as more people lived alone and women had, on average, fewer children.

procedures contain stem cells, unspecialized cells that can be induced to become cells with specialized functions. For example, stem cells might become insulin-producing cells of the pancreas—and thus a cure for diabetes; or they might become dopamine-producing neurons, offering therapy for Parkinson's disease, a progressive disorder of the nervous system affecting over 1 million Americans. President Bush, in 2001, acknowledged the "tremendous hope" promised by this research but called embryonic stem cell research "the leading edge of a series of moral hazards," including the possibility of cloning humans for spare body parts. In a highly controversial decision, Bush limited federally funded research to the existing seventy-eight stem cell lines, not all of which are **viable** for research.

TABLE 33.1 | U.S. MILITARY PERSONNEL ON ACTIVE DUTY IN FOREIGN COUNTRIES, 2001[1]

Region/Country[2]	Personnel	Region/Country	Personnel
United States and Territories		Singapore	160
Continental U.S.	947,955	Thailand	114
Alaska	15,926	**North Africa, Near East,**	
Hawaii	33,191	**and South Asia**	
Guam	3,398	Bahrain	1,280
Puerto Rico	2,525	Diego Garcia	537
Europe		Egypt	665
Belgium*	1,554	Israel	38
Bosnia and Herzegovina	3,109	Kuwait	4,300
France*	70	Oman	560
Germany*	71,434	Qatar	72
Greece*	526	Saudi Arabia	4,802
Greenland*	153	United Arab Emirates	207
Iceland*	1,713	**Sub-Saharan Africa**	
Italy*	11,854	Kenya	50
Macedonia	346	South Africa	30
Netherlands*	696	**Western Hemisphere**	
Norway*	187	Brazil	40
Portugal*	992	Canada	165
Russia	88	Chile	30
Serbia (includes Kosovo)	5,200	Colombia	59
Spain*	1,778	Cuba (Guantanamo)	461
Turkey*	2,170	Honduras	426
United Kingdom*	11,361	Peru	40
East Asia and Pacific		Venezuela	30
Australia	188	Total foreign countries[2]	255,065
China (includes Hong Kong)	54	Ashore	212,262
Indonesia (includes Timor)	48	Afloat	42,803
Japan	39,691	Total worldwide[2]	1,384,812
Korea, Rep. of	37,972	Ashore	1,242,524
Philippines	31	Afloat	142,288

*NATO countries

[1] Only countries with 30 or more U.S. military personnel are listed.

[2] Includes all regions/countries, not simply those listed.

Source: U.S. Department of Defense. *Selected Manpower Statistics*, Annual

CENTURY OF CHANGE

For middle-aged and older Americans, the stem cell debate was another indicator of the rapid pace of scientific advancement during their lifetime. The twentieth century had seen more **momentous** change than any previous century: change for better; change for worse; change that brought enormous benefits to human beings; change that threatened the very existence of the human species. Research in the physical and biological sciences had greatly broadened horizons and had provided deep insight into the structure of matter and of the universe. Technology—the application of science—had made startling advances that benefited tens of millions of Americans in nearly every aspect of life: better health, more wealth, more mobility, less drudgery, greater access to information.

12   As a result, Americans at the start of the new century were more connected to the rest of humankind. This interconnectivity of people was perhaps the most powerful product of globalization. A commodities trader in Chicago in March 2003 could send an e-mail to his fiancée in Tokyo while he spoke on the phone to a trader in Frankfurt and kept one eye on CNN's real-time coverage of the air war over Baghdad; within a minute or two he could receive a reply from his fiancée saying she missed him too. If he felt sufficiently lovesick, he could board an airplane and be in Japan the following day.

13   The world had shrunk to the size of an airplane ticket. In 1955, 51 million people a year traveled by plane. By the turn of the century 1.6 billion were airborne every year, and 530 million crossed international borders—or about 1.5 million each day. For our Chicago trader and for millions of other Americans, this **permeability** of national boundaries brought many benefits, as did the integration of markets and the global spread of information that occurred alongside it.

INFECTIOUS DISEASES

14   But there was a flip side to this growing connectivity that even many advocates of globalization perceived. For one thing, whereas people still needed passports and sometimes visas to travel from one country to another, infectious diseases did not. The rapid increase in international air travel was a particularly potent force for global disease **dissemination**, as flying made it possible for people to reach the other side of the world in far less time than the incubation period for many ailments. Thus in early 2003, a respiratory illness known as severe acute respiratory syndrome (SARS) spread from Guangdong Province of China to Hong Kong to various other countries in the world, chiefly via air passengers who **unwittingly** carried the disease in their lungs. Public health officials also warned that increased human mobility promised more trade in illegal products and contaminated foodstuffs, with negative implications for the world's population.

15   Environmental degradation was another powerful contributor to pressing global health threats. In 2003, the World Health Organization (WHO) estimated that nearly a quarter of the global burden of disease and injury was related to environmental disruption and decline. For example, some 90 percent of diarrheal diseases (such as cholera), which were killing 3 million people a year, resulted from contaminated water. WHO also pointed to globalization and environmental disruption as contributing to the fact that, in the final two decades of the twentieth century, more than thirty infectious diseases were identified in humans for the first time— including AIDS, Ebola virus, hantavirus, and hepatitis C and E. Environmentalists, meanwhile, continued to insist that the growing interaction of national economies was having a **deleterious** impact on the ecosystem through climate change, ozone depletion, hazardous waste, and damage to fisheries.

INTERNATIONAL RESPONSE TO DISEASE

But if the interaction between national economies and the rapid increase in person- 16
to-person contacts were responsible for many health and other problems, they also
were essential in mobilizing the world to find solutions. Whereas it took centuries to
identify the cause of cholera and two years to identify the virus that caused AIDS, in
the case of SARS, thirteen labs in ten countries put everything else aside and in a
matter of weeks determined that the coronavirus was responsible. Within a month,
laboratories from Vancouver to Atlanta to Singapore had mapped the **genome**,
whereupon efforts to devise a diagnostic test for the virus began. Thus although the
disease spread internationally with unprecedented speed, so did the response. Speed
of communication allowed for a coordinated international effort at finding the cause
of SARS and also allowed individual countries, including the United States, to adopt
measures that succeeded, in the early months at least, in keeping the epidemic out.

Even in the interconnected world of the new millennium, then, national borders 17
still mattered. There were limits to their permeability. In the wake of 9/11, indeed,
the process of integration was to some degree reversed. To prevent future terrorist
attacks, the United States and other countries imposed tighter security measures on
air travelers, imported goods, immigration, and information flows. Some economists predicted these measures would stall the global movement toward integration
of markets; in the short term they certainly did, but the long-term outlook was less
clear. Trade and investment shrank in 2001, but they were falling before September
11 as a result of economic slowdowns in the world's biggest economies, including
the United States, Europe, and Japan. Moreover, the falloff in international economic activity in the months after the attacks was not massive.

CONFRONTING TERRORISM

In military and diplomatic terms, though, 9/11 made a deep and lasting impression. 18
The attacks that day brought home what Americans had only dimly perceived before then: that globalization had shrunk the natural buffers that distance and two
oceans provided the United States. Al Qaeda, it was clear, had used the increasingly
open, integrated, globalized world to give themselves new power and reach. They
had shown that small cells of terrorists could become true transnational threats—
thriving around the world without any single state sponsor or home base. According to American intelligence, Al Qaeda operated in more than ninety countries—
including the United States.

How would one go about vanquishing such a foe? Was a decisive victory even 19
possible? These remained open questions two years after the World Trade Center
collapsed. Unchallenged militarily and seeing no rival great power, the United States
no longer felt constrained from intervening in sensitive areas like the Middle East or
Central Asia should national security interests demand it. Yet the nation took little
comfort from this superiority. It continued to spend vast sums on its military, more
indeed than the next twenty-five nations combined. (In 2003, the Pentagon spent
about $400 billion, or roughly $50 million dollars per hour.) America had taken on
military commitments all over the globe, from the Balkans and Iraq to Afghanistan
and Korea. Its armed forces looked colossal, but its obligations looked even larger.

Comprehension Check

Purpose and Main Idea

1. What is the author's topic?
   a. American life today
   b. Americans in the new millennium
   c. the new millennium
   d. twenty-first-century trends
2. Which one of the following best states the central idea?
   a. Some have argued that September 11, 2001, was the real beginning of the twenty-first century.
   b. Changes in population and demographics are characteristic of the new millennium.
   c. From television shows to lifestyles, twenty-first-century changes have fragmented our society.
   d. Twenty-first-century Americans not only are more diverse but also face new challenges and possibilities.
3. The authors' *primary* purpose is to:
   a. broaden your understanding of who Americans are now and where they are headed in the new millennium.
   b. provoke an emotional reaction to twenty-first-century challenges to the American family and national security.
   c. express their own views about national and global developments in the new millennium.
   d. make the case that in every century people will regard some development as good and some as bad.

Details

4. Population growth among people of color is mainly due to immigration and birth rates.
   a. True
   b. False
5. "At a Dairy Queen in the far southern suburbs of Atlanta ... teenage children of immigrants from India and Pakistan serve Blizzards and Mister Mistys." The author uses this example to support which one of the following general ideas?
   a. Immigrants have settled in all parts of the United States.
   b. Demographic changes have altered the face of America.
   c. Fast-food restaurants are equal-opportunity employers.
   d. Employment opportunities for American teenagers are few.
6. During the 1990s, approximately how many children were born outside of marriage?
   a. one-third of all children
   b. two-thirds of all children
   c. half of all children
   d. more than half of all children

7. The authors cite biogenetics as "the most powerful product of globalization."
    a. True
    b. False
8. What is the authors' *dominant* organizational pattern?
    a. sequence
    b. comparison
    c. cause and effect
    d. generalization and example

Inferences

9. Explain in your own words what the authors mean by this statement from paragraph 13: "The world had shrunk to the size of an airplane ticket."
10. According to the authors, "For middle-aged and older Americans, the stem cell debate was another indicator of the rapid pace of scientific advancement during their lifetime." What is one indicator of rapid scientific advancement in *your* lifetime?

Working with Words

Complete sentences 1–10 with these words from Word Alert:

proliferation	homogenizing	permeability	momentous	viable
dissemination	deleterious	unwittingly	genome	clout

1. People complain that despite the _____ of channels available through satellite and cable TV, there is still nothing to watch.
2. Too much alcohol is known to have _____ effects on health, causing liver disease and other conditions.
3. Scientists hail the mapping of the human _____ as the key to cures for cancer and other diseases.
4. Media such as radio and television once had the _____ effect of creating a shared culture, but the Internet and cable networks have reversed that trend.
5. Because of its _____ to odors, the plastic wrap covering the fish did not conceal its bad smell.
6. People who _____ leave the oven on while they are at work may be surprised to see an increase in their electric bill.
7. People join interest groups in order to have more _____ with politicians, who will have to listen to their demands.
8. Some of the cells in Dr. Zonas's Petri dishes had died, but others were still _____ .
9. Rosa Parks and Martin Luther King, Jr. were two Americans who had a _____ effect on the Civil Rights Movement.
10. Most businesses discourage the _____ of leaflets and other advertising on their premises.

Write your own sentences, using any two of the words from Word Alert.

11. _____

12. _____

Thinking Deeper

Ideas for reflection, discussion, and writing

Make Inferences from Your Reading

1. The authors say that American society has experienced the reverse of homogenization, meaning that we no longer have a shared culture. Do you agree or disagree? What examples can you cite to support your opinion?
2. Use the PRT strategy (page 00) to interpret Figure 33.3 "The Changing American Family." Then answer these questions in a class discussion: What is the graphic's purpose? What relationships are shown in the pie charts and bar graph? What does the text tell you about the significance of these figures?
3. What are some of the major changes in America's population, demographics, family life, technology, and relations with other nations that the author discusses? Which one of these changes has affected your life the most?
4. One way to get a feel for a subject is to read books or articles by known authorities. Choose a subject from this selection that grabs your attention. Go to Amazon.com or a similar site where you can search for book titles by subject, or search your library's online indexes for articles in periodicals. Ask your instructor or librarian for suggestions. Subjects that some students have found interesting are *the changing family, globalization, the new economy, the genome project, stem cell research*, and *the rise of the Internet*.

Write About It

5. Go back to questions 1 and 2 in First Thoughts at the beginning of this selection. Choose one of the questions as the basis for a short essay.
6. What is one value, belief, or tradition handed down from your family that you will pass on to your children?

PERSONAL CHALLENGES   PART   3

We humans are resilient creatures. We are able to bounce back from hardship and disaster with grace and dignity. We surmount obstacles, conquer our fears, reach milestones, and move on to accept new challenges. We are survivors.

We are inventors and trailblazers, too. Tell us it can't be done, and we will do it. Tell us we can't win, and we will set records. We may not live in a perfect world, but we believe that a better life is within our grasp.

We are the ordinary people who cope with disabilities, break bad habits, learn new skills, and strive to open doors that others have closed. These actions define, in part, who we are.

The Part 3 selections are about people who have met personal challenges with optimism, persistence, and a willingness to take risks. As you read each selection, ask yourself these questions: What is the challenge, the goal to reach, or the obstacle to overcome? What is risked and what is won? What is the lesson for me?

FIRST THOUGHTS

To build background for the reading selection, answer the following questions, either on your own or in a group discussion.

1. What stories have your grandparents or other family members told you about their past?
2. What do you know or have you read about the Jews who were sent to concentration camps during World War II?
3. Preview the title, headnote, and first one or two paragraphs. What do you think will follow?

WORD ALERT

Each word below is followed by its paragraph number. Preview the words and definitions before reading. Then review them as necessary during reading. Use context clues and your dictionary to define any additional unfamiliar words.

reflection (1) careful consideration, mental concentration
transit (2) passage, passing through or across
extermination (2) getting rid of by complete destruction
coincidence (3) events that are accidental but seem planned
typhus (5) an infectious disease carried by fleas, lice, or mites
gruel (6) a thin, watery food made by boiling oats or another type of meal in water or milk
reassured (7) restored confidence

◈ I Saw Anne Frank Die

IRMA SONNENBERG MENKEL

In this selection, which the author wrote at the age of 100, she recalls her experiences in the Bergen-Belsen concentration camp, where she was imprisoned by the Germans during World War II. The article appeared in *Newsweek* in 1997.

I TURNED 100 YEARS old in April and had a beautiful birthday party surrounded by my grandchildren, great-grandchildren and other family members. I even danced a little. Willard Scott mentioned my name on television. But such a time is also for **reflection**. I decided to overcome my long reluctance to revisit terrible times. Older people must tell their stories. With the help of Jonathan Alter of *Newsweek*, here's a bit of mine:

I was born in Germany in 1897, got married and had two children in the 1920s. Then Hitler came to power, and like many other Jews, we fled to Holland. As the Nazis closed in, we sent one daughter abroad with relatives and the other into hiding with my sister and her children in The Hague. My husband and I could not hide so easily, and in 1941 we were sent first to Westerbork, a **transit** camp where we stayed about a year, and later to Bergen-Belsen, a work and transit camp, from where thousands of innocent people were sent to **extermination camps.** There were no ovens at Bergen-Belsen; instead the Nazis killed us with starvation and disease. My husband and brother both died there. I stayed for about three years before it was liberated in the spring of 1945. When I went in, I weighed more than 125 pounds. When I left, I weighed 78.

After I arrived at the Bergen-Belsen barracks, I was told I was to be the barracks leader. I said, "I'm not strong enough to be barracks leader." They said that would be disobeying a command. I was terrified of this order, but had no choice. It turned out that the Nazi commandant of the camp was from my home town in Germany and had studied with my uncle in Strasbourg. This **coincidence** probably helped save my life. He asked to talk to me privately and wanted to know what I had heard of my uncle. I said I wanted to leave Bergen-Belsen, maybe go to Palestine. The commandant said, "If I could help you, I would, but I would lose my head." About once every three weeks, he would ask to see me. I was always afraid. It was very dangerous. Jews were often shot over nothing. After the war, I heard he had committed suicide.

There were about 500 women and girls in my barracks. Conditions were extremely crowded and unsanitary. No heat at all. Every morning, I had to get up at 5 and wake the rest. At 6 a.m., we went to roll call. Often we had to wait there for hours, no matter the weather. Most of the day, we worked as slave labor in the factory, making bullets for German soldiers. When we left Holland, I had taken only two changes of clothes, one toothbrush, no books or other possessions. Later I had a few more clothes, including a warm jacket, which came from someone who died. Men and women lined up for hours to wash their clothes in the few sinks. There were no showers in our barracks. And no bedding. The day was spent working and waiting. At 10 p.m., lights out. At midnight, the inspection came—three or four soldiers. I had to say everything was in good condition when, in fact, the conditions were beyond miserable. Then up again at 5 a.m.

5   One of the children in my barracks toward the end of the war was Anne Frank, whose diary became famous after her death. I didn't know her family beforehand, and I don't recall much about her, but I do remember her as a quiet child. When I heard later that she was 15 when she was in the camps, I was surprised. She seemed younger to me. Pen and paper were hard to find, but I have a memory of her writing a bit. **Typhus** was a terrible problem, especially for the children. Of 500 in my barracks, maybe 100 got it, and most of them died. Many others starved to death. When Anne Frank got sick with typhus, I remember telling her she could stay in the barracks—she didn't have to go to roll call.

6   There was so little to eat. In my early days there, we were each given one roll of bread for eight days, and we tore it up, piece by piece. One cup of black coffee a day and one cup of soup. And water. That was all. Later there was even less. When I asked the commandant for a little bit of **gruel** for the children's diet, he would sometimes give me some extra cereal. Anne Frank was among those who asked for cereal, but how could I find cereal for her? It was only for the little children, and only a little bit. The children died anyway. A couple of trained nurses were among the inmates, and they reported to me. In the evening, we tried to help the sickest. In the morning, it was part of my job to tell the soldiers how many had died the night before. Then they would throw the bodies on the fire.

7   I have a dim memory of Anne Frank speaking of her father. She was a nice, fine person. She would say to me, "Irma, I am very sick." I said, "No, you are not so sick." She wanted to be **reassured** that she wasn't. When she slipped into a coma, I took her in my arms. She didn't know that she was dying. She didn't know that she was so sick. You never know. At Bergen-Belsen, you did not have feelings anymore. You became paralyzed. In all the years since, I almost never talked about Bergen-Belsen. I couldn't. It was too much.

8   When the war was over, we went in a cattle truck to a place where we stole everything out of a house. I stole a pig, and we had a butcher who slaughtered it. Eating this—was bad for us. It made many even sicker. But you can't imagine how hungry we were. At the end, we had absolutely nothing to eat. I asked an American soldier holding a piece of bread if I could have a bite. He gave me the whole bread. That was really something for me.

9   When I got back to Holland, no one knew anything. I finally found a priest who had the address where my sister and daughter were. I didn't know if they were living or not. They were. They had been hidden by a man who worked for my brother. That was luck. I found them and began crying. I was so thin that at first they didn't recognize me.

10   There are many stories like mine, locked inside people for decades. Even my family heard only a little of this one until recently. Whatever stories you have in your family, tell them. It helps.

Comprehension Check

Purpose and Main Idea

1. What is the author's topic?
   a. World War II
   b. Anne Frank
   c. the Jewish religion and traditions
   d. memories of the concentration camps
2. What is the central idea of this selection?
   a. The horrors of life in a concentration camp should not be forgotten.
   b. Many Jews were sent to be exterminated in concentration camps.
   c. Anne Frank died of typhus in a concentration camp.
   d. Being a barracks leader helped save the author's life.
3. The author's *primary* purpose is to
   a. express her viewpoint about war.
   b. persuade older people to tell their stories.
   c. inform us about life in a concentration camp.
   d. explain what it is like to starve.

Details

4. The transit camp to which the author was sent first was Bergen-Belsen.
   a. True
   b. False
5. The author was married around
   a. 1897.
   b. 1920.
   c. 1941.
   d. 1945.
6. The author worked for the Nazis, making bullets.
   a. True
   b. False
7. At different times in the concentration camps, the author had all but which one of the following to eat?
   a. bread
   b. coffee
   c. meat
   d. soup
8. The organizational pattern in paragraph 2 is
   a. sequence.
   b. comparison and contrast.
   c. cause and effect.
   d. definition.

Inferences

9. What is one reason that the author may not have wanted to talk about her story?
10. Why do you think that the author was ordered to be barracks leader?

Working with Words

Complete sentences 1–7 with these words from Word Alert:

extermination	reflection	transit	gruel
coincidence	reassured	typhus	

1. At first, Barbara's grandmother, Amanda Burton, did not want to tell her story, but on _____, she decided that she would.
2. At the orphanage where she grew up, the children were fed _____ and little else.
3. Some of the children in the orphanage died of _____ as a result of the unsanitary conditions.
4. When Amanda was a young woman, she took a job with a company whose business was the _____ of mice and insects.
5. She spent several hours each day in _____ from home to work.
6. By an amazing _____, Amanda met a woman who turned out to be her long-lost sister.
7. The meeting _____ both women that they had a family after all and were not alone in the world.

Write your own sentences, using any two of the words from Word Alert.

8. _____
9. _____

Thinking Deeper

Ideas for reflection, discussion, and writing

Make Inferences from Your Reading

1. Discuss what the Holocaust means to you. What do you know about this historical event? What inference can you make about the likelihood that something like the holocaust could happen today, in any part of the world?
2. Do you think people who have endured great suffering should be encouraged to tell their stories? Do you believe that it is important to remember terrible events? Why or why not? What other stories and memories should older people be encouraged to tell their children and others?
3. Six million Jews were killed in concentration camps, but there were survivors like Irma Sonnenberg Menkel. Discuss any Holocaust survivors or wartime survivors you know or have read about. What were their challenges? What kept them going? What became of them after the war was over?

4. To learn more about the Holocaust, do an online search in your library. Find a book on the Holocaust or Nazi Germany, find an article written by or about a Holocaust survivor, or find photographs taken in concentration camps at the end of WWII. Your librarian will have suggestions on where to begin and how to narrow your search. Take notes on what you find for sharing in a class discussion.

Write About It

5. Write about a hardship that you or someone close to you endured. What did you learn from the experience?
6. The author says, "Whatever stories you have in your family, tell them." Tell one of your family stories in writing.

FIRST THOUGHTS

To build background for the reading selection, answer the following questions, either on your own or in a group discussion.

1. What is one thing you remember about your first day at school?
2. Was your first-day experience good or bad, and why?
3. Preview the title, headnote, and first one or two paragraphs. What do you think will follow?

WORD ALERT

Each word below is followed by its paragraph number. Preview the words and definitions before reading. Then review them as necessary during reading. Use context clues and your dictionary to define any additional unfamiliar words.

defiance (2) resistance to force or authority, open hostility
counsel (2) advice, guidance
defective (3) faulty, abnormal
explicitly (4) fully and clearly expressed
illiterate (5) unable to read or write, having no formal education
naught (6) nothingness, nonexistence, insignificance
precariously (9) dangerously
cascaded (9) fell, tumbled
resolve (13) determination, firmness of purpose

◈ Back to School

TOM BODETT

The first day of school is a traumatic experience for some children. For others, it is a time of great expectations. In this selection, the author remembers his first day at school. Tom Bodett has been a commentator on National Public Radio's *All Things Considered* and the host of *The End of the Road Review*, a radio variety show. He is the author of several books, including *Small Comforts*, from which this selection is taken.

HE COULDN'T HAVE weighed much more than his new raincoat. It was so new, in 1 fact, that it wouldn't let his arms hang the way they should. They stuck out from his sides at an odd angle, and he could no more scratch his nose than he could turn his head strapped into the hood. He stood stiffly beside the road and watched me coming from a long way. As I passed him he looked at me with his lip curled under his front teeth in fear.

When I found him again in my rear-view mirror, I saw it wasn't me he'd been 2 looking at at all, but the big yellow school bus behind me. "Oh, that's right," I thought. "First day of school." I wanted to turn around and go comfort him, but was called off by something remembered in his expression. Yes, the kid was scared, but his eyes were fixed on the bus with such **defiance** that I knew he didn't need any **counsel**. He was going through with it. Brave as any soldier, he was going to get on that bus for the very first time. I drove on while a similar bus in a similar rain charged out of my memory in fourth gear.

I hadn't been to kindergarten. That's what had me worried. I knew my colors 3 and I could count past a hundred, but I couldn't spell at all. My mother assured me I didn't need to spell to go to first grade. That's what they wanted to teach me. But I wasn't so sure. My older brother was way up in the third grade, and he could spell like crazy. He had me convinced I was a mental **defective** and the nuns at our small parochial school would serve me for hot lunch the first day if I didn't get my act together.

Determined to measure up, I asked my brother what it took to spell. "Lots of 4 paper and some pencils," he said. The pencils were covered. I'd already sharpened the life out of all three fat number ones in my Roy Rogers pencil box, and their big pink erasers were good and broken in. It was the paper that had me worried. Mom had told me the school would give me what I needed, but I couldn't trust her. She wasn't going to school, and my brother, who was, had **explicitly** mentioned paper. So I stole the whole stack of typing paper from the kitchen drawer and slipped it under my brand-new yellow raincoat.

Standing by the mailboxes with my brother, I was probably as scared as I ever 5 have been since. Six years old and functionally **illiterate**. Buckled into an impossible raincoat I wasn't sure I could find my way out of without maternal assistance. The only thing I had going for me was a Roy Rogers pencil box, a Davy Crockett lunch pail, and over four hundred sheets of stolen typing paper. The hardest thing I ever did in my life was step onto that bus.

6   I'd like to be able to say that all my worrying was for **naught**, but it wasn't. Actually, as I reached this mythical place called Saint Sebastian's Elementary, my worst fears were realized.

7   Upon approaching the first-grade classroom I was greeted by Sister Antonio. I'd never been so close to a nun before and wasn't sure just how to act. When she smiled and said "Good morning," it was as if a burning bush had spoken. Until that moment I had never heard a nun speak. My only experience of them had been watching them in church in their mysterious black-and-white robes. I had some twisted notion that they were all related to Saint Peter—a good friend of Jesus'—and none of these people were to be taken lightly. I nearly swallowed my tongue as I stumbled past her into the room. That's where the real trouble started.

8   All the desks were in neat rows, and each one had a little folded card on top. "Find the desk with your name on it and take your seat, Tommy," I heard her say from the door. Other kids I'd never seen before were gracefully finding their places and admiring their name cards. I didn't even know what my name looked like. I stalled around the aisles until there were only two empty seats. Taking my best shot, I marched up, plopped down my Davy Crockett lunch pail, and collapsed with relief into Tammy Beech's chair.

9   The details are fuzzy from there, but I think I was found out during roll call. I vaguely remember Sister Antonio looming over my desk and saying something like, "You don't even know your own name?" This was the last thing I needed pointed out in the presence of my very first peer group. Still in my raincoat, I clumsily got out of my chair and dislodged the four hundred–odd sheets of paper that were **precariously** stashed underneath. They **cascaded** across the floor in an impressive display and proceeded to soak up the mud and water left by thirty first-graders. First-graders being how they are about wiping their feet, it's a good thing I brought as much paper as I did.

10   To say I could've died would be an understatement. I blushed so hard my ears rang. The thing I remember most about picking up that paper was the presence of the burning bush right behind me in eternal silence, the cruel giggles of my class-mates, and the pounding of my broken little heart.

11   Of course, I lived through all this and went on to finish my first year of school. I got used to Sister Antonio and, believe it or not, she even taught me how to spell. I was never served up for hot lunch, and I played Joseph in the Christmas play.

12   All these memories came back to me when I passed that little guy on the road. All the fear and uncertainty that come with a strange new land. All the pain and humiliation that go with screwing it up. And everything we learn in the process. It never stops, and it never seems to get any easier.

13   I must say, though, how encouraged I was by that small face along the road. Biting his lip in terror, but with pure **resolve** in his eye, he reminded me all over again of the best lesson I ever learned. If you want to go somewhere, you gotta get on the bus.

Comprehension Check

Purpose and Main Idea

1. What is the author's topic?
   a. education
   b. teaching
   c. problems in school
   d. first day of school
2. What is the central idea of this selection?
   a. Education is the most important life experience a child can have.
   b. Parochial schools differ from public schools in a number of important ways.
   c. Looking back on our first day of school, we recall the fear we felt and the lessons we learned.
   d. Children today use many of the same school supplies as did children of the past.
3. The author's *primary* purpose is to
   a. express what it was like to be a first grader.
   b. persuade us to make the first day of school easier for kids.
   c. inform us about what first grade is like in a parochial school.
   d. entertain and amuse us with his memories of his first day of school.

Details

4. Before the author went to first grade, he knew how to spell.
   a. True
   b. False
5. The author felt confident about all of his school supplies except his
   a. pencils.
   b. paper.
   c. pencil box.
   d. lunch pail.
6. The author says that he never got used to Sister Antonio.
   a. True
   b. False
7. Recalling his first day of school, the author says that he remembers all of the following except which one?
   a. his classmates' names
   b. the fear and uncertainty
   c. his classmates' giggles
   d. the pounding of his heart
8. The organizational pattern in paragraph 3 is
   a. definition.
   b. cause and effect.
   c. comparison and contrast.
   d. sequence.

Inferences

9. Why was the author unable to find the right seat?
10. How effective do you think Sister Antonio was as a teacher, and why? Support your inference with details from the selection.

Working With Words

Complete sentences 1–9 with these words from Word Alert:

precariously	defective	resolve
illiterate	defiance	counsel
explicitly	cascaded	naught

1. The high diver balanced _____ on his toes before plunging into the pool.
2. Despite the fact that education is available for everyone in the United States, many people are still _____ .
3. This electric pencil sharpener may be _____ because I cannot make it work.
4. The angry driver shook his hand in _____ at the flagger who was directing traffic during road construction.
5. Marta had been having trouble outlining her research paper, but with new _____ she tried again.
6. During the spring thaw, waterfalls _____ down the mountainside.
7. When you are struggling with a problem, it may help to seek the _____ of those who have had experience with similar problems.
8. Before trying to assemble the toy, read the directions, which are _____ stated on the box.
9. Although the time you spend studying may seem for _____ , when you score high on a test, you know it was worth it.

Write your own sentences, using any two of the words from Word Alert.

10. _____
11. _____

Thinking Deeper

Ideas for reflection, discussion, and writing

Make Inferences from Your Reading

1. Discuss what the author means by "If you want to go somewhere, you gotta get on the bus." Do you think this is good advice? Why or why not?
2. Compare your first day at school with the author's first day. What similarities and differences do you see? Discuss first-day or first-time experiences in general—for example, your first day at college or your first day at work. What do they all have in common? What inference can you make about the lessons learned from first-day or first-time experiences?

3. Put yourself in the place of a child on the first day of school. If you are apprehensive and fearful, just getting on the bus is a big step. In taking that risk, you meet the challenge, overcoming your fear to find self-confidence. Throughout school or college, what are some of the academic or social challenges that students must face and overcome to reach their goals?

4. If you like this selection, search your library's online catalog for a collection of essays by Tom Bodett. Scan the list of titles and read one or two essays that appeal to you. Based on your reading, what inference can you make about this author's themes and topics? If you have difficulty finding an essay collection, go to Tom Bodett's official website, www.tombodett.com, to learn more about this author.

Write About It

5. In the last paragraph, the author says that seeing the little boy waiting for the bus made him remember all over again the best lesson he ever learned. What is the best lesson you ever learned in school?

6. Write about a first-time experience—a first date or a first job, for example. Describe the experience, what happened, how you felt, and what you learned about yourself or others.

13

FIRST THOUGHTS

To build background for the reading selection, answer the following questions, either on your own or in a group discussion.

1. Are you a smoker or a nonsmoker?
2. Have you ever tried to quit smoking? Describe your experience.
3. Preview the title, headnote, and first one or two paragraphs. What do you think will follow?

WORD ALERT

Each word below is followed by its paragraph number. Preview the words and definitions before reading. Then review them as necessary during reading. Use context clues and your dictionary to define any additional unfamiliar words.

raging (2) moving or speaking with great violence or anger
grope (9) to search blindly or uncertainly
intervals (10) amounts of time between events
oxygenate (12) treat, combine, or infuse with oxygen
combatting (12) fighting, opposing
vivid (13) bright, lifelike, realistic
abstinence (13) self-denial, the act of refraining from indulging an appetite

◈ How I Quit Smoking, If I Really Did

HELEN PARRAMORE

Helen Parramore retired from Valencia Community College as a humanities professor. In this selection, she explains her struggles with a smoking habit. The selection ran in the *Orlando Sentinel*'s "My Word" column in April 1998.

ON AUG. 27, 1967, at 3:30 in the afternoon, with my five kids in the station wagon on 1
the way to the pound to pick out a puppy in Gainesville, I quit smoking.

The only other date I remember with certainty is 1066, when the Battle of 2
Hastings occurred. That's because my high-school history teacher had a **raging** fit in class one day, quite as memorable as the battle itself, when everyone missed the question on a test. In my mind, quitting smoking is associated with the Battle of Hastings.

In 1967, everybody smoked. Nobody talked about quitting. I don't know why I 3
thought I should. Nobody encouraged me. I had quit six or seven times before this memorable date, but that was the last time I quit.

To do it, I had to figure out how to live in a world of smokers. 4

How could I take a coffee break without a cigarette? 5

How could I keep others from blowing smoke in my face? 6

Would I never be able to have a drink or socialize with friends? 7

After dinner in the evening or when chatting on the phone, what could I do 8
instead of smoking?

I chose Life Savers. I had to **grope** to find the roll in my purse, then unravel the 9
wrapper, offer one to a friend, pry one loose and pop it into my mouth. I had to suck, then wrap up the rest and put the roll away. The sugar gave me a little lift and reward—the same motions and effects of smoking.

I learned that my craving was as predictable as the clock. Every 20 minutes, 10
when I wanted to smoke, I popped a Life Saver and promised myself to wait 10 minutes. Ten minutes later, I had forgotten about it and was content until the craving hit again. So, actually, I quit smoking forever in 10-minute **intervals**.

In the following weeks, the time between cravings gradually increased. Every 11
time I waited, I gained a few seconds. Within three months, cravings were down to about four times a day—a manageable problem.

I began bicycling and swimming because I found that physical exercise eased 12
my cravings. Years later, I read that exercise gets rid of the sticky, brown gunk that coats the lungs of smokers and helps **oxygenate** our body and brains. Exercise is a natural "upper." Without knowing what I was doing, I was **combatting** the depression that accompanies withdrawal while helping my lungs to heal.

After the worst was over, I began having **vivid** dreams about smoking. In these 13
dreams, I would light a cigarette, telling myself I could have one occasionally. Then I would light another and another, and I would see that both of my hands held a full pack of cigarettes. I awoke from these dreams depressed and confused. Had I really quit? Or had I lied to myself all along? I still occasionally have that dream—a reminder to myself that, despite 31 years' **abstinence**, I am still a smoker.

14   If you've tried to quit and can't, try again. Remember, nobody does it the first time. You're battling true addiction. It isn't easy, but you can do it 10 minutes at a time.

Comprehension Check

Purpose and Main Idea

1. What is the author's topic?
   a. addiction
   b. bad habits
   c. smoking
   d. cigarettes
2. Which one of the following best expresses the author's central idea?
   a. I quit smoking at 3:30 p.m. on August 27, 1967.
   b. In the 1960s, smoking was accepted behavior.
   c. Smoking, like drinking, is a true addiction.
   d. Quitting smoking is a battle that I must keep fighting.
3. The author's *primary* purpose is to
   a. inform us about the effects of smoking.
   b. entertain us with the ways others have quit smoking.
   c. persuade smokers to keep trying to quit.
   d. express how difficult it is to quit smoking.

Details

4. The author cites her friends' encouragement as the reason she quit smoking in 1967.
   a. True
   b. False
5. To live in a world of smokers, the author had to figure out how to do all of the following except which one?
   a. Continue smoking when under stress.
   b. Take a coffee break without a cigarette.
   c. Keep others from blowing smoke in her face.
   d. Have a drink or socialize without a cigarette.
6. To quit smoking, the author tried bicycling, swimming, and eating Life Savers.
   a. True
   b. False
7. The author says that the time between cravings for cigarettes
   a. gradually increased.
   b. gradually decreased.
   c. stayed the same.
   d. stopped suddenly.
8. The overall organizational pattern in this selection is
   a. definition: the author explains what addiction means.
   b. cause and effect: the author explains the dangers of smoking.

   c. comparison and contrast: the author compares smoking with alcohol addiction.

   d. process: the author explains how she quit smoking.

Inferences

9. What underlying meaning can you infer from the title of this selection?
10. When the author says you can stop smoking "10 minutes at a time," she probably means what?

Working with Words

Complete sentences 1–7 with these words from Word Alert:

abstinence	oxygenate	vivid	raging
combatting	intervals	grope	

1. The tornado was _____ outside, rooting up trees and tearing houses off their foundations.
2. Smoking interferes with your lungs' capacity to _____ the blood.
3. Tourists visit New England in the fall to see the _____ leaves and enjoy the cool weather.
4. Rain fell off and on, but we were able to walk to the library during one of the dry _____ .
5. In the dark, I had to _____ for the light switch.
6. A smoker's lungs will heal themselves after a long _____ from smoking.
7. If you do not get enough sleep, you will be spending most of your time in class _____ the urge to doze.

Write your own sentences, using any two of the words from Word Alert.

8. _____
9. _____

Thinking Deeper

Ideas for reflection, discussion, and writing

Making Inferences from Your Reading

1. Discuss various forms of addictive behavior, including smoking. What do you infer as reasons that people engage in addictive behavior?
2. Discuss the steps in the process the author went through to quit smoking. How does her experience compare either to your own or to that of someone you know who has tried to quit smoking?
3. The author suggests that battling addiction may be a lifelong process, which means that those who succeed do so at great personal risk and will continue to face challenges. What success stories do you know about people who battled their addictions and won?

4. Smoking is a highly addictive habit. Search the Internet to access information on smoking and health. Visit several sites to compare viewpoints and offerings. Here are some sites to try. Because websites come and go, ask a librarian if you need help finding URLs.

    -   www.ash.org. ASH stands for Action on Smoking and Health. ASH is a charitable organization for antismoking activists.
    -   www.cdc.gov/tobacco. The Center for Chronic Disease Prevention and Health is a division of the U.S. Center for Disease Control and Prevention. The site provides information and statistics on smoking.
    -   www.web.md.com. This site provides information on a variety of health issues and concerns. Advice on smoking and health and on smoking cessation is available on this site.
    -   www.epa.gov/smokefree/pub/etsfs. Go to this site for a fact sheet on respiratory health and the effects of passive smoking.

Write About It

5. Have you ever tried to break a bad habit or to battle an addiction? Were you successful? What strategies did you use? Describe your experience.
6. Write about the benefits of some activity that you do regularly.

FIRST THOUGHTS

To build background for the reading selection, answer the following questions, either on your own or in a group discussion.

1. Do you know or can you imagine what it would be like to be blind?
2. What are some of the things you do as a sighted person that you think you would not be able to do as a blind person?
3. Preview the title, headnote, and first one or two paragraphs. What do you think will follow?

WORD ALERT

Each word below is followed by its paragraph number. Preview the words and definitions before reading. Then review them as necessary during reading. Use context clues and your dictionary to define any additional unfamiliar words.

reckon (1) to think or assume

retinal (2) of or relating to the membrane lining the inner eyeball

perceive (2) to become aware of through the senses, to understand

coddle (4) to treat with indulgence

Braille (6) a system of writing and printing in which raised dots represent letters and numerals

taunts (7) jeers, gibes, words meant to ridicule

dorsal (12) toward, on, or near the back

◈ The Boy Who Sees with Sound

ALEX TRESNIOWSKI AND RON ARIAS

Alex Tresniowski is a senior writer for *People* magazine. He writes on topics of human interest, business, crime, entertainment, and other subjects. Ron Arias, author of several books, is a staff correspondent for *People*.

1   THERE WAS THE time a fifth grader thought it would be funny to punch the blind kid and run. So he snuck up on Ben Underwood and hit him in the face. That's when Ben started his clicking thing. "I chased him, clicking until I got to him, then I socked him a good one," says Ben, a skinny 14-year-old. "He didn't **reckon** on me going after him. But I can hear walls, parked cars, you name it. I'm a master at this game."

2   Ask people about Ben Underwood and you'll hear dozens of stories like this— about the amazing boy who doesn't seem to know he's blind. There's Ben zooming around on his skateboard outside his home in Sacramento; there he is playing kickball with his buddies. To see him speed down hallways and make sharp turns around corners is to observe a typical teen—except, that is, for the clicking. Completely blind since the age of 3, after **retinal** cancer claimed both his eyes (he now wears two prostheses), Ben has learned to **perceive** and locate objects by making a steady stream of sounds with his tongue, then listening for the echoes as they bounce off the surfaces around him. About as loud as the snapping of fingers, Ben's clicks tell him what's ahead: The echoes they produce can be soft (indicating metals), dense (wood) or sharp (glass). Judging by how loud or faint they are, Ben has learned to gauge distances.

3   The technique is called echolocation, and many species, most notably bats and dolphins, use it to get around. But a 14-year-old boy from Sacramento? While many blind people listen for echoes to some degree, Ben's ability to navigate in his sightless world is, say experts, extraordinary. "His skills are rare," says Dan Kish, a blind psychologist and leading teacher of echomobility among the blind. "Ben pushes the limits of human perception."

4   Kish has taught echolocation to scores of blind people as a supplement to more traditional methods, such as walking with a cane or a guide dog, but only a handful of people in the world use echolocation alone to get around, according to the American Foundation for the Blind. A big part of the reason Ben has succeeded is his mother, who made the decision long ago never to **coddle** her son. "I always told him, 'Your name is Benjamin Underwood, and you can do anything,'" says Aquanetta Gordon, 42, a utilities-company employee. "He can learn to fly an airplane if he wants to."

5   Ben plays basketball with his pals, rides horses at camp and dances with girls at school events. He excels at PlayStation games by memorizing the sounds that characters and movements make. "People ask me if I'm lonely," he says. "I'm not, because someone's always around or I've got my cell phone and I'm always talking to friends. Being blind is not that different from not being blind."

Ben was just 2 years old when doctors discovered his retinal cancer. Ben's first 6
Braille teacher, Barbara Haase, believes the boy's ability to see during his first two
years helped him develop "a sort of map of the physical world," she says. Growing
up, Ben got help from his brothers Joe, now 23, and Derius, 19, and sister Tiffany,
18. (His father, Stephen, died in 2002.) "They taught him how to find the seams on
his clothes so he puts them on right side out, stuff like that," says Aquanetta. "But
they didn't overdo it."

Aquanetta sent Ben to mainstream schools, where professionals on staff gave 7
him individual attention and taught him to overlook **taunts** from classmates who
waved their hands in his face or snatched food off his tray. "The hardest thing for
me to accept is rejection," says Ben, who starts ninth grade in the fall. "I can tell
when someone rejects me in some way." At home his mother let him play with no
restrictions. "If he fell, she would just say, 'Oh, he fell,' and he'd get up and try
again," says his kindergarten teacher Ann Akiyama. "I've seen him run full speed
into the edge of a big brick column and get back up. He was fearless."

Ben learned how to read Braille and walk with a cane, but when he was 3, he 8
also began teaching himself echolocation, something he picked up by tossing objects
and making clicking sounds to find them. His sense of hearing, teachers noticed,
was exceptional. "One time a CD fell off his desk and I was reaching for it when
he said, 'Nah, I got it,'" says Kalli Carvalho, his language arts instructor. "He went
right to it. Didn't feel around. He just knew where it was because he heard where it
hit." Haase took walks with Ben to help him practice locating objects. "I said,
'Okay, my car is the third car parked down the street. Tell me when we get there,'"
she says. "As we pass the first vehicle, he says, 'There's the first car. Actually, a
truck.' And it was a pickup. He could tell the difference."

Ben was 6 when he decided he wasn't going to use a cane—he calls it a stick— 9
to get around. "You go to school and you're the only one with a stick, what's the
first thing some kid's going to do? Break it in two," he says. "And then where are
you? You're helpless." At times he was even able to come to the aid of people with
normal sight. "I remember taking him to the park with my son, sister and my
nieces, and it got dark," says Akiyama. "But Ben had figured out the park's layout,
and he led the way out. He was in his element."

Still, Ben's zone of maximum comfort remains his family's three-bedroom 10
stucco home—where he lives with his mom and brother Isaiah, 11—and the quiet
streets around it. Some professionals who work with Ben worry that his near-
complete reliance on echolocation could hurt him when he finds himself in unfamiliar settings. Haase wishes he would use a cane to help him gauge, for instance, the
depth of a hole. But Ben is sticking to his guns. "He's a rebellious traveler," says
Kish, who despite teaching echolocation around the world still occasionally uses a
cane. "Ben puts himself at risk."

Others believe Ben's remarkable abilities will make it easier for him to face new 11
challenges and conquer new surroundings. "The world is not going to change for
these kids; they need to adapt to it," says Ben's eye doctor James Ruben, a Kaiser
Permanente ophthalmologist. "His mother understood that plenty of sighted people
have miserable lives and plenty of unsighted people have happy lives."

Last month Ben widened his horizons even further. "The thing I'm most scared 12
of is water," he says. "But if I had eyes, it's what I'd most like to see." So on June 25

he took a trip to San Diego's Sea World Adventure Park to swim with dolphins and hear how they use echolocation. Waist-deep in a saltwater pool, he immersed one ear as Sandy, a bottle-nosed dolphin, swam toward him. "Man," he said, "she clicks fast!" Ben spent 45 minutes playing with Sandy, touching her teeth and stroking her **dorsal** fin. Bob McMains, supervisor of Sea World's dolphin program, says that in his 23 years there, few people have listened so intently to the sounds the dolphins make. "He's got a gift with dolphins; he's truly unique," says McMains. "I told him, once he's 18 he's got a job here anytime."

13   McMains can get in line. Ben's world may be dark, but the most amazing surprises are just a click away. He might become a math teacher or a pro skateboarder— or, as his mother believes, just about anything. And wouldn't that make for a truly amazing Ben Underwood story? "I tell people I'm not blind," he says. "I just can't see."

Comprehension Check

Purpose and Main Idea

1. What is the topic of this selection?
   a. overcoming disabilities
   b. how Ben Underwood sees
   c. animals that navigate with sound
   d. technologies for the blind
2. Which one of the following best states this selection's central idea?
   a. Blindness, like other disabilities, can have many causes.
   b. Many animals use a navigational system called echolocation.
   c. One boy has found an extraordinary way to navigate in his sightless world.
   d. Various organizations exist that help the disabled to lead productive lives.
3. The *primary* purpose of this selection is to
   a. persuade readers to help the disabled.
   b. inform readers about echolocation.
   c. entertain readers by lifting their spirits.
   d. arouse readers' sympathy.

Details

4. Echolocation is, more often than not, a supplement to traditional methods of mobility for the blind.
   a. True
   b. False
5. Which one of the following best explains how echolocation works?
   a. Every noise or sound that people or animals make creates an echo.
   b. Everyone has a natural instinct for getting around in the absence of sight.
   c. Sounds bounce off surfaces, creating echoes that help species gauge distances.
   d. Blind people learn to recognize the natural sounds in their environments.

6. Ben Underwood has been blind since birth.
   a. True
   b. False
7. What has been the hardest thing for Ben to accept?
   a. limitations
   b. taunts
   c. blindness
   d. rejection
8. What is the organizational pattern in paragraph 5?
   a. Ideas are compared.
   b. Examples support a generalization.
   c. A term is defined.
   d. A process is explained.

Inferences

9. Explain in your own words what Ben means by "Being blind is not that different from not being blind" (paragraph 5).
10. In paragraph 9, what does the sentence "He was in his element" mean? Give an example from your own experience of someone who fits that description.

Working with Words

Complete sentences 1–7 with these words from Word Alert:

taunts	perceive	coddle	dorsal
retinal	Braille	reckon	

1. Books, computer keyboards, and other materials printed in _____ have made information accessible to visually impaired people.
2. The use of a _____ scan has helped ophthalmologists to find diseases of the eye so that they can be treated.
3. Critics of the prison system say that providing criminals with too much comfort will serve only to _____ them when they should be dealt with more strictly.
4. Beachgoers scan the ocean for a _____ fin that will alert them of an approaching shark.
5. Despite First Amendment guarantees of free speech, controversial speakers may be shouted down by the _____ of an angry crowd.
6. Ben Underwood's sense of sound enables him to _____ objects and to navigate his world.
7. When asked whether she thought that her child would like to have an ice cream cone, she said, "I _____ so."

Write your own sentences, using any two of the words from Word Alert.

8. _____
9. _____

Thinking Deeper

Ideas for reflection, discussion, and writing

Making Inferences from Your Reading

1. Before reading this selection, what images or ideas did you have about blindness itself or about people who are blind? How has your reading either supported or changed your ideas?
2. As you read Ben's story, what effect did it have on you? For example, did you find it entertaining or inspirational? Can you think of another word to describe the story's effect? Cite specific examples or quotations from the selection that provoked your response.
3. What legislation and attitude changes have improved life and working conditions for people with disabilities? What should we do to show our support as such people struggle to meet life's challenges and achieve their dreams?
4. In paragraph 4, the authors mention the American Foundation for the Blind. Visit its website at www.afb.org, where you can find facts and statistics on blindness, learn about careers that involve working with the blind, and access links to other topics such as Braille or the life of Helen Keller. Share the results of your search in a class discussion.

Write About It

5. Using this selection as an example, write about someone you admire who has a disability, and explain why this person inspires you.
6. If you were to become blind due to an illness or an accident, what aspect of being sighted would you miss most?

FIRST THOUGHTS

To build background for the reading selection, answer the following questions, either on your own or in a group discussion.

1. Is math an easy or difficult subject for you?
2. Do you believe that skill in mathematics is inborn or learned?
3. Preview the title, headnote, and first one or two paragraphs. What do you think will follow?

WORD ALERT

Each word below is followed by its paragraph number. Preview the words and definitions before reading. Then review them as necessary during reading. Use context clues and your dictionary to define any additional unfamiliar words.

analogue (2) the representation of data by a measurable variable such as a number (U.S. spelling of this term is "analog.")

dyscalculia (3) an inability to associate a set of objects with the numerical symbol that represents it

dyslexia (3) a learning disability involving reading

fluency (4) ease of using a language; in this case, the language of mathematics

entails (5) requires

relevant (7) having to do with the matter at hand

magnitudes (7) large numbers or quantities

ratio (10) relation in degree or number between two things

foraging (14) searching for food or provisions

perseverance (22) sticking to an idea or a task despite obstacles

◈ When Numbers Don't Add Up

LAURA SPINNEY

The author is a writer based in Lausanne, Switzerland. In this article, which appeared in *New Scientist* magazine on January 24, 2009, she answers the question "What makes otherwise intelligent people useless at mathematics?"

1   JILL, 19, FROM MICHIGAN, wants to go to university to read political science. There is just one problem: she keeps failing the mathematics requirement. "I am an exceptional student in all other subjects, so my consistent failure at math made me feel very stupid," she says. In fact, she stopped going to her college mathematics class after a while because, she says, "I couldn't take the daily reminder of what an idiot I was."

2   Last November, Jill got herself screened for learning disabilities. She found that while her IQ is above average, her numerical ability is equivalent to that of an 11-year-old because she has something called dyscalculia. The diagnosis came partly as a relief, because it explained a lot of difficulties she had in her day-to-day life. She can't easily read a traditional, **analogue** clock, for example, and always arrives 20 minutes early for fear of being late. When it comes to paying in shops or restaurants, she hands her wallet to a friend and asks them to do the calculation knowing that she is likely to get it wrong.

3   Welcome to the stressful world of **dyscalculia,** where numbers rule because inhabitants are continually trying to avoid situations in which they have to perform even basic calculations. Despite affecting about 5 percent of people—roughly the same proportion as are dyslexic—dyscalculia has long been neglected by science, and people with it incorrectly labelled as stupid. Now, though, researchers are starting to get to the root of the problem, bringing hope that dyscalculic children will start to get specialist help just as youngsters with **dyslexia** do.

4   For hundreds of millions of people this really matters. "We know that basic mathematical **fluency** is an essential prerequisite for success in life, both at the level of employment and in terms of social success," says Daniel Ansari, a cognitive neuroscientist at the University of Western Ontario in London, Canada. A report published in October 2008 by the British government claimed that dyscalculia cuts a pupil's chances of obtaining good exam results at age 16 by a factor of 7 or more, and wipes more than £100,000 from their lifetime earnings. Early diagnosis and remedial teaching could help them avoid these pitfalls.

5   People with dyscalculia, also known as mathematics disorder, can be highly intelligent and articulate. Theirs is not a general learning problem. Instead, they have a selective deficit with numerical sets. Put simply, they fail to see the connection between a set of objects—five walnuts, say—and the numerical symbol that represents it, such as the word "five" or the numeral 5. Neither can they grasp that performing additions or subtractions **entails** making stepwise changes along a number line.

This concept of "exact number" is known to be unique to humans, but there is   6
long-standing disagreement about where it comes from. One school of thought
argues that at least some elements of it are innate, and that babies are born with an
exact number "module" in their brain. Others say exact number is learned and that
it builds upon an innate and evolutionary ancient number system which we share
with many other species. This "approximate number sense" (ANS) is what you
use when you look at two heavily laden apple trees and, without actually counting
the apples, make a judgement as to which has more. In this view, as children acquire speech they map number-words and then numerals onto the ANS, tuning it
to respond to increasingly precise numerical symbols.

The debate over exact number is directly **relevant** to dyscalculics, as tackling   7
their problem will be easier if we know what we are dealing with. If we have an
innate exact number module that is somehow faulty in people with dyscalculia,
they could be encouraged to put more faith in their ability to compare **magnitudes**
using their ANS, and learn to use calculators for the rest. However, if exact number
is learned, then perhaps dyscalculia could be addressed by teaching mathematics in
ways that help with the process of mapping numbers onto the ANS.

So how do the two models stand up? The innate number module theory makes   8
one obvious prediction: babies should be able to grasp exact numbers. This was
explored in the early 1990s. Using dolls, a screen and the fact that babies stare for
longer at things that surprise them, developmental psychologist Karen Wynn, then
at the University of Arizona in Tucson, showed that five-month-old infants could
discriminate between one, two and three. They look for longer if the number of dolls
that come out from behind the screen does not match the number that went in.

Some teams have taken a different approach to show that we are born with a   9
sense of exact number. They argue that if exact number is learned, it ought to be
influenced by language. Brian Butterworth from University College London recently
did tests of exact number on children aged 4 to 7 who spoke only Warlpiri or
Anindilyakwa, two Australian languages that contain very few number words. He
found no difference in performance between the indigenous children and a control
group from English-speaking Melbourne (*Proceedings of the National Academy of
Sciences,* vol 105, P 13179). This, he says, is evidence that "you're born with a
sense of exact number, and you map the counting words onto pre-existing concepts
of exact numbers."

Both of these approaches, however, have been criticised. Neuroscientist Stan   10
Dehaene of the Collège de France in Paris points out that Wynn's finding also fits
the rival theory—that babies enter the world with only an intuition about approximate number. This is because the ANS is concerned with **ratios**, so is reasonably
reliable when the numbers involved are small, but falls off as the proportional size
difference shrinks. A size ratio of 1:2 is more easily discernable than 9:10. Wynn
tested babies on small numbers and, as Dehaene points out, "one versus two is a
large ratio."

COUNT ON LEARNING

11　What is more, Dehaene has worked with an Amazonian tribe whose language only contains words for numbers up to five, and says it provides good evidence for the idea that exact number is learned (see "One, two, lots").

12　Supporters of the idea that exact number is learned also point to research showing how young children actually acquire an understanding of numbers. First they learn what the number word "one" means, then "two" and soon until, around the age of 4, they suddenly grasp the underlying concept of the number line and counting. "There is something very special occurring in development with exact numbers, and with the understanding of number words," says Dehaene.

13　For now, the idea that exact number is learned has the upper hand, suggesting that dyscalculia is a learning problem. To complicate things further, however, new research indicates that this may only be part of the story.

14　It was long thought that the ANS contributes little to performance in mathematics. As it is essential for survival skills such as **foraging**, it was assumed that everyone would have comparable abilities with approximate number. This myth was exploded in 2008 when Justin Halberda of Johns Hopkins University in Baltimore, Maryland, tested the ANS in 64 14-year-olds and was "blown away" by the variability he found (*Nature*, vol 455, p 665).

15　The teenagers, all of whom fell within the normal range for numeracy, watched an array of dots made up of two colours flash onto a computer screen. In each case, they had to say which colour was more numerous. As expected, their judgements became less accurate as the size ratio of the two sets shrank towards 1:1.The surprise was how much faster accuracy fell off in some kids than in others, with the poorest performers having difficulty with ratios as large as 3:4.

16　There was a further surprise in store when the team compared the teenagers' ANS scores with their mathematics test results from the age of 5 and up. "I literally jumped out of my seat when I saw the correlation going all the way back to kindergarten," says Halberda. The link remained even after IQ, working memory and other factors had been controlled for, and it only held for mathematics, not for other subjects. A subsequent larger study, including some children with dyscalculia, confirmed the suspicion that those with the number disorder had markedly lower ANS scores than children with average ability. This implicates a faulty ANS in dyscalculia.

17　Case closed? Not quite. The problem is that two other groups have come up with conflicting findings. In 2007, Laurence Rousselle and Marie Pascale Noël of the Catholic University of Louvain (UCL) in Belgium reported that dyscalculic children, when asked to compare the magnitude of collections of sticks—say, five sticks versus seven—performed no worse than controls. However, they struggled when asked to circle the larger of two numerals, such as 5 and 7. Ansari's team has obtained a similar result. Both teams conclude that in dyscalculic children the ANS works normally, and the problem comes in mapping numerical symbols onto it.

One, Two, Lots

Amazonian hunter-gatherers called the Mundurucú only have words for numbers up to 5. Does this affect the way they think about mathematical problems? Experts who think that the human concept of exact number is innate would predict not. However, Stan Dehaene of the Collège de France in Paris is among a growing number who believe that exact number is learned and therefore affected by our culture. He decided to test this idea with the Mundurucú.

Working with his colleague in the field, Pierre Pica, and others, Dehaene has found that the Mundurucú can add and subtract with numbers under 5, and do approximate magnitude comparisons as successfully as a control group. But last year the team discovered a big cultural difference. They asked volunteers to look at a horizontal line on a computer screen that had one dot at the far left and 10 dots to the right. They were then presented with a series of quantities between 1 and 10, in different sensory modalities—a picture of dots, say, or a series of audible tones—and asked to point to the place on the line where they thought that quantity belonged.

English-speakers will typically place 5 about halfway between 1 and 10. But the Mundurucú put 3 in the middle, and 5 nearer to 10 (*Science*, vol. 320, p. 1217). Dehaene reckons this is because they think in terms of ratios—logarithmically—rather than in terms of a number line. By the Mundurucú way of thinking, 10 is only twice as big as 5, but 5 is five times as big as 1, so 5 is judged to be closer to 10 than to 1.

The team conclude that "the concept of a linear number line appears to be a cultural invention that fails to develop in the absence of formal education." With only limited tools for counting, the Mundurucú fall back on the default mode of thinking about number, the so-called "approximate number system" (ANS). This is logarithmic says Dehaene. When it comes to negotiating the natural world—sizing up an enemy troop or a food haul—ratios or percentages are what count. "I don't know of any survival situation where you need to know the difference between 37 and 38," he says. "What you need to know is 37 plus-or-minus 20 per cent."

How to account for these contradictory findings? Halberda, Ansari and Dehaene believe that there may be different types of dyscalculia, reflecting different underlying brain abnormalities. So in some dyscalculic individuals, the ANS itself is damaged, while in others it is intact but inaccessible so that individuals have problems when it comes to mapping number words and numerals onto the innate number system. 18

The existence of such subtypes would make dyscalculia harder to pin down, and make it difficult to design a screening programme for schoolchildren. At the moment, the condition goes widely unrecognised, and testing is far from routine. But where it is tested for, the tests are relatively crude, relying on the discrepancy between the child's IQ or general cognitive abilities and their scores in mathematics. Nevertheless, perhaps one day all children entering school will be assessed for various types of dyscalculia. Then teachers may be able to start intervention programmes based on teaching tools that are currently being tested. 19

20   One such tool, called The Number Race, in which children compete against a computer for rewards in a series of treasure hunts and other games, has been created by Dehaene and his colleague Anna Wilson. It assumes that the problem lies with the exact number system, so begins with tasks that the ANS is good at, involving numerical comparison, and gradually moves to more difficult tasks such as addition and subtraction. Testing of its effects is ongoing, but early indications are that it may help to bolster dyscalculic children's concept of number and simple transformations of numerical sets.

21   Even those researchers who remain convinced that dyscalculia is caused by a faulty exact number module believe that intervention could help. "After all, genetics isn't destiny—well, not entirely—and the brain is plastic," says Butterworth. His team is testing a piece of software that it designed in collaboration with the London Knowledge Lab to strengthen dyscalculic schoolchildren's basic number concepts. He suspects this will not be enough, however: "It may be the case that the best we can do is teach them strategies for calculation, including intelligent use of calculators, and get them onto doing more accessible branches of mathematics, such as geometry and topology."

22   Ansari also points out that children with dyscalculia could be helped immediately by practical measures already in place in schools for pupils with dyslexia, such as extra time in exams. And, of course, simply recognising dyscalculia as a problem on a par with dyslexia would make a huge difference. As Jill says, now that she knows what her problem is, "It's easier to have the confidence and the **perseverance** to keep working until I get it." That, in turn, means the condition becomes less damaging to her self-esteem and perhaps, ultimately, to her chances in life.

Comprehension Check

Purpose and Main Idea

1. What is the author's topic?
    a.   dyscalculia
    b.   mathematics
    c.   numerical systems
    d.   performance in math
2. Which one of the following sentences *best* states the author's central idea?
    a.   Dyscalculia is a stressful condition that affects some students' ability to perform simple calculations.
    b.   Researchers are beginning to solve the problem of dyscalculia in the hope that those affected may get the help they need.
    c.   There are several competing theories that explain dyscalculia.
    d.   Dyscalculics are, nevertheless, able to solve certain kinds of mathematical problems.
3. The first two paragraphs of the article serve what *primary* purpose?
    a.   define the meaning of the term "dyscalulia"
    b.   entertain readers with an example of one student's struggle
    c.   introduce a difficult topic with a story that readers can relate to
    d.   persuade readers that a debate about the causes of dyscalculia exists

Details

4. All of the following except which one are typical of people who have dyscalculia?
   a. consistent failure in math
   b. difficulty in calculating payments
   c. an inability to recognize letters when reading
   d. avoidance of situations requiring basic calculating
5. According to the author, dyscalculia in schoolchildren is a widely recognized problem.
   a. True
   b. False
6. Discalculia is also known as which one of the following?
   a. math anxiety
   b. a general learning problem
   c. mathematics disorder
   d. a fear of numbers
7. Researchers disagree about where the concept of "exact number" comes from.
   a. True
   b. False
8. The author's details consist mainly of
   a. facts and theories about the causes and treatment of dyscalculia.
   b. opinions about the psychological damage caused by dyscalculia.
   c. reasons why it is difficult to test for dyscalculia.
   d. examples of people who have dyscalculia and their struggles.

Inferences

9. In paragraph 21, the author quotes Butterworth as saying "genetics isn't destiny" and "the brain is plastic." What meaning do you infer from these statements? What do they tell you about your ability to do math or to perform any other skill?
10. In your own words, what are the two competing theories about the causes of dyscalculia? Find details in the article to support your explanation.

Working with Words

Complete sentences 1–10 with these words from Word Alert:

perseverance	magnitudes	analog	dyscalculia	relevant
dyslexia	foraging	entails	fluency	ratio

1. I have always preferred _____ clocks to digital clocks.
2. A person who constantly struggles to learn math may have _____.
3. Those who have _____ in mathematics or in languages are more likely to excel in areas requiring the use of these skills.

4. People may apply for a job without knowing the extent of the skills it _____.

5. Instructors often supplement their lectures with _____ personal experiences to build students' interest in the topic.

6. Most people have difficulty relating to dollar amounts in _____ of millions or higher.

7. The bill was so unpopular with legislators that they rejected it by a _____ of 2 to 1.

8. Earth's earliest humans spent much of their time _____ for food.

9. A person who has trouble distinguishing between the words "unite" and "untie" might have _____ and not know it.

10. When it comes to studying, persistence and _____ will pay off in the long run.

Write your own sentences, using any two of the words from Word Alert.

11. _____

12. _____

Thinking Deeper

Ideas for reflection, discussion, and writing

Make Inferences from Your Reading

1. The author says that basic mathematical fluency is essential to success in life. Do you agree or disagree? Based on your own experience, what are the social or economic benefits of fluency in mathematics?

2. Based on the author's details, what inference can you make about the possibility that you or someone you know has dyscalculia? On what do you base this inference?

3. One challenge for researchers is to develop strategies that will help students with dyscalculia to fuction better in a world of numbers. Imagine that you are a student with dyscalculia. What are some everyday things involving numbers or calculations that you might not be able to do?

4. To find out more about dyscalculia, do an Internet search. Share the results of your search with the rest of the class, and comment on the usefulness of the sites you visited. What did you learn? Did the information support what you read in Selection 15? Ask a librarian or your instructor if you need help with finding URLs.

Write About It

5. Describe a strategy that has helped you achieve success in a math course or another course that gave you difficulty.

6. Find a statement in the article with which you strongly agree or disagree. Explain your reasons.

FIRST THOUGHTS

To build background for the reading selection, answer the following questions, either on your own or in a group discussion.

1. What does the term "friendship" mean to you?
2. In what ways are online pals the same or different from your other friends?
3. Preview the title, headnote, and first one or two paragraphs. What do you think will follow?

WORD ALERT

Each word below is followed by its paragraph number. Preview the words and definitions before reading. Then review them as necessary during reading. Use context clues and your dictionary to define any additional unfamiliar words.

pruning (3) removing, cutting back

superficial (4) shallow, trivial, concerned only with the obvious

networked (7) connected by computer so as to facilitate online interaction with others

aloof (14) distant, reserved in social interaction

touted (17) promoted, praised

utopian (19) impractical, idealistic

fraught (39) upsetting, marked by distress

pallbearers (58) Those carrying a coffin at a funeral

◈ Friends Indeed?

JOEL GARREAU

Joel Garreau is a reporter. In this selection, which ran in the *Washington Post* on April 20, 2008, he examines the effect of social networking on our relationships, and invites us to ponder whether those people we call "friends" are friends indeed.

1   SHADEE MALAKLOU HAS lots of friends. A whole lot—1,295, according to her latest Facebook count. But whom exactly can she count on?

2   Malaklou, 22, acknowledges that if she ran into some of her "friends" on the street, she might not remember their names. When she went to Duke, where "I was quote unquote popular," social life was so competitive that sometimes invitations were based only on online determinations of how hot a person was, and whether her "friends" were cool.

3   Now that she is working at a Washington nonprofit, Malaklou is planning on **pruning** her "friends" as a rite of spring cleaning, defriending people who have come to mean little to her.

4   She does stay Facebook friends, however, with professors who might be good for letters of recommendation to graduate school. "The biggest value-added is that it helps maintain relationships—somewhat **superficial** but not worth getting rid of," she says.

5   The word "friend" has long covered a broad range of relationships—roommates, army buddies, pals from the last law firm, old neighbors, teammates, people you used to smoke dope with in back of your high school, people you see once a year at the Gold Cup, scuba instructors and carpool members, along with fellow gun collectors, Britney fans and cancer victims. The Oxford English Dictionary traces "freondum" back to "Beowulf" in 1018, and "to be frended" to 1387.

6   But MySpace and all the hundreds of other social networking Web sites, from Flickr to Twitter to Bebo, have caused us to think afresh about the boundaries and intensities of these relationships. Never before in history has it been so easy to keep up with so many people with whom you otherwise would have lost contact. These new electronic meshes are more than mere improvements over alumni magazines, holiday cards with pictures of families and those horrible letters about their lives, Rolodexes, yearbooks, organizational newsletters, and birth and death notices in the newspaper.

7   Summer friendships, for example, have been transformed. The ritual of meeting again at the beach after a long winter was once marked by hours of catching up. Not today. **Networked** people who haven't seen each other in forever already know about the new boyfriend, and what happened to the old one—in very great detail. They also know about the old school and the new job. They have known, every day, no matter where in the world they roamed, the instant that emotional change occurred. Now, after the initial squeals and swaying hugs, conversations pick up in mid-sentence. It's a mind-meld uncanny to watch.

This is a world of "participatory surveillance," says Anders Albrechtslund of 8
Denmark's Aalborg University in the online journal *First Monday*.

Real online friends watch over each other—mutually, voluntarily and enthusi- 9
astically, in ways that can be endearing.

Others have referred to it as "empowering exhibitionism," Albrechtslund says. 10
Call it Friends Next. 11

YOU CAN PICK YOUR FRIENDS, BUT . . .

Life was once so simple. "I'll be there for you, when the rain starts to pour," went 12
the *Friends* theme. "I'll be there for you, 'cause you're there for me too."

Today, when you join a social network, the first thing you start questioning is 13
if you really want to embrace *every* "friend" request. Such promiscuity's down-
side quickly becomes obvious. Do you really want every petitioner—no matter
how unclear his identity or intent—to see your revealing personal information?
Much less those pictures of Ashley, Courtney and Jason from last Saturday
night?

There's this girl at school "who won't even say 'hi' in the hallway," says a 14
16-year-old junior at a Washington high school who desires anonymity for fear of
social ostracism. The **aloof** girl keeps asking to be a virtual "friend" on Facebook,
arguably the most sophisticated popular site, no matter how often the answer
is no.

This junior struggles with the relationship dilemma, "Why would I want to 15
be 'friends' with this person? I occasionally smile at her. I guess it's kind of
really impersonal to me, if she's not even going to say 'hi.'" The high schooler
says she's "selective in acceptance of friends"—she has "only" 131 on Facebook.
But if she had a relationship blow up, on the shoulders of how many could
she *cry*?

"Probably like 20," she says. 16

For two decades, online social networks have been **touted** as one of the finest 17
flowerings of our new era. But what is the strength of ties so weak as to barely exist? Who will lend you lunch money? Who will bail you out of jail? Who's got your
back?

A remote Wyoming cattle ranch was home to Internet pioneer John Perry 18
Barlow when he was a boy in the '50s. In the '80s, when he encountered the first
settlers of online communities such as the Well, he felt like he was back in the small
towns he once knew. He reveled in the throngs "gossiping, complaining . . . com-
forting and harassing each other, bartering, engaging in religion . . . beginning and
ending love affairs, praying for one another's sick kids," he once wrote. "There
was, it seemed, about everything one might find going on in a small town, save
dragging Main or making out on the back roads."

He has since developed a more jaundiced view of the Internet's **utopian** promise 19
to dissolve barriers between people—"the reason I got involved in that stuff" in the
first place, he says. Barlow hoped for "a distinctly 19th-century understanding of
what community was. Where it was not just bail you out of jail, but stand behind

you with a loaded gun—the Wyoming version." Instead, he sees people collecting and displaying enormous numbers of "friends" on MySpace, "for the same reason that elk grow antlers, I expect."

20 As part of his firm's "online strategy," James C. Courtovich, 42, managing partner of a Washington lobbying and public relations outfit, recently joined Facebook and had a small team take the 3,000 names in his address book and cross-reference them with everyone there. The overlap was "shocking," he reports. "I expected my niece, but not the chairman of *The Washington Post*. At my age I expected a tenth of a percent." Instead, he found 7 percent of his world there: "Capitol Hill types, journalists, friends I'd not seen in years."

21 Do you consider these people your friends? "Some friends are more equal than others," Courtovich says. To him, this network is no more than Washington business-as-usual—"an online cocktail party without having to stay up late or drink alcohol."

22 Some encounters can be novel and strange. Jessica Smith, 23, remembers the time someone she'd never heard of from Vassar tried to friend her. It happened when Smith was an undergraduate at George Washington University and had just started dating her boyfriend. Peter. Turned out the stranger was Peter's ex.

23 "There was nothing friendly about this," she says. "She only wanted to know about me." When Smith didn't fall for this probe—like it was the ex's business how cute she might be, or clever—"a friend of hers friended me. Like that would trick me—'Ooo, a new friend from Vassar!' It was weird. Really creepy." Before social networks, "she wouldn't have called me, or written me a letter."

Worlds Colliding

24 You know all those separate lives you lead? When you're not being the FTC lawyer, or the hair-metal band freak, you're the wife of a glassblower and mother of two who likes to spend every vacation she can on the black-sand beaches of Dominica?

25 Forget about keeping those lives neatly partitioned in Friends Next.

26 "It's the postmodern nightmare—to have all of your selves collide," says Rebecca G. Adams, a sociologist at the University of North Carolina at Greensboro who edits *Personal Relationships*, the journal of the International Association for Relationship Research.

27 In villages of the agrarian age, you wouldn't even have developed those various personalities. In Friends Next you can't escape them. "If you really welcome all of your friends from all of the different aspects of your life and they interact with each other and communicate in ways that everyone can read," Adams says, "you get held accountable for the person you are in all of these groups, instead of just one of them."

28 This became dramatically clear in September 2003, on an early site called Friendster. Two 16-year-old students approached a young San Francisco teacher with two questions: Why do you do drugs, and why are you friends with pedophiles? So reports danah boyd, a PhD candidate at the University of California at Berkeley's School of Information who has become renowned for her research into

online social networks, and who insists on rendering her name without capital letters.

The teacher's profile was nothing extraordinary or controversial. Her picture 29 showed her hiking. But she had a lot of friends who were devotees of Burning Man—the annual weeklong festival in the Nevada desert that attracts tens of thousands of people experimenting with community, artwork, self-expression, self-reliance, absurdity and clothing-optional revelry.

"The drug reference came not from her profile but from those of her Friends, 30 some of whom had signaled drug use (and attendance at Burning Man, which for the students amounted to the same thing)," Boyd writes. "Friends also brought her the pedophilia connection—in this case via the profile of a male Friend who, for his part, had included an in-joke involving a self-portrait in a Catholic schoolgirl outfit and testimonials about his love of young girls. The students were not in on this joke."

In Friends Next, all your lives and circles of relationships are collapsed. 31 Extreme cases of friend mash-ups resemble the barroom scene in "Star Wars."

"You can be friends with someone you know well and don't like," reports 32 Susannah Clark, a sophomore at the University of Mary Washington. "You read their profiles and blogs and are well aware of their life. It's a love-to-hate type arrangement."

"I even agreed to be one person's friend because he's so psychotic I was scared 33 of what would happen if I said no," writes blogger Dan Kaufman.

STITCHED TOGETHER

We're inventing Friends Next every day. 34

"For most people, when they thought of their close friends, it was people with 35 whom they would share personal things," says Sherry Turkle, a sociologist and psychologist at MIT who has studied online social networks from their beginnings. "What's changing now is that people who are not in the other person's physical life meet in this very new kind of space. It is leaving room for new hybrid forms."

The weirdness of Friends Next is that it comes at you like a melodrama: "Is he 36 married yet?" "Is he still straight?" "She's changed her religious views to 'rain dancing'? I thought she had a cross tattooed on her hip."

Facebook is more about entertainment than work," says Nicholas A. Christa- 37 kis, a physician and sociologist who studies social networks at Harvard. "Instead of watching soap operas, they're watching soap operas of people they sort of know."

"It sucks you in," says Mary Washington's Clark. "The public conversations— 38 it's digital eavesdropping."

Losing friends in this new world is as **fraught** as making them. "Real-world 39 friendships are not usually intentionally ended," Adams says. "Folks just let things naturally cool off. On Facebook, decisive action has to be taken." Defriending cements that a friendship is over.

The best soap operas occur when a couple breaks up. Change your profile from 40 "In a Relationship" to "Single"—or even more ominously, "It's Complicated"—and little press releases blast out to all your gossip-hound "friends." Massive e-mailing and tongue-wagging ensues.

41 It's futile to try to erase latent traces of Friends Next. "The digital trails of an online friendship—true or not—really do last forever," Albrechtslund says. Its evidence is stored on servers indefinitely, beyond the control of the persons involved.

42 While many are still trying to figure out how to make Friends Next work for us, Todd Huffman is trying to harness this new social form to save us.

43 The Phoenix software developer is creating a company called sStitch. In times of crisis, like the recent San Diego wildfires, Huffman notes, there are vast quantities of useful information buzzing among Friends Next. They turn to their social tech—text-messaging, blogs, e-mail, Web networks— to announce: "I'm okay." "I'm evacuating to this city." "This freeway is shut down." "That road is flooded." They send pictures on the fly. Their cell phones' global positioning locates them precisely.

44 This is all instant bottom-up information from hundreds of thousands of eyes not now available to the people trying to manage the disaster. How great would it be, Huffman thinks, if you could aggregate all that into a comprehensive and sensible God's-eye picture of what's going on that would allow instantaneous and effective response?

45 Huffman, 28, sees the potential in this because Friends Next is at the heart of his personal life. "I'm one of the first in that generation of people very defined by friends obtained and maintained through social technologies," he says. "Almost all my close friends, I originally met over the Internet. They're *very* geographically spread out."

46 The one thing he's learned is Friends Next is not enough to sustain relationships. "A lot of friendship is sharing experiences, not necessarily planned. It's people going through the world, negotiating a pathway together."

47 But Huffman has discovered Friends Next can be a gateway to genuine intimacy.

48 Recently he organized a ski trip to British Columbia with his core group of buddies, and for the hell of it announced on Facebook that anybody who could read his profile was invited to come along. To his surprise, an acquaintance from Texas took him up on it. Houston-boy started off not knowing anybody else, but intense bonds ensued. "Now he's going with us to Burning Man—he's become a de facto member of the core group," Huffman says.

49 The novel ties of Friends Next have caused Huffman to think hard about what the word "friend" means.

50 "You can maintain a friendship over a distance. Once the person is a friend, it takes *very* little data to communicate very complex things. You can send a five-word e-mail" that, for someone else, "would take a two-hour conversation."

51 "A friend," however, he has decided, "is someone who you like a lot who understands you at a pretty deep level."

THE REAL THING

52 So in Friends Next, what matters? Is being good company enough? Is trust a key ingredient? Or loyalty? Or self-sacrifice?

"Go through your phone book, call people and ask them to drive you to the airport," Jay Leno once said. "The ones who will drive you are your true friends. The rest aren't bad people; they're just acquaintances." 53

It's the friends you can call up at 4 a.m. that matter," said Marlene Dietrich. 54

While Facebook will allow you as many as 5,000 "friends," enduring realities impose far more significant limits. 55

No matter how thick your soup of constant communication, sooner or later you may have to decide who will be your bridesmaid. 56

No matter how easily you can get Facebook on your iPhone, sooner or later you may have to decide who will be the godfather of your child. 57

And no matter how extensive your profile, it is certain that someday, someone is going to have to decide who will be your **pallbearers**. 58

Comprehension Check

Purpose and Main Idea

1. What is the author's topic?
   a. human relationships
   b. networking websites
   c. friendship in the digital age
   d. real friends vs. online "friends"
2. Which of the following sentences *best* states the author's central idea?
   a. Online networks are a big improvement over the more traditional alumni magazines and newsletters.
   b. The word "friend" covers a broad range of relationships from acquaintances to close friends.
   c. Because of sites like MySpace and Facebook, it has never been so easy to keep up with so many people.
   d. Networking websites have caused us to rethink the boundaries and intensities of our friendships.
3. The author's *primary* purpose is to
   a. inform us about the ways social networks have expanded our friendships.
   b. persuade readers that online friendships have their limits.
   c. entertain us with examples of real-world networking experiences.
   d. explain the advantages and disadvantages of having online "friends."

Details

4. The author calls which one of the following "arguably the most sophisticated popular site"?
   a. Friends Next
   b. MySpace
   c. Facebook
   d. Twitter

5. The world of social networking has been called a world of "participatory surveillance."
    a. True
    b. False
6. The students who questioned their teacher's drug use and choice of friends illustrates which one of the following points about social networking?
    a. Some friends are more equal than others.
    b. The Internet is a postmodern nightmare.
    c. You can't expect to keep your separate lives private.
    d. Social networks were supposed to dissolve barriers between people.
7. Although a real-world friendship may naturally fade away, losing friends in the digital world may require decisive action.
    a. True
    b. False
8. The author's details consist mainly of
    a. generalizations followed by examples
    b. quotations and explanations
    c. items compared and contrasted
    d. questions and answers

Inferences

9. Does the author seem to have a generally favorable or unfavorable attitude toward social networking?
10. What meaning do you infer from this quotation: "The digital trails of an online friendship—true or not—really do last forever" (paragraph 41). What might be the advantage or disadvantage of leaving behind a "digital trail?"

Working with Words

Complete sentences 1–8 with these words from Word Alert:

superficial	networked	fraught	touted
pallbearers	utopian	pruning	aloof

1. Some movies are not as good as they are _____ to be.
2. People who have too many online friends to keep up with may end up _____ those friendships.
3. The _____ at a funeral are often close friends or relatives of the deceased.
4. Because the wound was only _____, it did not require any stitches.
5. In the movie *Avatar*, the setting is a _____ society: what some would call a perfect world.
6. A person who is _____ may have a more difficult time making friends than someone who is outgoing.

7. Adjusting to life in a new town can be as _____ as moving from a place you love.
8. Because the friends were _____, they were able to keep up with each other even though they lived far apart.

Write your own sentences, using any two of the words from Word Alert.

9. _____

10. _____

Thinking Deeper

Ideas for reflection, discussion, and writing

Make Inferences from Your Reading

1. Discuss the social networking websites with which you are familiar. Do your experiences affirm or contradict what the author and the people he quotes have to say about online friendships?
2. Discuss the author's use of quotations in this selection. Are the quotations used effectively? Do you find the author's ideas more or less convincing because of these references, and why? What other purpose do the quotations serve?
3. Some researchers believe that social networking technology is bringing people closer together because it erases the physical distance between them, making it easier for them to stay in touch. Others believe that because online friendships are superficial and the ties between online "friends" are weak, this will only serve to drive people further apart and make it more challenging for them to find real-world friends. With which point of view do you agree, and why?
4. Explore several networking websites such as Facebook, MySpace, or others. If you already use these sites, choose one to explore that you have not visited. Your instructor or librarian may have suggestions. Then discuss with the class the advantages and disadvantages of these sites and their potential usefulness to you.

Write About It

5. Write about the way you use technology (websites, text messaging, cell phone, twitter, etc.) in your relationships with others.
6. What qualities do you seek in a real-world friend? Write about a friend of yours who has these qualities, and explain why you value the relationship.

FIRST THOUGHTS

To build background for the reading selection, answer the following questions, either on your own or in a group discussion.

1. Do you know a senior citizen who is learning to read for the first time or is attending college for the first time?
2. Looking back on your life so far, is there anything you didn't do when you were younger that you would like to do now?
3. Preview the title, headnote, and first one or two paragraphs. What do you think will follow?

WORD ALERT

Each word below is followed by its paragraph number. Preview the words and definitions before reading. Then review them as necessary during reading. Use context clues and your dictionary to define any additional unfamiliar words.

inspiration (2) stimulation of the mind or emotions to a higher level
huddle (3) gather closely together
vowed (4) promised solemnly, pledged
urged (5) advocated, insisted
stunned (6) dazed, astounded, shocked senseless
toting (7) carrying
septuagenarian (9) a person between the ages of 70 and 79
anchor (9) source of security or stability

◈ A First-Grader at Age 70

ALICIA DENNIS

Alicia Dennis has written numerous articles of human interest for *People* magazine. In this selection, she tells the inspiring story of Alferd Williams, a first-grader at the age of 70.

CHEEKS RED FROM the wind, the first graders bounce into Alesia Hamilton's class on 1 a recent Friday morning. Peeling off their mittens, they exchange excited greetings with a student, already seated, at the back of the room. "Good morning, Alferd!" one child sings. "Look, Alferd, I got new boots!" another calls out. "Are you ready for school, Alferd?" a third asks. Alferd Williams smiles back at his classmates and declares, "I'm ready."

And how. At 70, Willams, who joined Hamilton's class at Edison Elemen- 2 tary School in St. Joseph, MO., in September 2005, is fulfilling a promise he made to his mother, and himself, six decades ago. He is learning to read. Sitting in a circle with 25 six- and seven-year-olds, singing the class good morning song as he sips his cup of coffee, the world's oldest first grader couldn't be happier. "I lived all my life without knowing words," he says. "But now my life is changing." So too is the school that has supported Wiliams in pursuing his dream and, in return, has found a source of **inspiration**. "He is a powerful force in the building," says principal Jennifer Patterson. "I can't imagine life here without him."

For the soft-spoken Williams, it took a giant leap of imagination, and faith, 3 to get to Edison Elementary. Born in 1937 to Samuel and Lilly Williams of Eudora, AR., the fourth of nine children, Williams was just 8 when he went to work in the field, helping his sharecropper father pick cotton, corn, potatoes and cabbage until the sun went down. At night the family would **huddle** with blankets to shield themselves from the wind that whipped through cracks in the walls, papered-over with flour, water and pages of the Montgomery Ward catalogue; there was no reading hour. "We were just too tired to learn anything," Williams recalls.

His mother could read, but his father could not and paid a price for it. "People 4 took advantage of him his whole life," Williams says, recalling how, at the end of every harvest season, landowners would show Samuel "proof" that he owed them money. Williams **vowed** his life would turn out differently. But even as his twin brother, Jesse, sneaked off to school, Williams stayed in the fields. "Someone had to work so we could eat," he says. "Mama cried that I couldn't go to school. She made me promise that someday I would learn to read."

Married at 18, Williams and his wife would have eight children (they would 5 later separate and Williams would have two more children in another relationship); he couldn't help with much homework, but says he **urged** his kids to take school seriously. Employed as a metal worker and roofer in his 20s and 30s, he tried going to a reading tutor once, but quit, humiliated, after the guy chewed him out for showing up late. In 1998, alone, broke and in poor health, he spent a few weeks in a St. Louis homeless shelter; his brother Albert, a preacher, took him in and eventually helped him find a basement flat, where he lives today on $825 in monthly Social Security and disability pay. (His relationships with his adult children are mixed; he is close to a few and estranged from several. Admits Williams: "I could have been there more.")

6   Walking a friend's kids to Edison Elementary one day in 2005, he noticed Alesia Hamilton, a veteran teacher with a gentle manner. "She called students 'friends'; never did she raise her voice," he recalls. "I thought, 'Maybe she could teach me.'" Hamilton was **stunned** by his request. "I thought, 'How do I teach him?'" she says.

7   But she agreed to try. For two hours every afternoon that summer, Hamilton and Williams sat in the library, poring over picture books with one or two words to a page. "He didn't know words or letters," Hamilton, 43, recalls. "But, unlike a child, he had this wealth of knowledge that comes with living your life and he understood words in a way that young children can't." Impressed with his dedication, Hamilton persuaded principal Patterson to let Williams join her class for the 2006 academic year; after clearing a background check, Williams showed up that August for the first day of school, **toting** the lone worn leather duffel bag in a sea of brightly colored backpacks.

8   Attending daily from 9 a.m. to noon (he eats in the cafeteria with the kids once a week), Williams now is in his second year in Hamilton's class. Using a finger roughened by years of physical labor to follow the words as he reads, he counts his accomplishments by the books in his reading nook—*The Three Little Pigs*, Bill Cosby's *The Best Way to Play: A Little Bill Book for Beginning Readers* and a children's bible. On this recent morning, Williams and his two reading buddies Denisse Rubio and Jessica Lord sit at a table—Williams on an adult-size bench that Hamilton brought in—and start on a new book, *Too Many Puppies*. "What did you say that word was?" Williams asks Denisse. "I think it's 'yikes,'" Denisse says. Jessica agrees. "I don't hear that one very often," Williams says.

9   The help goes both ways. At Edison, where 87 percent of kids get free lunch and one-parent families are the norm, the **septuagenarian** first grader has become a beloved grandfather figure, school district officials say. "Alferd," adds Hamilton, "is an **anchor**. He lifts kids up." Drayke Collins, 7, recently diagnosed with ADHD, "had a horrible kindergarten year and didn't want to go to first grade," says his mom, Amber Jones, 26. "Then there was Alferd. Drayke loves reading and talking with him. Now I can't keep him away." Sydney Bauer's daughter Leah, 8, and now a second-grader, was in class with Williams last year. "Leah would come home every day with stories about Alferd," says Bauer, a cook. "He's teaching kids you can learn at any age." Says Leah: "He showed me how to stretch out words if you couldn't figure it out. He's helped so many of us. He's a great person to have in your class."

10   Williams' lesson to his young classmates is simple: "I tell the kids they can have anything they want in life if they stay in school," he says.

11   As for himself, Williams plans to stay in Hamilton's class, year after year, until he gets his GED, a goal Hamilton is convinced he'll achieve, just as surely as he finished his first book—*Little Bear,* by Else Holmelund Minarik, about a mother

bear caring for her cub. "I'll never forget it," Williams says. "That was like saying to my mother, 'I did it. I did what I promised I would do. I learned to read.'"

Comprehension Check

Purpose and Main Idea

1. What is the author's topic?
   a. first-grade memories
   b. literacy
   c. Alferd Williams
   d. learning to read
2. Which one of the following sentences from the selection states the author's central idea?
   a. Alferd Williams is learning to read and inspiring others in the process.
   b. At age 70, Williams is the world's oldest first-grader.
   c. You are never too old to learn how to read.
   d. It is not unusual for a senior citizen to return to elementary school.
3. The author's *primary* purpose is to
   a. persuade readers to support literacy education.
   b. express her admiration for Alferd Williams.
   c. explain what it is like to be a 70-year-old attending school for the first time.
   d. entertain us with an inspiring story about a man who is learning to read.

Details

4. Williams was not encouraged to go to school when he was young.
   a. True
   b. False
5. All of the following are true of Alferd Williams except which one?
   a. He worked as a roofer and a metal worker
   b. Williams is a sharecropper's son.
   c. He has never been married.
   d. Williams was homeless for a time.
6. The children at Edison Elementary School have reacted favorably to Williams's presence there.
   a. True
   b. False
7. Hamilton agreed to teach Williams for all but which one of the following reasons?
   a. Hamilton was impressed with his dedication.
   b. His wealth of knowledge came from life experience.
   c. He understood words in a way that the children did not.
   d. Hamilton felt sorry that he had missed out on school.

8. The author's primary pattern of organization is
   a. sequence.
   b. cause and effect.
   c. comparison and contrast.
   d. classification.

Inferences

9. In paragraph 5, what is the meaning of the phrase "chewed him out?" What specific words or examples help you make this inference?
10. Using the context, determine the meaning of "estranged" in paragraph 5. What clues do you find in the sentence in which this word appears, or in surrounding sentences?

Working with Words

Complete sentences 1–8 with these words from Word Alert:

septuagenarian	stunned	anchor	vowed
inspiration	huddle	toting	urged

1. When choosing a topic for a research paper, look to your own areas of interest for the _____ to write.
2. The students hurried to _____ under an awning to get out of the rain.
3. Alferd Williams _____ that he would one day learn to read.
4. Doctors _____ their patients to get their flu vaccines early.
5. Some parents are _____ by the outlandish outfits today's teenagers wear.
6. It would take less time to load passengers on an airplane if they weren't _____ so much carry-on baggage.
7. The grocery clerk looked at the driver's license of the _____ and said "You don't look like a 70-year-old."
8. We all need someone to lean on, someone to be the _____ in our lives.

Write your own sentences, using any two of the words from Word Alert.

9. _____
10. _____

Thinking Deeper

Ideas for reflection, discussion, and writing

Make Inferences from Your Reading

1. What would you infer are the costs to society when millions of adults do not have basic literacy; that is, they are unable to read simple instructions on food packages or the inserts that come with prescriptions? What is the likely future of children born to adults who cannot read?

2. The author suggests that the students in his class help Williams and he helps the students. How does this help go both ways, as the author says in paragraph 9? What inferences can you make from Williams's story about the value of having people of different ages in any class at any level?

3. Alferd Williams is one of *People* magazine's "Heroes Among Us," a regular feature in this periodical. Based on your reading of the selection, what makes Alferd Williams a hero?

4. Search the Internet to learn more about literacy in the United States. How many adults in the United States are unable to read? What are some of the reasons for poor reading or lack of reading ability? What conclusions can you draw about ways to combat this problem? Share your search results with the class. Some websites to try are www.proliteracy.org and www.nifl.gov. Because URLs and website content change frequently, ask your instructor or librarian for help if needed.

Write About It

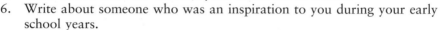

5. Write about someone who fits your definition of a hero.

6. Write about someone who was an inspiration to you during your early school years.

FIRST THOUGHTS

To build background for the reading selection, answer the following questions, either on your own or in a group discussion.

1. Have you ever made New Year's resolutions?
2. Can you think of a resolution, either for New Year's or otherwise, that you have kept?
3. Preview the title, headnote, and first one or two paragraphs. What do you think will follow?

WORD ALERT

Each word below is followed by its paragraph number. Preview the words and definitions before reading. Then review them as necessary during reading. Use context clues and your dictionary to define any additional unfamiliar words.

disgruntled (1) ill-humored, discontented
apathy (1) lack of interest or concern
forum (3) a public place, a medium for open discussion
grudge (3) feeling of resentment
bygones (4) old grievances or complaints that have long past
accountable (6) responsible, answerable
malice (8) a desire to harm others or to see others suffer

◈ Real Resolutions

TARA L. TEDROW

Tara L.Tedrow was a Presidential Scholar for Debate and captain of the Mock Trial Team at Wake Forest University in North Carolina. Her articles have appeared in the *Orlando Sentinel*. This article was written in anticipation of the new year and holds an empowering message for all of us who face challenges.

MAKING NEW YEAR'S resolutions is about as common as breaking them, leaving 1 most Americans **disgruntled** with their newly required gym memberships or nicotine patches. The list of broken pledges is endless, and the reasons we made them in the beginning are lost when feelings of guilt or **apathy** are all that remain. This year should be different. America enters [next year] with big problems and big decisions ahead. Here are resolutions that I think people should try to live by…

You can't take it with you when you go. Bill Gates has set a wonderful example 2 of helping others with his fortune while he's alive. In every community there's a family struggling. You don't have to be rich to do a simple act of kindness. I took part of my summer job money and bought groceries for a family last week I'd never seen before and will never see again. I'm not rich, but it made me feel like a million dollars.

Take personal responsibility. This seems to be my generation's greatest fault. 3 If you wrong someone, say you're sorry. If you made a mistake, don't try to cover it up by blaming others. You don't need Judge Judy to tell you this, but it seems that Court TV is the popular **forum** for battling out a **grudge**. Trust me, once you apologize and put the past behind you, you'll be entering next year with one less enemy.

Realize that nobody's perfect. We're all sinners, and we all make mistakes. 4 Count to 10 before you react in anger. Truly let **bygones** be bygones, and you'll immediately feel that stress lifting off your shoulders. But keep in mind that what you find a fault is not the fault in the eyes of others—try to see things from other perspectives. Don't hold everyone to the same standard of perfection that you might hold yourself to—and especially don't hold others to it if you don't even hold yourself to it.

Treat others like you want to be treated. Think how much the tone in this 5 country would change if we all took a step back and began smiling more. Hold the door for an elderly person at the grocery. Say thank you to waitresses who are struggling to get by and leave an extra tip. We were all taught this when we were little, but we've lost this simple, but so important, aspect of our lives that could lower tempers and raise the livability of every community in this country.

Register to vote and vote like your life depended on it. America desperately 6 needs more citizen participation. Get involved and learn the facts, because it's wrong to believe that our leaders know more than we do. Think of the mess in Iraq or the scandal at the Orlando-Orange County Expressway Authority. Politicians need to be

accountable, and that means following the way they vote and voting against them if you don't like it. I've about had it with people my age and older who complain about our country yet haven't even seen what a voter-registration card looks like. People have risked and still are risking their lives for freedom that we constantly take for granted—show respect for their hard work and for what our country is supposed to stand for.

7   **When you see the flag, give it a nod.** Put your hand over your heart when you say the pledge. Take your ball cap off when the National Anthem is sung at a Magic game. There are brave American soldiers dying in faraway places who are willing to give up their lives for you and that flag, so respect it and you respect them.

8   **Get a life.** Work to live; don't live to work. Spend time with your children; they grow up before you realize it. Wet a line and rediscover the magic of catching a fish, as I did two weeks ago. If you're lonely, get a pet. Learn to laugh without **malice**. Take a daily walk and look for the simple things around you, and you'll find that there truly is a higher power that has brought all this together.

9   **Open your heart.** Stop this moment, pick up the phone and call your mom or dad and tell them you love them. Send a card to your grandma just to say you're thinking about her. I wrote my grandpa a long letter out-of-the-blue last month, remembering some of the fun times we'd had together, and he called and we talked and laughed for an hour. If you're divorced and your kids are living away from you, call those kids every week, and with sincerity, thank the man or woman who has taken your place.

10   Next year could be life changing for each of us if we open our hearts to each other. I'm going to do my best to end this year with a smile on my face, with memories in my mind's eye about a few simple good deeds that I've done. I hope you'll make a resolution to do the same.

Comprehension Check

Purpose and Main Idea

1. What is the author's topic?
    a. types of resolutions
    b. New Year's resolutions
    c. meaningful resolutions
    d. keeping resolutions
2. Which sentence from the aritcle *best* states the author's central idea?
    a. paragraph 1, first sentence
    b. paragraph 1, last sentence
    c. paragraph 10, first sentence
    d. paragraph 10, last sentence
3. What is the author's *primary* purpose?
    a. inform readers about the history of making resolutions
    b. define the concept of New Year's resolutions
    c. express a viewpoint about New Year's resolutions in general
    d. persuade readers to make and keep resolutions

Details

4. "Let bygones be bygones" is an example of which resolution?
   a. Take personal responsibility.
   b. Realize that nobody's perfect.
   c. Treat others like you want to be treated.
   d. Open your heart.
5. The author believes that resolutions are meant to be broken.
   a. True
   b. False
6. The author uses incidents from her personal life to add support to all but which one of the following resolutions?
   a. You can't take it with you.
   b. Open your heart.
   c. Treat others like you want to be treated.
   d. Get a life.
7. The author thinks the failure to take personal responsibility is her generation's greatest fault.
   a. True
   b. False
8. Which one of the following is the author's *dominant* pattern of organization?
   a. contrast
   b. process
   c. cause and effect
   d. generalization then example

Inferences

9. What inference can you make from the title? What makes the author's resolutions "real?"
10. Apart from being "real resolutions," what is one more thing that all the author's resolutions have in common?

Working with Words

Complete sentences 1–7 with these words from Word Alert:

accountable	bygones	grudge	apathy
disgruntled	malice	forum	

1. It is better to forgive than to hold a _____ toward someone who has wronged you.
2. Don't we all wish that our elected officials were more _____ to the voters?
3. A _____ person will most certainly have fewer friends than one who is good humored.
4. Many couples have a tendency to bring up _____ when they are having an argument.

5. My mother is a kindhearted person who has no _____ in her heart.
6. Ideally, the editorial pages of newspapers serve as a _____ where people can express different opinions.
7. When your team isn't winning, you may have to work at maintaining school spirit so that you do not sink into _____.

Write your own sentences, using any two of the words from Word Alert.

8. _____
9. _____

Thinking Deeper

Ideas for reflection, discussion, and writing

Make Inferences from Your Reading

1. To support the resolution "You can't take it with you when you go," the author gives several examples. Based on these details, what additional examples can you give of people helping others, including examples from your own life?
2. "Treat others like you want to be treated" is a paraphrase of the Golden Rule. Review the author's examples of following the Golden Rule rule in paragraph 5. What inference can you make about the Rule as it applies in your daily life? Who follows the rule? Who breaks it?
3. In paragraph 1, the author says that America faces "big problems and big decisions" in the coming year. There is probably no year in which this statement would not be true. In your opinion, what big challenges face America? What big decisions are you facing?
4. In paragraph 2, the author praises Bill Gates for sharing his fortune while he is still alive. People who help others in this way are called philanthropists. Is there someone in public life that you admire for his or her public service? Research this person on the Internet. Find out what charities, groups, or causes he or she supports. Then share your results with the class.

Write About It

5. Evaluate the author's list of resolutions. Write about the one that you think is most important and why.
6. Write your own list of "real resolutions" that you think people should live by and explain your reasons.

FIRST THOUGHTS

To build background for the reading selection, answer the following questions, either on your own or in a group discussion.

1. What do you know about parables, fables, or folktales?
2. What is the purpose of such a story?
3. Preview the title, headnote, and first one or two paragraphs. What do you think will follow?

WORD ALERT

Each word below is followed by its paragraph number. Preview the words and definitions before reading. Then review them as necessary during reading. Use context clues and your dictionary to define any additional unfamiliar words.

fetlocks (1) tufts of hair above and behind a horse's hooves

anlage (1) foundation for a future development, potential

threshed (2) beat, stomped, tossed about

embankment (2) mound of earth or stone built to hold back water or a roadway

parapet (2) a low protective wall or railing

peered (2) looked intently or searchingly

fraction (4) fragment, small amount or part

From *The Grapes of Wrath*

JOHN STEINBECK

John Steinbeck is one of our great American authors. His novel *The Grapes of Wrath*, from which this selection is taken, is about the plight of migrant workers who fled the dust bowl during the Depression to find work picking fruit and vegetables in California. This selection is Chapter Three of the book, and many have called it a parable, or instructive tale.

1   THE CONCRETE HIGHWAY was edged with a mat of tangled, broken, dry grass, and the grass heads were heavy with oat beards to catch on a dog's coat, and foxtails to tangle in a horse's **fetlocks,** and clover burrs to fasten in sheep's wool; sleeping life waiting to be spread and dispersed, every seed armed with an appliance of dispersal, twisting darts and parachutes for the wind, little spears and balls of tiny thorns, and all waiting for animals and for the wind, for a man's trouser cuff or the hem of a woman's skirt, all passive but armed with appliances of activity, still, but each possessed of the **anlage** of movement.

2   The sun lay on the grass and warmed it, and in the shade under the grass the insects moved, ants and ant lions to set traps for them, grasshoppers to jump into the air and flick their yellow wings for a second, sow bugs like little armadillos, plodding restlessly on many tender feet. And over the grass at the roadside a land turtle crawled, turning aside for nothing, dragging his high-domed shell over the grass. His hard legs and yellow-nailed feet **threshed** slowly through the grass, not really walking, but boosting and dragging his shell along. The barley beards slid off his shell, and the clover burrs fell on him and rolled to the ground. His horny beak was partly open, and his fierce, humorous eyes, under brows like fingernails, stared straight ahead. He came over the grass leaving a beaten trail behind him, and the hill, which was the highway **embankment,** reared up ahead of him. For a moment he stopped, his head held high. He blinked and looked up and down. At last he started to climb the embankment. Front clawed feet reached forward but did not touch. The hind feet kicked his shell along, and it scraped on the grass, and on the gravel. As the embankment grew steeper and steeper, the more frantic were the efforts of the land turtle. Pushing hind legs strained and slipped, boosting the shell along, and the horny head protruded as far as the neck could stretch. Little by little the shell slid up the embankment until at last a **parapet** cut straight across its line of march, the shoulder of the road, a concrete wall four inches high. As though they worked independently the hind legs pushed the shell against the wall. The head upraised and **peered** over the wall to the broad smooth plain of cement. Now the hands, braced on top of the wall, strained and lifted, and the shell came slowly up and rested its front end on the wall. For a moment the turtle rested. A red ant ran into the shell, into the soft skin inside the shell, and suddenly head and legs snapped in, and the armored tail clamped in sideways. The red ant was crushed between body and legs. And one head of wild oats was clamped into the shell by a front leg. For a long moment the turtle lay still, and then the neck crept out and the old humorous frowning eyes looked about and the legs and tail came out. The back

legs went to work, straining like elephant legs, and the shell tipped to an angle so that the front legs could not reach the level cement plain. But higher and higher the hind legs boosted it, until at last the center of balance was reached, the front tipped down, the front legs scratched at the pavement, and it was up. But the head of wild oats was held by its stem around the front legs.

Now the going was easy, and all the legs worked, and the shell boosted along, 3 waggling from side to side. A sedan driven by a forty-year-old woman approached. She saw the turtle and swung to the right, off the highway, the wheels screamed and a cloud of dust boiled up. Two wheels lifted for a moment and then settled. The car skidded back onto the road, and went on, but more slowly. The turtle jerked into its shell, but now it hurried on, for the highway was burning hot.

And now a light truck approached, and as it came near, the driver saw the tur- 4 tle and swerved to hit it. His front wheel struck the edge of the shell, flipped the turtle like a tiddly-wink, spun it like a coin, and rolled it off the highway. The truck went back to its course along the right side. Lying on its back, the turtle was tight in its shell for a long time. But at last its legs waved in the air, reaching for something to pull it over. Its front foot caught a piece of quartz and little by little the shell pulled over and flopped upright. The wild oat head fell out and three of the spearhead seeds stuck in the ground. And as the turtle crawled on down the embankment, its shell dragged dirt over the seeds. The turtle entered a dust road and jerked itself along, drawing a wavy shallow trench in the dust with its shell. The old humorous eyes looked ahead, and the horny beak opened a little. His yellow toe nails slipped a **fraction** in the dust.

Comprehension Check

Purpose and Main Idea

1. What is the author's topic?
   a. the desert landscape
   b. desert weather conditions
   c. a busy highway
   d. a land turtle's journey
2. Which sentence *best* states the central idea of the selection?
   a. A desert highway is a dangerous place for both animals and people.
   b. A turtle crosses a highway, carrying on nature's processes.
   c. The desert landscape is filled with life.
   d. Dust and heat are characteristic of desert weather.
3. The author's *primary* purpose is to
   a. express his feelings about nature.
   b. teach readers facts about turtles.
   c. describe desert life.
   d. relate an instructive story.

Details

4. The turtle in this story is old.
   a. True.
   b. False.
5. In the first paragraph, the author describes the process of
   a. plant growth.
   b. fertilization.
   c. seed dispersal.
   d. soil erosion.
6. What did the turtle do when he came to the embankment?
   a. He stopped and remained at the foot of it.
   b. He walked in the opposite direction.
   c. He crawled parallel to it.
   d. He climbed to the top of it.
7. A head of wild oats became lodged under the turtle's shell.
   a. True
   b. False
8. The author's details are mainly
   a. facts.
   b. examples.
   c. descriptions.
   d. reasons.

Inferences

9. Based on the details in paragraph 4, what do you conclude has happened to the oat seeds?
10. What do you infer as an underlying message of this tale?

Working with Words

Complete sentences 1–7 with these words from Word Alert:

embankment	fraction	anlage	parapet
fetlocks	threshed	peered	

1. The little boy _____ from between the blinds, watching his dad leave for work.
2. We live in a beautiful city where even the _____ below the interstate highway is planted with flowers.
3. Don't tempt me with even a _____ of a slice of that pie because I am trying to watch my weight.
4. The telephone line workers _____ through my yard in their heavy hoots, smashing my flowers.
5. Holding the small egg that had fallen out of the nest, Tina knew that it possessed the _____ of life.

6. We climbed to the top of the tower and stood along a _____ looking out across a wide valley.
7. After the race, the horse's _____ were wet with sweat.

Write your own sentences, using any two of the words from Word Alert.

8. _____
9. _____

Thinking Deeper

Ideas for reflection, discussion, and writing

Make Inferences from Your Reading

1. Trace the turtle's journey. Where is he going, and what happens along the way?
2. Discuss Steinbeck's use of descriptive details. Identify passages in the story that create especially vivid images in your mind.
3. Life is a struggle for all living things—including humans. If tales are meant to be instructive, then what does this one teach us by the example of the turtle's journey and the oat seed's progress?

4. Search your library's online catalog for a book of folktales. Most such tales are short, like this one. Find a tale that you enjoy and that you think has an important message for readers. Share the tale in a class discussion.

Write About It

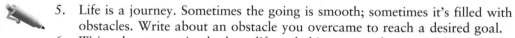

5. Life is a journey. Sometimes the going is smooth; sometimes it's filled with obstacles. Write about an obstacle you overcame to reach a desired goal.
6. Write about an animal whose life or habits can teach us something about our own lives.

FIRST THOUGHTS

To build background for the reading selection, answer the following questions, either on your own or in a group discussion.

1. Does the thought of giving a speech before a group make you anxious?
2. What strategies for reducing speech anxiety do you know?
3. Preview the title, headnote, and first one or two paragraphs. What do you think will follow?

WORD ALERT

Each word below is followed by its paragraph number. Preview the words and definitions before reading. Then review them as necessary during reading. Use context clues and your dictionary to define any additional unfamiliar words.

In a textbook chapter, the words to watch may appear in boldface, italics, or a special color.

speech anxiety (1) fear of speaking in front of an audience
apprehension (4) anxiety, fear about the future
peers (5) equals; those who have equal standing with each other
vantage (7) strategic position; a position offering a comprehensive view or perspective
spotlight effect (9) a belief that others are observing you more carefully than they actually are
itinerary (10) account or record of an experience or a journey
visualization (15) formation of a mental image
relabeling (17) assigning positive words or phrases to physical reactions
diaphragm (20) a muscular membrane that functions in breathing

◈ What Is Speech Anxiety?

STEPHANIE J. COOPMAN AND JAMES LULL

This textbook reading from the discipline of speech communication is excerpted from Chapter 2 of *Public Speaking, The Evolving Art.* The authors examine the problem of speech anxiety and offer hope for its sufferers.

WHAT IS SPEECH ANXIETY?

In the simplest terms, **speech anxiety** refers to fear of speaking in front of the audi-   1
ence. Speech anxiety begins with uncertainty.[6] For most people, speaking in public is not an everyday situation. You communicate with others every day, but probably not in a situation as formal and structured as a speech. The change in context from your regular everyday interactions with others to an unfamiliar, public interaction naturally makes you nervous.

Sources of Speech Anxiety

Speech anxiety stems from seven different sources of uncertainty: the speaker's   2
role, your speaking abilities, your ideas, the audience's response, the setting, the technology used, and how others will evaluate you. Those sources are summarized in **Table 2.1.**

UNCERTAINTY ABOUT YOUR ROLE AS A SPEAKER

Like most people, you're probably much more familiar with listening than with   3
speaking in public. In the speaker role, you may wonder, Will they understand me? How should I use notes? What does the audience expect? Those uncertainties can begin long before you present a speech—even in the early stages of preparation you might feel your heart rate go up as you think about your speech.[8] The less certain you are about your role as speaker, the more nervous you will feel about presenting a speech.

UNCERTAINTY ABOUT YOUR SPEAKING ABILITIES

A second uncertainty associated with public speaking concerns your speaking abili-   4
ties. You may wonder, What am I able to do as a speaker? You likely haven't had many opportunities to test your skills as a communicator in formal, structured situations. You may lack confidence in your abilities as a public speaker; you may not be sure you have the skills you need to speak effectively. If English is not your first language, you may also feel uncertain of your ability to make your message clear. The less confidence you have in your speaking skills, the more **apprehension** you will feel about public speaking.[9]

TABLE 2.1 | Uncertainties and Questions about Public Speaking

UNCERTAINTY ABOUT ...	QUESTION SPEAKERS ASK THEMSELVES
the speaker's role	What should I do?
my speaking abilities	What am I able to do?
my ideas	How well do I know my topic?
the audience's response	How will others react?
the setting	How familiar/unfamiliar is the space?
the technology	Will the technology work?
how others will evaluate me	What impression will I make?

UNCERTAINTY ABOUT YOUR IDEAS

5 In everyday conversations you don't expect people to thoroughly research every topic they talk about. In contrast, your public speaking audience expects you to be an authority on your subject. Nobody wants to appear foolish, and certainly not in front of a group of **peers**. You may ask yourself, "How well do I know my topic?" The less sure you are about your knowledge of your topic, the more nervous you will feel about giving the speech.

UNCERTAINTY ABOUT THE AUDIENCE'S RESPONSE

6 When you have a pretty good idea about what will happen in a given situation, you feel fairly comfortable. In public speaking, you don't know exactly how audience members will respond to your message.[11] You might ask yourself, "Will they understand my point? Will they respect me and my ideas? Will they agree or disagree with me? Will they find my speech interesting, or think it's boring?" When you present a speech, you risk having your ideas rejected. The less you believe you can predict the audience's response to your speech, the more anxious you will feel.

UNCERTAINTY ABOUT THE SETTING

7 As a student, you're used to the instructor standing in the front of the room. As a speaker, you're the one up there in front. The room seems very different from this **vantage** point—and even more intimidating when you face an auditorium filled with 500 people. While you may be accustomed to public settings as an audience member, you're probably less used to such settings as a speaker.[12] The more unfamiliar the setting, the more nervous you may feel about your speech.

UNCERTAINTY ABOUT TECHNOLOGY

8 You instant message and chat with friends from your home computer. If you lose your internet connection, you may be annoyed and frustrated, but not embarrassed. In contrast, when the laptop you're using for your speech freezes, you panic and

your anxiety level soars. When thinking about giving a speech, you'll probably ask, "Will the technology work?" Lack of familiarity with technical equipment and concerns about it working increase a speaker's nervousness.

UNCERTAINTY ABOUT EVALUATION

Fear of negative evaluation plays a major role in students' anxiety about public speaking and contributes to physical symptoms such as elevated heart rate and queasiness. Even after you learn how your instructor grades speeches, you may feel nervous about how your classmates will respond. In other public speaking situations, such as giving an oral report at work or nominating someone at a meeting, speakers are also concerned about how others view them.[13] Research shows, however, that the **spotlight effect** leads a speaker to *think* people observe her or him much more carefully than they actually do.[14] Many of the little things you may do when speaking—stumbling over a word, briefly losing your train of thought, skipping to the wrong digital slide—are far more noticeable to you than to the audience. Of course, listeners will evaluate your presentation, but the spotlight probably isn't nearly as bright as you might think. 9

STRATEGIES FOR BUILDING YOUR CONFIDENCE

The remainder of this chapter travels through the whole **itinerary** of the public speaking experience—from the weeks before the speech to the hours afterward—to identify what you can do at each stage to effectively manage speech anxiety and build your confidence. You'll learn about specific strategies for managing your speech anxiety as public speaking becomes a more familiar and comfortable activity. 10

MAINTAINING A POSITIVE ATTITUDE

Research shows that taking a positive attitude truly helps lessen your anxiety about speaking in front of others, while negative thoughts increase anxiety.[15] 11

Think of speech anxiety as intelligent fear, a natural response that can serve a positive purpose. With intelligent fear, you use the responses associated with fear, such as heightened emotions, increased sensitivity to your surroundings, and greater attention to sensory information, to give a better presentation.[16] Taking a positive attitude toward public speaking also can become a self-fulfilling prophecy in which you define the situation as a positive one, leading you to act in ways that move you toward a positive outcome. If you have a positive attitude toward public speaking, you: 12

- Look forward to sharing information with your audience.
- View public speaking as an opportunity to influence others ethically.
- Welcome the chance to entertain others with humor and stories.
- Listen eagerly to what others have to say in their speeches and during discussion.

13   Feeling more positive about public speaking takes time; it won't happen overnight. Developing a positive attitude toward public speaking provides a first step toward managing your speech anxiety.

VISUALIZATION, RELABELING, AND RELAXATION

14 Visualization, relabeling, and relaxation are three methods you can use to view public speaking in a more positive way and improve your effectiveness when you speak.

VISUALIZATION

15 When you apply **visualization** to public speaking, you think through the sequence of events that will make up the speech in a positive, detailed, concrete, step-by-step way. Visualize the place, the audience, and yourself successfully presenting your speech. Focus on what will go right, not what will go wrong.[17] Use all your senses to really *feel* what will happen. Visualize yourself:

- Gathering your notes, standing up, and walking to the front of the room.
- Facing the audience, making eye contact, smiling, and beginning the speech.
- Observing audience members nodding, jotting down a few notes, and listening intently.
- Presenting each main point.
- Incorporating effective presentation resources.
- Giving the conclusion and listening to audience members clapping.
- Answering questions readily.
- Thanking the audience, walking back to your seat, and sitting down.
- Congratulating yourself on giving an effective speech.

16   Psychologists, teachers, athletes, actors, and many others emphasize the importance of controlling your feelings when facing the challenge of a public presentation. You may already have visualized success in challenging situations. When you visualize your speech going well, you will reduce your anxiety and build your confidence.[18]

RELABELING

17 **Relabeling** involves assigning positive words or phrases to the physical reactions and feelings associated with speech anxiety. You stop using negative words and phrases like *fearful* and *apprehensive,* and instead use positive words like *thrilled* and *delighted.* When your voice quavers a bit and your hands shake, attribute those sensations to your body and mind gathering the energy they need to prepare for and present the speech. Say to yourself, "I'm really excited about giving this speech!" rather than, "I'm so nervous about this speech." Skeptical? Try it! Your anxiety won't magically disappear, but relabeling puts your response to public speaking in a positive light and can increase your ability to manage your anxiety.

RELAXATION TECHNIQUES

Relaxation techniques help reduce the physical symptoms of stress, such as in- 18 creased heart rate and tense muscles. Developing good breathing habits provides the foundation for relaxing. Three exercises increase breathing efficiency, reduce nervousness, and help you relax.[19]

The first exercise, *diaphragmatic breathing,* relies upon smooth, even breathing 19 using your diaphragm. Sit or stand with your feet flat on the floor, shoulder width apart. With your hands just below your rib cage, breathe in with an exaggerated yawn while pushing your abdomen out. Exhale slowly and gently, letting your abdomen relax inward.

The second exercise, *meditation breathing,* helps your body relax. Begin by 20 breathing with your **diaphragm**, but this time focus on every aspect of the breathing process and how it feels. Clear your mind of all thoughts and concentrate on the rhythm of your breathing: in breath, out breath, in breath, out breath.

The last exercise, *tension-release breathing,* combines diaphragmatic breathing 21 with relaxing specific parts of your body. Begin by finding a comfortable position and breathing naturally. While you're breathing, identify tense muscle areas. Then inhale fully, using your diaphragm. As you slowly exhale, relax one tense muscle area. Continue this process until you feel completely relaxed. This exercise can be done systematically by starting at your head and progressing to your toes, or vice versa.[20]

Managing speech anxiety begins with developing a positive attitude toward 22 public speaking. Visualizing a successful presentation, relabeling anxious feelings, and using relaxation techniques are three proven ways to increase your positive feelings and reduce your anxiety. **Table 2.2** summarizes these strategies.

TABLE 2.2 | VISUALIZATION, RELABELING, AND RELAXATION

STRATEGY	BRIEF DEFINITION	EXAMPLE
Visualization	Imagining successful presentation	Envision audience's positive response to speech introduction.
Relabeling	Assigning positive words to anxious feelings	Use "lively" or "energetic" instead of "nervous."
Relaxation techniques	Reducing physical symptoms of stress	Engage in meditation breathing by focusing on how it feels to breathe.

Comprehension Check

Purpose and Main Idea

1. What is the authors' topic?
   a. improving speeches
   b. public speaking
   c. speech anxiety
   d. presentations

2.   Which sentence from the textbook excerpt states the central idea?
    a.   paragraph 1, first sentence
    b.   paragraph 2, first sentence
    c.   paragraph 3, last sentence
    d.   Paragraph 22, first sentence
3.   The authors' *primary* purpose is to
    a.   entertain readers with interesting facts about speaking.
    b.   inform readers about the causes of speech anxiety.
    c.   persuade readers to improve their speaking.
    d.   express an opinion about public speaking.

Details

4.   Which one of the following is *not* one of the authors' seven sources of speech anxiety?
    a.   the speaker's role
    b.   your speaking ability
    c.   inherited traits
    d.   audience response
5.   According to the authors, speech anxiety stems from uncertainty.
    a.   True
    b.   False
6.   Which one of the following is a question to ask yourself about how others will evaluate you as a speaker?
    a.   What am I able to do?
    b.   How will others react?
    c.   What impression will I make?
    d.   How well do I know my topic?
7.   According to the authors, speech anxiety is a natural response.
    a.   True
    b.   False
8.   The authors define speech anxiety primarily by which one of the following?
    a.   comparing several types of speech anxiety
    b.   providing examples of anxiety-provoking situations
    c.   classifying the uncertainties that cause speech anxiety
    d.   explaining a process for overcoming speech anxiety

Inferences

9. Based on the details in paragraph 12, what do you infer as the meaning of the term "self-fulfilling prophecy"?
10. In paragraphs 15 and 16, the authors explain visualization, a technique that can help you reduce speech anxiety. Based on the information presented in these paragraphs, for what other activities might visualization be a useful technique?

Working with Words

Complete sentences 1–9 with these words from Word Alert:

spotlight effect	visualization	relabeling	itinerary	peers
speech anxiety	apprehension	diaphragm	vantage	

1. When exercising, you should breathe deeply from your _____.
2. Based on our _____ for this trip, we will visit five countries over the next two weeks.
3. According to the United States Constitution, an accused criminal is entitled to a trial by a jury of his or her _____.
4. Feeling nauseated before making a presentation is one sign of _____.
5. To improve performance in any activity, use a _____ technique to help you see yourself being successful.
6. Replacing the phrase "I can't" with the phrase "I can" is one example of the _____ process.
7. From the _____ point of the observation deck on the building's highest floor, we could see out across the entire city.
8. Believing that people are paying more attention to you than they actually are is one example of the _____.
9. It is common to feel feelings of _____ whenever you try an activity for the first time.

Write your own sentences, using any two of the words from Word Alert.

10. _____
11. _____

Thinking Deeper

Ideas for reflection, discussion, and writing

Make Inferences from Your Reading

1. Read through the list of uncertainties and questions listed in Table 2-1. In terms of your own experiences with public speaking, which one of the uncertainties gives you the most trouble and why?
2. What is your reaction to this sentence from paragraph 7: "The more unfamiliar the setting, the more nervous you may feel about your speech." Do you agree or disagree? From your own experience, what inference can you make about the effect of the setting on performing any other activity?
3. Speech anxiety is a personal challenge for many students. What personal academic challenges have you encountered in college so far? Which one of the authors' suggestions about how to reduce speech anxiety might also help you to meet your challenge?

4. What else can you do to reduce speech anxiety or to ensure that you will make an effective speech? Search the Internet for ideas. Toastmasters is one site to try. Ask your instructor or librarian for more URLs.

Write About It

5. The authors explain several ways to reduce speech anxiety. Write about one of these techniques that you have tried and explain whether it was successful.
6. Write about a fear that you overcame and explain how you did it.

HARD QUESTIONS FOR ALL

Most days begin with questions: What kind of weather are we having? What should I wear to class or to work? What do I want for breakfast? These are easy questions that you can answer without giving them much thought. However, life is filled with harder questions that require critical thinking and whose answers may have personal, national, or global consequences.

Education, social and cultural values, race relations, the economy, immigration, global terrorism, homeland security, disease epidemics, and natural disasters raise hard questions for which the answers are often complex or elusive.

The Part 4 selections are about confronting life's hard questions and searching for answers. As you read each selection, ask yourself: What is the issue? What is the author's perspective? What are the opposing perspectives? What questions are raised, and what answers are offered? As a final question, ask yourself: What do I think?

FIRST THOUGHTS

To build background for the reading selection, answer the following questions, either on your own or in a group discussion.

1. Do you believe that educators have correctly determined your needs as a student?
2. Do you think that male and female students have different needs?
3. Preview the title, headnote, and first one or two paragraphs. What do you think will follow?

WORD ALERT

Each word below is followed by its paragraph number. Preview the words and definitions before reading. Then review them as necessary during reading. Use context clues and your dictionary to define any additional unfamiliar words.

unfathomable (1) not understandable, incomprehensible

cues (4) signals, hints, suggestions

procreation (7) sexual reproduction

agitation (12) emotional disturbance, restlessness

implicit (15) implied, suggested, not directly expressed

succinctly (17) expressing much in few words, concisely

tainted (22) morally corrupted

adulation (22) excessive flattery or admiration

exuberance (24) enthusiasm, joy

◆ Have Today's Schools Failed Male Students?

PATRICIA DALTON

Patricia Dalton is a Washington, D.C., clinical psychologist. In this selection she suggests that in our attempt to overcome the disadvantages of female students, we may have shortchanged male students.

FOR ALL THE **unfathomable** horror of the shootings at Columbine High School, there 1 was one thing that came as no surprise to me.

It was boys who fired the guns in Littleton, Colo. Just as it was boys who 2 fired the guns in the school shootings in Pearl, Miss., in West Paducah, Ky., in Jonesboro, Ark., in Springfield, Ore., and in Conyers, Ga.

It seems clear to me, both as a psychologist and as the mother of two daughters 3 and a son, that we should be concerned about how we are failing our boys.

I'm not suggesting that every boy is a potential killer. Far from it. But from 4 observing my patients and my son's friends, I think we are missing **cues**.

I can recall a teenage boy I saw some time ago in therapy. He had changed 5 schools after his parents divorced. His dad was concerned that he was not interested in sports and was not hanging around with the other guys. I knew that the boy was unhappy, but the underlying problem was that his behavior simply didn't fit his father's picture of being a man. His dad seemed surprised—even embarrassed— that his son was going through a hard time, as if real guys shouldn't have doubts and worries. What his son needed, I realized, was for his father to understand that real guys do have doubts and worries.

To really help boys, we need to think not only about issues such as the violence 6 they are exposed to and the availability of weapons; we also need to widen the lens and look at their daily lives, both in and out of school, and examine the expectations and messages they get from us.

Because of legitimate concerns about gender discrimination, for years we tended 7 to play down differences between boys and girls, even though research and common sense tell us they exist. Ask any parent who has raised children of both sexes. The differences show up at a young age, they persist, and they are probably there for good evolutionary reasons: They bring the sexes together and promote **procreation**.

More recently, as we've begun to acknowledge gender differences, we've 8 focused our attention on girls. Think of Mary Pipher's bestseller, *Reviving Ophelia*, which catalogued problems such as anorexia nervosa, bulimia and self-mutilation that girls are likely to exhibit. Think of Harvard professor of education Carol Gilligan and her research team as they described girls who are confident at 11 but confused by 16. And think of all the recent studies of single-sex education that have addressed almost exclusively the special needs of girls.

Where does all this leave boys? 9

The statistics that cross my desk are not encouraging. They suggest that boys 10 may be the more fragile sex. Approximately three out of every four children identified as learning disabled are boys. Boys are much more likely than girls to have drug and alcohol problems. Four of every five juvenile-court cases involve crimes committed by boys. Ninety-five percent of juvenile homicides are committed by boys. And while girls attempt suicide four times more often, boys are seven times as likely to succeed as girls—usually because they choose more lethal methods, such as guns.

11   While girls tend to internalize problems, taking their unhappiness out on themselves, boys externalize them, taking their unhappiness out on others. Boys have more problems than girls in virtually every category you can think of with the exception of eating disorders.

12   The signs of depression my colleagues and I are likely to see in girls are typically straightforward—sadness, tearfulness and self-doubt. In boys, depression is generally hidden behind symptoms such as irritability, **agitation** and explosiveness.

13   Since our kids spend the majority of their day in the structured setting of school, that's where problems are most likely to come to light. Many boys think that their grade schools are boy-unfriendly. I well remember my son bursting into the kitchen one day after school, yelling "They want us to be girls, Mom, they want us to be girls!" A seventh-grader once told me he was planning that night to write a book report that was due the next day—"not like the perfect girls who did theirs three weeks ago."

14   We all know that boys mature more slowly than girls, and that they reach the cognitive milestones essential for doing well at school later than girls do. Take reading, for example. Girls are usually ready to read earlier than boys. This means that average boys wind up feeling less successful, and learning-disabled boys can feel easily defeated.

15   What have schools done to accommodate these well-documented differences in rates of maturity? Very little. Schools, like researchers, have been concentrating on girls. In recent years, some parents have been holding their boys back voluntarily, because they don't seem ready for first grade. Maturity differences persist through adolescence, although adults sometimes seem to ignore them. Teenagers seem to have an **implicit** understanding of them, though; boys are often a year or two older than the girls they date.

16   So here's a radical proposal: Have boys start school a year later than girls so that the two sexes are more evenly matched.

17   Besides their different maturity rates, boys are more active than girls and slower to develop control of their impulses. I'm not the first one to suggest this; even Plato observed that of all the animal young, the hardest to tame is the boy. A young boy put the matter to me **succinctly:** "I figured it out. I'm bad before recess."

18   But many schools have not accommodated boys' need to work off excess energy. Instead, many have shortened lunch and recess periods in order to cram more class time into the day, as the pressure to become more competitive and test-oriented has increased.

19   A fifth-grade boy once told me, "School just sucks the fun out of everything." And my high-school-age son, who enjoyed preschool and kindergarten so much that he left for first grade one day saying, "Ready to rock and roll," had changed his tune by middle school. "Mom," he said, "it's like going to prison."

20   While parents and schools have often failed to respond to these signals, popular culture has picked up on them. Matt Groening once said that he created *The Simpsons* because of all the teachers who, when he was enjoying himself, would shoot him a look that said, "Take that stupid grin off your face right now."

Groening has it right. I hear a lot about *The Simpsons* from the kids I see in 21 therapy. Girls like *The Simpsons*; boys love the show.

One of the ways boys can blow off steam is sports. Yet even this outlet is 22 **tainted** by the student and adult **adulation** of athletes that pervades many of the big high schools. That's a problem for several reasons: It gives athletes an inflated idea of themselves and nonathletes feelings of inferiority and resentment. The boys I see in my office often tell me how sports provide an arena in which they can test themselves, and many feel like failures when they get cut from a team—something that is increasingly likely to happen in our highly competitive mega-schools. All kids need to exercise and play sports, and not just for the short time they have physical education. It would be good to see all schools offering intramural after-school sports to all students.

There's no question in my mind that, in our haste to make up for the disadvan- 23 tages that girls have historically suffered, we've tended to overlook the needs of ordinary boys.

Like everyone else, boys of all ages need adults to love them, appreciate them 24 and enjoy them, so that they can come to value and have faith in themselves. We need to help them find outlets for their natural **exuberance**, vitality and even devil-ishness. One of my favorite sights is the look on boys' faces on the baseball field as they steal bases—when it's good to be bad.

Comprehension Check

Purpose and Main Idea

1. What is the author's topic?
   a. differences between boys and girls
   b. ways to help boys in school
   c. academic performance of boys and girls
   d. how we are failing boys
2. The central idea of this selection is stated in
   a. paragraph 1 "For all the unfathomable...."
   b. paragraph 3 "It seems clear to me...."
   c. paragraph 6 "To really help boys...."
   d. paragraph 23 "There's no question...."
3. The author's *primary* purpose is to
   a. entertain readers with a discussion of gender differences.
   b. inform readers of the ways in which schools are meeting the needs of female students.
   c. persuade readers that schools should address the needs of male students.
   d. express concern that girls are being overlooked in school.

Details

4. According to the author, we can really help boys by thinking about the messages and expectations they get from us.
   a. True
   b. False

5. According to the author, boys—not girls—may be the more fragile sex for all but which one of the following reasons?
   a. Boys attempt suicide four times more often than girls.
   b. Three out of every four learning-disabled children are boys.
   c. Boys are more likely than girls to have drug and alcohol problems.
   d. Boys commit 95 percent of juvenile homicides.
6. Which one of the following is a sign of depression in boys?
   a. self-doubt
   b. tearfulness
   c. irritability
   d. eating disorders
7. The author suggests that boys should start school a year later than girls because boys mature faster than girls.
   a. True
   b. False
8. The author's organizational pattern in paragraphs 14 through 17 is
   a. comparison and contrast.
   b. cause and effect.
   c. sequence.
   d. definition.

Inferences

9. According to the author, schools have failed to address boys' needs, but popular culture has picked up on them. Give one example to support this conclusion.
10. Based on what you can infer from the author's details, how might a boy externalize his unhappiness? Give an example from your experience.

Working with Words

Complete sentences 1–9 with these words from Word Alert:

unfathomable	exuberance	implicit
procreation	agitation	tainted
succinctly	adulation	cues

1. Taking her _____ from her friends, who were dressed informally, Janet changed into jeans and a T-shirt.
2. Ron's red face and restlessness showed his _____ over not being able to find his keys.
3. The instructor said, "Your paper is too long and wordy; you need to express your ideas more _____."
4. In their _____, some fans go to extremes, such as attending every personal appearance of a favorite celebrity.
5. On Oscar night, winners cannot conceal their _____ at being selected.

6. Some crimes, such as those involving kids who kill their classmates, seem _____ to otherwise knowledgeable people.
7. In a zoology class, you will study the _____ and behavior of various animal species.
8. An attitude of disrespect is _____ in the behavior of drivers who swear at or make obscene gestures to others on the road.
9. While some people enjoy betting on the outcome of a game, others refrain, believing that gambling has _____ professional sports.

Write your own sentences, using any two of the words from Word Alert.

10. _____
11. _____

Thinking Deeper

Ideas for reflection, discussion, and writing

Make Inferences from Your Reading

1. The author says that in focusing their attention on girls, the schools have failed male students. What evidence does she offer to support this statement? Based on your own experience in school, would you reach the same conclusion or not? Explain your reasons.
2. In paragraph 24 the author says, "One of my favorite sights is the look on boys' faces on the baseball field as they steal bases—when it's good to be bad." What other examples can you think of to illustrate "when it's good to be bad"?
3. Once we asked the question, "How have schools failed girls?" Having made the classroom more comfortable for girls, now we seem to be shortchanging boys. What do you think schools can or should do to accommodate the needs of both sexes?
4. Search the Internet for an article on one of the school shootings that has occurred over the past several years. Read the article, write a brief summary of it, and draw your own conclusion as to what the school could have or should have done to prevent the shooting. Share your opinions in a class discussion. Begin your search with "Columbine" and "school shootings." Your instructor or librarian may also suggest some search words and phrases or sites to browse.

Write About It

5. In paragraphs 11 and 12, the author compares the ways boys and girls handle problems. Does your own experience support the idea that girls internalize problems while boys externalize them? Write a short essay in which you compare the way you and a friend or family member of the opposite sex handle problems.
6. Imagine that you are the teacher of a fourth grade class. What would you do to make sure that neither boys nor girls feel they are being shortchanged or treated unfairly?

FIRST THOUGHTS

To build background for the reading selection, answer the following questions, either on your own or in a group discussion.

1. What constitutes domestic abuse?
2. Who are the victims of domestic abuse, and how widespread is this problem?
3. Preview the title, headnote, and first one or two paragraphs. What do you think will follow?

WORD ALERT

Each word below is followed by its paragraph number. Preview the words and definitions before reading. Then review them as necessary during reading. Use context clues and your dictionary to define any additional unfamiliar words.

galvanizes (3) arouses to awareness or action
coercive (3) dominating or controlling forcefully
frustrated (4) discouraged or baffled
devastating (6) overwhelming, destructive
perpetrated (6) committed
mobilize (9) prepare for, set in motion
equitably (9) fair and just
discord (10) lack of agreement

◆ Ask New Questions about Domestic Abuse

FRANCINE GARLAND STARK

Francine Garland Stark is the executive director of the *Battered Women's Project*. This organization provides support services to victims of domestic violence in Aroostook County, Maine. In the following selection, Stark invites readers to think afresh about domestic abuse.

A WOMAN CAME into my office recently after everyone else had left for the day. It 1 was late, and I was busy, but she had seen the light on and came to get a purple ribbon for Domestic Violence Awareness Month. I found one and gave her some to share with others. She commented that she never forgets and wants to be sure to help everyone else remember, too.

I am overwhelmed by the numbers. More than 1,200 people called the Battered 2 Women's Project for help in the past year; more than 10 times that number received services from the member projects of the Maine Coalition to End Domestic Violence collectively. Every day so many people in our towns, close at hand, are suffering, afraid for their lives, struggling for their dignity, grasping for hope.

While we work to help victims of abuse to find safety, the gruesome truth of 3 homicide **galvanizes** our sense of urgency. In Maine, since last October, two men killed children. Five men killed women. Two women killed men. These were not random crimes but crimes against family, the results of unimpeded patterns of **coercive**, controlling behavior where there was to have been love.

We—all of us—often are **frustrated** when victims of domestic abuse and violence 4 continue to care about the people who abuse them and hold on to hope that the abuse will stop. We pay little attention to the reality that victims of abuse leave (or try to leave) abusive partners every day. Most of the time, when men kill women, it is to stop them from ending their relationship, to prove their ultimate control.

Why don't victims leave? Why do they continue to love the person who abuses 5 them? Why do they give their controlling partners another chance? Why do they marry these people? Why don't the victims stop being victims and get on with building better lives for themselves?

I wish we would stop asking these questions. No one enters into an intimate 6 relationship, a marriage, or a live-in partnership thinking that it is going to be a **devastating** and pain-filled experience. Really. Love begins with hope and, when tangled with the obligations and interdependent reality of living in partnership, hope remains a binding force through even the outrageous acts **perpetrated** by abusers, until the fear of staying outweighs the fear of leaving. A 74-year-old woman who left her abusive husband of more than 40 years taught me that.

It is important also for us to recognize that leaving does not end a relationship 7 as long as the abusive person continues to demand compliance from his or her former partner. Abusers will use whatever methods remain available to assert their power, frequently involving the children; they often stalk their former partner, maintaining a climate of fear and intimidation.

8   Imagine how differently we would all think about domestic abuse and violence if we asked a different set of questions: What gives abusers the idea that they can rule over their partners, their children and anyone who tries to help them? Am I doing anything that supports the idea that some people have the right to treat other people horribly, as if they were less worthy of respect than I believe myself to be? What will stop them?

9   What if we all acted on the belief that it is wrong to treat others in any way other than how we wish to be treated? What if we all acted on the belief that violence among people is wrong? Would we **mobilize** all our resources to teach one another how to live peacefully and **equitably**? Imagine what it would be like if no one made excuses for domestic abuse and violence.

10   Having come back to live and work in the community where I was born and grew up, I am again frequently in the treasured places where I learned about respect, trust, love and safety. Healthful relationships and happy homes are wonderful things, full of humor, **discord**, strength, confusion, love and hope, anger and forbearance, but there is no place for abuse and violence.

11   Nearly all of us know someone who is or has been a victim of abuse. Remember them. Remember what they taught you about surviving, about loving, about injustice and about the work we need to do together. Take time to think about how you talk about domestic abuse and violence. Do you focus on the responsibility of perpetrators to stop the abuse or blame the victims for being there?

12   All of us need to silence the violence—not the victims, the violence. Over the past 35 years, we have brought the reality of abuse out of dark silence. Now we must replace that darkness with the light of hope and joy.

Comprehension Check

Purpose and Main Idea

1. What is the author's topic?
   a. the causes of violence
   b. stopping domestic abuse
   c. fair treatment for women
   d. abusers and their victims
2. Which one of the following sentences *best* states the author's central idea?
   a. We must learn how to live with each other equitably.
   b. The relationship between abuser and victim is a complicated one.
   c. To stop domestic abuse, we need to first change the way we talk about it.
   d. The causes of domestic violence are rooted in ignorance and poverty.
3. The author's primary purpose is to
   a. entertain readers with stories about survivors of domestic abuse.
   b. inform readers about the causes of domestic violence.
   c. express a personal feeling about domestic relationships.
   d. persuade readers to take action to end domestic abuse.

Details

4. Abusers use all but which one of the following to assert their power in a relationship?
    a. involving the children
    b. stalking their partner
    c. creating a climate of fear
    d. engaging in self-blame
5. The author thinks that we have tended to blame the victims of abuse rather than focusing on the perpetrators' responsibility for their crimes.
    a. True
    b. False.
6. According to the author, we should be asking which one of the following questions about domestic abuse?
    a. Why do victims give their abusers another chance?
    b. Why do victims continue to love their abusers?
    c. What makes abusers think they can rule over their partners?
    d. Why don't the victims stop being victims and get on with their lives?
7. The reality is that most victims of abuse either don't try to leave or don't want to leave.
    a. True
    b. False
8. The details that support the main idea in paragraph 2 consist mainly of
    a. facts.
    b. reasons.
    c. examples.
    d. personal opinions.

Inferences

9. What purpose does the first paragraph serve? What meaning do you infer from the last sentence?
10. What makes someone an abuser? What makes someone a victim of abuse? The author doesn't answer these questions directly, but what answers can you infer from the details in the reading selection?

Working with Words

Complete sentences 1–8 with these words from Word Alert:

devastating	galvanizes	equitably	coercive
perpetrated	frustrated	mobilize	discord

1. In a healthy relationship, there is room for both harmony and _____, but no room for violence.
2. The _____ effects of the 2010 earthquake in Haiti will continue to be felt long after rebuilding has begun.
3. The algebra students were _____ because they did not understand the example problem that the instructor wrote on the chalkboard.

4. We must begin now to _____ campaign workers before the next election.
5. The case of the Boston Strangler is one of the most famous crimes ever _____.
6. A natural disaster is one of those events that quickly _____ people who previously may have been unconcerned.
7. When a partner's behavior becomes _____ or threatening, it is time to end the relationship.
8. A boss and employees should work together _____, in an atmosphere of mutual trust and respect.

Write your own sentences, using any two of the words from Word Alert.

9. _____

10. _____

Thinking Deeper

Ideas for reflection, discussion, and writing

Make Inferences from Your Reading

1. Is it a valid inference to say that the author thinks domestic abuse is everyone's business? Find specific details in the reading selection to support the inference.
2. The author's details consist of two sets of questions: those we should stop asking and those we should begin asking. Find the paragraphs where these questions are stated and read them again. What is the fundamental difference between the two sets of questions? Do you agree with the author that the questions you ask determine not only the answers you get but may act as a force for change? Explain your reasoning.
3. What to do about domestic abuse—both from a victim's point of view and the public who has to provide the support services needed to help victims—is a hard question. What are your thoughts on domestic violence? Is there more of it today than in previous generations? What is being done in your community to help victims of abuse?
4. Visit the author's website, www.batteredwomensproject.org, to build background for exploring similar sites. Then search the Internet for a site that offers services to abuse victims in your home state. What services are available? What other information is provided? Based on your search, what inferences can you make about the prevalence and types of abuse either in your state or nationwide? Ask your instructor or librarian if you need help finding URLs.

Write About It

5. Write about a time when you stood up to someone who was mistreating you in some way. What did you do, and what did you learn about yourself in the process?
6. Choose a statement from the reading selection that you agree or disagree with strongly. Explain your reasons.

FIRST THOUGHTS

To build background for the reading selection, answer the following questions, either on your own or in a group discussion.

1. What does the term racial profiling mean?
2. Under what conditions do you think that police officers should question or search individuals?
3. Preview the title, headnote, and first one or two paragraphs. What do you think will follow?

WORD ALERT

Each word below is followed by its paragraph number. Preview the words and definitions before reading. Then review them as necessary during reading. Use context clues and your dictionary to define any additional unfamiliar words.

stammered (4) spoke in a way marked by uncontrollable pauses and repetitions
cheeky (8) bold, impertinent
seething (10) violent, excited, or agitated
concocted (10) devised, contrived, prepared by mixing ingredients
stark (12) harsh, grim, blunt
railed (14) expressed objection or criticism in bitter, harsh, or abusive language
chastens (16) restrains, subdues, punishes
nexus (19) means of connection, link, tie, connected series or group
disproportionate (19) out of proportion, as in size, shape, or amount
incessant (19) continuing without interruption

◈ Black & Middle Class: Both a Victim of Racial Profiling—and a Practitioner

STEVEN A. HOLMES

> Steven A. Holmes writes for *The New York Times*. In this selection, he suggests that the police are not the only ones who use the tactic of racial profiling.

1 THE SPRING DAY was bright and sunny enough for sunglasses, yet cool enough to require a sweatshirt and baggy sweat pants.

2   As I walked along a busy street in the predominantly white northwest Washington neighborhood where I lived, I hardly thought that my clothing or, more important, my dark skin would attract the attention of the police.

3   But sure enough, after a few blocks, a brown and white cruiser from the Capital Police suddenly pulled alongside. A white police officer jumped out and demanded to know what I was doing there.

4   I live here, I **stammered**, somewhat stunned.

5   Incredulous, he asked to see some identification.

6   I produced a driver's license verifying that I lived a few blocks away—that this was, indeed, my neighborhood. He seemed satisfied.

7   I was not. "Why are you stopping me?" I asked.

8   "There was a burglary in the area, and you fit the description of the suspect," he answered, sounding surprised at what he clearly regarded as a **cheeky** question.

9   "Oh, yeah?" I replied. "Where?"

10   He quickly gave me the name of a street where the crime allegedly had occurred and departed, leaving me standing on the sidewalk, **seething**. I later called the local police precinct to check out this supposed burglary and was not surprised to find out that there was no report of any break-in on that street. The officer's explanation, I assumed, had been **concocted** to cover up what really had happened—a random stop of a black man who to the officer's eye did not fit the area.

11   The issue of whether the police target minorities for questioning and searches has been thrust onto center stage. Figures compiled by the New York City police show that in the 20 precincts where the Street Crimes Unit has been most active, 63 percent of the people stopped and frisked were minorities. Recently, investigators in New Jersey announced that a two-year study of random stops on the New Jersey Turnpike showed that roughly three-fourths of the people whose cars were halted and searched by state troopers were black or Hispanic.

12   The numbers are **stark**, and to civil-rights leaders and liberal politicians the numbers are proof of the use of racial profiling by police. But the figures give little sense of the depth of anger of people like me singled out evidently because of race or ethnicity.

13   The incident left me frustrated and irate. I thought: I'm a middle-class black man who works hard, pays his taxes, keeps out of trouble and tries to treat people with dignity and respect. Why should I be an object of suspicion?

14   I **railed** at the injustice of it all. Yet, as my anger cooled, I asked myself a harder question: Hadn't I done the same thing myself?

I thought back to the time back in the early 1970s when, as a college student in 15
New York City, I supported myself by driving a taxi at night. In many ways, it was
a great job for a student—flexible hours, good pay, a way to meet interesting people, especially women. It could also be dangerous. In three years, I was held up
twice. Both times the perpetrators were young black men.

Fear **chastens** you. I did not quit driving a taxi. But I became more choosy 16
about who I let in my cab. I still picked up black women, older men, couples, families and men dressed in suits. But my sense of tolerance and racial solidarity was
tested every time a casually dressed young black man tried to hail my cab. Most
times, I drove right by.

Like it or not, I was engaging in my own form of racial profiling. What I was 17
doing was playing the odds, playing it safe, taking no chances. Looking back, I realized that those I declined to pick up looked remarkably like I did when the cop
stopped me as I walked down a Washington street.

As I contemplated this, my anger spread to many targets: the police officer who 18
had confronted me, and the young black hoodlums whose criminal behavior had
made the officer suspicious of all African-American men in the first place. And I re-
sented the country's history of racism, which helped to ensure that the presence of a
black person in a leafy, affluent neighborhood of Washington was still a rare sight.

The **nexus** of race, crime and stereotyping raises difficult questions that 19
are often ignored. Even as crime rates tumble, young black men still commit a
disproportionate share of serious offenses, a fact that is driven home in metropolitan areas by television's seemingly **incessant** airing of crime news. And whether the
fear stems from real experience or media-driven perceptions, people—police and
civilian, white and black—play the odds all the time when it comes to how they
view and respond to young black men.

Too often the country fails to acknowledge how widespread the practice is. 20
Some years ago, at a town hall meeting on race in Akron, Ohio, then-President
Clinton asked a group of whites who had joined him onstage whether they felt
fear when they saw a young black man on the street who was not well dressed. A
number sheepishly raised their hands. Clinton thanked them for their honesty. I sat
there wondering, "Mr. President, why don't you ask the black participants the same
question?"

Even the seemingly clear-cut statistics on racial profiling don't tell the whole 21
story. New York's Street Crimes Unit did indeed stop and frisk a disproportionately
large number of black men. Yet in those same precincts, 71 percent of the suspects,
as described by their victims, were black men.

On the flip side, New Jersey state troopers arrested or seized contraband from 22
13.5 percent of the minorities whose cars were searched on the turnpike, compared
with 10.5 percent of the whites. At first blush that seems like a sizable difference.
But then consider that the troopers stopped three times as many non-whites or
Hispanics as others: Racial profiling hardly seems to be producing enough arrests
to justify the effort—or the heartache.

That may be the biggest argument against targeting some people as suspects 23
based on their race, beyond the constitutional argument of equal treatment before
the law. With crime rates tumbling in virtually every big city in the land, racial profiling may have outlived its usefulness. Perhaps if I were a young New York City

cab driver today I would not be as wary of young black men as I once was. With the streets safer, it could be time for the public and the police to shed the kind of attitude I held nearly three decades ago—the attitude that followed me into middle-aged respectability on a Washington street.

Comprehension Check

Purpose and Main Idea

1. What is the author's topic?
   a. racial profiling
   b. race relations
   c. race and ethnicity
   d. racial discrimination
2. Which one of the following is the *best* statement of the author's central idea?
   a. Racial profiling is only one crime-fighting method.
   b. Racial profiling is not as prevalent as people think.
   c. The reality of racial profiling is that we all do it.
   d. Racial profiling is unfair to those who are singled out.
3. The author's *primary* purpose is to
   a. inform readers that racial profiling exists.
   b. express concern about the number of crimes committed by African Americans.
   c. persuade readers to shed stereotypical attitudes.
   d. entertain readers with his experiences as a taxi driver.

Details

4. According to the author, racial profiling is a legitimate crime-fighting technique.
   a. True
   b. False
5. In the author's opinion, he was stopped and questioned because he
   a. was dressed casually.
   b. fit the suspect's description.
   c. was a black man in a white neighborhood.
   d. might have information for the officer.
6. The author says that he should not be an object of suspicion because he works hard and pays his taxes.
   a. True
   b. False
7. According to the author, what may be the biggest argument against racial profiling?
   a. The number of arrests doesn't justify the effort.
   b. It is an unfair tactic.
   c. Racial profiling may be unconstitutional.
   d. The country has a history of racism.

8. In paragraph 14, the word *yet* signals that the relationship between the first sentence and the second sentence is
    a. example.
    b. process.
    c. definition.
    d. contrast.

Inferences

9. What point does Clinton's question at the town meeting in Ohio (paragraph 20) and the author's response to it illustrate?
10. The author says that whether their fears are real or imagined, people fear black men. Do you agree or disagree, and what inference can you make about the source of these fears?

Working with Words

Complete sentences 1–10 with these words from Word Alert:

disproportionate	concocted	cheeky	nexus
stammered	seething	railed	
incessant	chastens	stark	

1. A good parent _____ a child for playing too near the street.
2. Some of the actors who won Oscars were so surprised that they _____ into the microphone, unable to speak clearly.
3. _____ with anger, Lyn shook her fist at the driver who had smashed into her car while she was stopped at a traffic light.
4. The instructor _____ at the students who were caught cheating on the exam.
5. The students thought the exam was too hard because a _____ number of them failed it.
6. When my horn got stuck, the _____ honking drove everyone crazy until I could get it stopped.
7. What is _____ behavior to one person may seem timid to another.
8. Only a person who is used to living in harsh conditions would appreciate a trip to Antarctica's _____ landscape.
9. The coastal town where we grew up is the _____ that draws me and my cousins together each summer.
10. I _____ a surprisingly good meal from the leftovers in my refrigerator.

Write your own sentences, using any two of the words from Word Alert.

11. _____
12. _____

Thinking Deeper

Ideas for reflection, discussion, and writing

Make Inferences from Your Reading

1. Discuss the author's arguments for and against racial profiling. Why do police use the tactic? Why do some people rail against it? Do you think racial profiling is or is not justified? Explain your inferences.
2. Racial profiling is a type of stereotyping. Have you observed instances of stereotyping, either in the classroom or on your campus at large? What individuals or groups of people were involved? Describe the situation and its outcome.
3. In paragraph 14, the author says about racial profiling, "I asked myself a harder question: Hadn't I done the same thing myself?" A hard question for you to discuss and answer is, "Have you engaged in racial profiling?"
4. At the time of this writing (1999), the author says that crime rates are tumbling and that racial profiling may have outlived its usefulness. Is this a valid inference now? Using your library's online resources, research crime statistics for your area. Have some types of crime increased or decreased since 1999?

Write About It

5. Write about a time when you felt singled out because of your race, or the way you were dressed, or for some other reason.
6. Write about the pros and cons of racial profiling. Include in your writing whether or not you think there is a circumstance in which racial profiling might be justified.

FIRST THOUGHTS

To build background for the reading selection, answer the following questions, either on your own or in a group discussion.

1. Do you think that reading poetry is different from reading other types of material? Why or why not?
2. What are some of the feelings that reading a poem may provoke?
3. Preview the title, headnote, and first two lines of the poem. What do you think will follow?

WORD ALERT

Each word below is followed by its line number. Preview the words and definitions before reading. Then review them as necessary during reading. Use context clues and your dictionary to define any additional unfamiliar words.

morbid (5) preoccupied with unwholesome matters, gruesome
amble (10) to walk slowly or in a leisurely way
blowsy (10) disheveled, disordered, especially in hair and clothing
hag (15) an ugly old woman
bore (15) past tense of *to bear*, meaning endured or carried on
sassafras (16) a type of tree, the bark of which is used as a flavoring

◈ Complaint

JAMES WRIGHT

James Wright (1927–1980) is the author of several books of poetry and translations of other poets' work. In 1972, he won the Pulitzer Prize for his *Collected Poems*. Wright taught at institutions around the country, including Hunter College in New York.

1   She's gone. She was my love, my moon or more.
2   She chased the chickens out and swept the floor,
3   Emptied the bones and nut-shells after feasts,
4   And smacked the kids for leaping up like beasts.
5   Now morbid boys have grown past awkwardness;
6   The girls let stitches out, dress after dress,
7   To free some swinging body's riding space
8   And form the new child's unimagined face.
9   Yet, while vague nephews, spitting on their curls,
10 Amble to pester winds and blowsy girls,
11 What arm will sweep the room, what hand will hold
12 New snow against the milk to keep it cold?
13 And who will dump the garbage, feed the hogs,
14 And pitch the chickens' heads to hungry dogs?
15 Not my lost hag who dumbly bore such pain:
16 Childbirth and midnight sassafras and rain.
17 New snow against her face and hands she bore,
18 And now lies down, who was my moon and more.

Comprehension Check

Purpose and Main Idea

1. What is the author's topic?
    a. loss
    b. death
    c. family
    d. love
2. What is the poem's central idea?
    a. Love conquers all.
    b. Death is the necessary end of life.
    c. The loss of a loved one raises questions.
    d. Raising a family is hard work.
3. The author's *primary* purpose is to
    a. inform readers about life on a farm.
    b. persuade readers to value what they have.
    c. entertain readers with a sad story.
    d. express a feeling about a personal loss.

Details

4. The *protagonist*, or voice, in this poem is most likely a man who is mourning the death of his wife.
   a. True
   b. False
5. The poem describes a family that lives in an urban setting.
   a. True
   b. False
6. Which word *best* describes the author's tone?
   a. mocking (making fun of)
   b. sentimental (overly sensitive or emotional)
   c. indignant (angry with feelings of injustice)
   d. intense (profound, showing depth of feeling)
7. All but which one of the following words are used to describe the wife?
   a. love
   b. moon
   c. hag
   d. friend
8. In line 18, "lies down" refers to which one of the following?
   a. sleep
   b. death
   c. childbirth
   d. grief

Inferences

9. Look up the word *dumb* in your dictionary. Then explain what the author means in line 15 by "dumbly bore such pain."
10. What is the author's meaning in lines 6 through 8?

Working with Words

Complete sentences 1–6 with these words from Word Alert:

sassafras	blowsy	morbid
amble	bore	hag

1. It is pleasant to _____ through a national park, enjoying the view.
2. Surprisingly, the child _____ the toothache pain without complaint.
3. Dressed in ragged clothing and made-up to look like a _____, the actress played the part of a witch in the film.
4. Disturbingly, horror films and other _____ tales of death and destruction draw large crowds.
5. Getting caught in rain and wind without protection is bound to give one a _____ appearance.
6. In the old days, people brewed tea from _____ as a cold remedy.

Write your own sentences, using any two of the words from Word Alert.

7. _____

8. _____

Thinking Deeper

Ideas for reflection, discussion, and writing

Make Inferences from Your Reading

1. What does the title "Complaint" mean in reference to the poem as a whole? What is the protagonist's complaint?
2. Read again the first and last lines. What is the purpose of ending these lines with a similar phrase? What is the difference in meaning between "my moon *or* more" in the first line and "my moon *and* more" in the last line?
3. Following a personal loss such as the death of a loved one, we are tempted to ask hard questions such as "Why me?" or "What will I do now?" What are some of the ways that people cope with personal losses and find the strength to carry on?
4. Learn more about James Wright's life and read another of his poems. One site to try is http://www.poets.org, the official site of the Academy of American Poets. Type the author's name in the search box to access a page that contains a biographical sketch and several poems to read. Based on your search, what inferences can you make about this author's choice of themes and topics?

Write About It

5. Describe a personal loss in your own life and explain what it has meant to you.
6. Write about someone you know who is "the moon and more" to his or her family.

FIRST THOUGHTS

To build background for the reading selection, answer the following questions, either on your own or in a group discussion.

1. What does the term binge drinking mean to you?
2. What would you guess is the percentage of college students who regularly engage in binge drinking nationwide?
3. Preview the title, headnote, and first one or two paragraphs. What do you think will follow?

WORD ALERT

Each word below is followed by its paragraph number. Preview the words and definitions before reading. Then review them as necessary during reading. Use context clues and your dictionary to define any additional unfamiliar words.

swilling (1) drinking greedily or grossly

binge (2) a drunken spree, a period of uncontrolled self-indulgence

pledged (11) promised

swigs (31) deep swallows, especially of liquor

metabolism (34) the functioning of a specific substance within the body

glint (38) a brief flash of light, a sparkle

◈ Death Shows Binge Drinking Still Plagues Many Campuses

ANGIE WAGNER

Based in Las Vegas, the author is the western regional reporter for the Associated Press. This article was inspired by Colorado State student Samantha Spady's death from alcohol poisoning at the Sigma Pi fraternity.

1   BY THE TIME THE rainy night stretched into early morning, Samantha Spady had been drinking and partying for hours. Earlier it was beer and shots of tequila. Now, inside a fraternity house, she was **swilling** vanilla vodka straight from the bottle.

2   The **binge** had gone on for 11 hours. When it was over, the Colorado State student's blood-alcohol level was more than five times the legal driving limit in Colorado. She was stumbling, unable to stand on her own.

3   Two students wrapped the 19-year-old's limp arms around their necks and walked her to a forgotten fraternity room.

4   They laid her on a couch, and a few minutes later, Sam blinked her eyes and nodded as the last person left the room.

5   She just needs to sleep it off, her friends thought.

ALMOST PERFECT

6   Sam grew up in Beatrice, Neb., about 35 miles from Lincoln. There, her father owned a car dealership, and everyone knew her.

7   It was hard not to. Senior-class president. Head cheerleader. Honor student. Homecoming queen.

8   Almost perfect.

9   On weekends, she and her friends would head to the country to hang out and sometimes drink beer. But Sam never drank to get drunk, said her best friend from high school, Kelleigh Doyle.

10   The business major hadn't really known anyone here but quickly made new friends. Her mother had always admired that about her, the way people were drawn to her.

11   Sam had **pledged** Chi Omega sorority as a freshman, but it took up a lot of time. There were functions to attend, and it was hard to balance with schoolwork. She longed for home-cooked meals and her bed at home, and by her second semester, she had dropped out of Chi Omega.

12   Mirna Guerra hadn't known Sam that long when the two decided to get together Sept. 4, the Saturday before Labor Day and the evening of the big Colorado State-Colorado football game.

13   Sam picked up Mirna, a freshman, just before 6 p.m., and they went to a house to watch the game. Sam drank a beer and two shots of tequila, ate a hot dog and munched on chips and dip. They left two hours later.

14   They watched the rest of the game at another house, where Sam drank a few beers.

They left around 10:30 p.m. 15

Friends told police Sam had been out partying the past three nights. It wasn't 16 unusual for her to drink three or four times a week. Sometimes, Sam vomited and later passed out.

"It's what everyone does," said Sam's roommate, Sara Gibson. "Some people 17 party every night."

It's college. Away from parents, often for the first time for any extended period, 18 college students can come and go as they please and are free to experiment with alcohol.

Parties come on the fly, and there's never a shortage of kegs to tap. In pubs and 19 bars near campus, drinks are cheap, and women often get them free.

All of it is an invitation for binge drinking, said Henry Wechsler, director of the 20 College Alcohol Studies at the Harvard School of Public Health. And there is no one to say "no."

Nationally, 44 percent of college students report binge drinking— five drinks in 21 a row for men, four for women—at least once in the previous two weeks. Half of those students do it more than once a week.

Members of fraternities and sororities tend to drink more than other students. 22

Nationally, there are more than 1,400 alcohol-related deaths each year among 23 college students, according to the National Institute on Alcohol Abuse and Alcoholism. Most are the result of automobile accidents.

"ALWAYS MADE PEOPLE SMILE"

It was raining hard, and Sam was having a hard time seeing through her windshield 24 because of the storm. She hit the median and ended up flattening two tires. Mirna didn't think Sam was drunk.

It didn't spoil the evening. Sam and Mirna still wanted to find a good party. 25 They soon found one.

For about two hours, they drank and danced to Michael Jackson. Sam downed 26 four or five cups of beer.

"By then, we had started drinking pretty fast," Mirna said. 27

Still, Sam seemed fine. She and Mirna were having a good time, talking about 28 music they liked and possibly rooming together next year.

About 2:30 a.m., Sam and Mirna were at the Sigma Pi house. Sam had lots of 29 friends in the fraternity and had dated a few members. Some considered her a little sister.

"She always made people smile," Sigma Pi President Darren Pettapiece said. 30

About 4 a.m., Sam and Mirna were doing **swigs** of Sam's favorite drink: vanilla 31 vodka. They put the bottles to their lips and tilted their heads back, as the room echoed: "Go, go, go!"

Minutes later, Sam was sitting on the front stoop, resting her head on her elbows. 32

She was unable to stand and fell back. Her head hung down, and she didn't 33 respond when friends spoke to her.

She should have been taken to a hospital then, said Dr. Charles Lieber, an expert 34 in alcohol **metabolism** at Mount Sinai School of Medicine in New York. But she wasn't.

35   About 5 a.m. Sigma Pi member Baylor Ferrier and a friend helped Sam upstairs and put her on a couch in an unused room.

36   She just wants to sleep, Mirna thought. She'll be fine. But the homecoming queen with the megawatt smile was dying.

37   She was likely in a coma, Lieber said. If she had gotten medical help, he said, even that late she might have lived. But there was no help in the Sigma Pi room.

38   As Sunday dawned and the **glint** of orange crept through the mountains, Sam's cell phone started ringing.

39   Her mother, Patty Spady, called and then waited. She called again. Still no Sam. She tried not to worry, but it was so unlike Sam not to call back.

BOOZE STILL FLOWS

40   Almost 13 hours after Sam had been left to sleep off the drunken night, a fraternity member was giving his mother a tour of the house.

41   When he opened the door to the social room that had been stuffed with extra couches, he saw Sam's alcohol-poisoned body, clad in jeans and a yellow T-shirt. Her long blond hair was pulled back. It looked like she was sleeping.

42   "Hello?" he asked. "Hello?"

43   He touched her leg. It was cold and stiff.

44   She had a blood alcohol level of 0.436 percent.

45   Since Sam's death, the parties continue, the booze still flows.

46   But the Sigma Pi house has been shut down. Fraternities have banned alcohol, and alcohol sales are banned inside the football stadium. Nineteen people were cited for alcohol-related offenses as part of the investigation into Sam's death.

47   "It's not just the students on that campus. It's not just the faculty. It's not just the bar owners. Everybody in the community has a responsibility for some changes to take place," Patty Spady said.

Comprehension Check

Purpose and Main Idea

1. What is the author's topic?
    a. preventing alcoholism
    b. the effects of binge drinking
    c. one student's alcohol-related death
    d. binge drinking on college campuses
2. Which sentence best states the author's central idea?
    a. Preventing binge drinking is everyone's responsibility.
    b. Alcoholism affects people of all ages and circumstances
    c. Samantha Spady's death illustrates the problem of binge drinking.
    d. College officials should do more to prevent student alcohol abuse.
3. What is the author's *primary* purpose?
    a. to express concern about alcohol abuse among college students
    b. to show by example that binge drinking continues to be a problem
    c. to inform readers about the physical effects of too much alcohol
    d. to persuade readers that they should support banning alcohol on campus

Details

4. Since Sam's death, the Sigma Pi house has been shut down, but the parties continue.
   a. True
   b. False
5. Most alcohol-related deaths among college students result from automobile accidents.
   a. True
   b. False
6. The author provides all but which one of the following details about Samantha Spady's life?
   a. She was the homecoming queen.
   b. She was the senior class president.
   c. She was the head cheerleader.
   d. She was an English major.
7. Sam's body was discovered when
   a. Patty Spady called Sam's cell phone.
   b. her friends noticed that she had not come home.
   c. a fraternity member gave his mother a tour of the house.
   d. an expert in alcohol metabolism was called.
8. What is the organizational pattern in paragraph 21?
   a. process
   b. definition
   c. sequence
   d. classification

Inferences

9. Was Sam's death inevitable? At what point do you think she might she have been saved?
10. About her daughter's death, Sam's mother says that everyone in the community has a responsibility for some changes to take place (paragraph 47). Do you agree or disagree, and why?

Working with Words

Complete sentences 1–6 with these words from Word Alert:

swilling	pledged	swigs
metabolism	binge	glint

1. Nicholas _____ to join a fraternity his second semester in college.
2. Exercise and diet affect the body's _____ of substances from food.
3. A _____ of sunlight shone through a tear in the curtain.
4. _____ large quantities of alcohol can cause drunkenness and death.
5. If you _____ on chocolate too often, you will gain weight.
6. After a hard workout, several _____ of water taste good.

Write your own sentences, using any two of the words from Word Alert.

7. _____

8. _____

Thinking Deeper

Ideas for reflection, discussion, and writing

Make Inferences from Your Reading

1. What inferences can you make about binge drinking among the students on your campus? About what percentage of students do you think engage in binge drinking? Who is most likely to engage in binge drinking?
2. In this selection, the author tells the story of one student's death as an example of the kind of problem many colleges face. How did the story affect you? Is this an effective way of dealing with the topic? Why or why not?
3. What to do about binge drinking among college students is a hard question for college officials and community members. What are your views on this topic? How much responsibility should a college take for the actions of students? What can colleges do to discourage alcohol abuse?
4. What are the facts about binge drinking? What is it, and how prevalent is it? To answer these and other questions about binge drinking, go to www.samhsa.gov and type "binge drinking" in the search frame to access a list of articles. Or do a Google search, using "binge drinking and college students" as your search phrase. This search will generate a long list of sites. Your best resources are those sponsored by the government or an educational institution. Look for a "fact sheet" that lists statistics on binge drinking. Be prepared to explain how the facts you have learned from your search either do or do not support your own inferences about the prevalence of binge drinking and the types of students who do it.

Write About It

5. At some point, every college student must make decisions about when, where, or whether to drink. What decisions have you made?
6. Write about the effects of alcohol use or abuse on the life of someone you know.

FIRST THOUGHTS

To build background for the reading selection, answer the following questions, either on your own or in a group discussion.

1. What does the term global warming mean to you?
2. Are you concerned about global warming? Why or why not?
3. Preview the title, headnote, and first one or two paragraphs. What do you think will follow?

WORD ALERT

Each word below is followed by its paragraph number. Preview the words and definitions before reading. Then review them as necessary during reading. Use context clues and your dictionary to define any additional unfamiliar words.

skeptic (1) one who habitually doubts, questions, or disagrees

permafrost (2) permanently frozen subsoil, occurring in cold regions such as the Arctic

meteorological (4) relating to the study of the atmosphere

opine (6) to state or hold an opinion

theoretical (8) based on theory or accepted but unproven knowledge and assumptions

murky (8) gloomy, dark, muddied, unclear

exacerbate (12) aggravate, worsen, increase the severity of

isotopes (18) atoms whose nuclei have the same number of protons but different numbers of neutrons

◈ Heat Wave

THE EDITORS OF *TIME*

> Heat Wave is taken from *Nature's Extremes*, a *Time* special edition. In this essay, the authors discuss the threat of global warming.

1   YOU SAY YOU'RE A SKEPTIC ON GLOBAL warming? Perhaps you don't live in Florida, along the Gulf Coast or in Shishmaref, Alaska: people who live in those parts tend to be believers. Florida was battered by four monster hurricanes in 2004, while Katrina swamped New Orleans and hammered the coast of Mississippi a year later. The extraordinary power of the past few hurricane seasons, many scientists believe, is due to global warming. The big storms beef up on the warm waters of the Gulf of Mexico, and those latitudes are growing warmer, year by year.

2   As for the tiny town of Shishmaref (pop. 600), it is an Inupiaq Eskimo village perched on a slender barrier island 625 miles north of Anchorage. When *Time* reporter Margot Roosevelt visited it in 2004, she discovered it was "melting into the ocean." It had lost 100 to 300 ft. of coastline—and half of that amount occurred since 1997. The **permafrost** beneath the beaches was thawing, and the sea ice was thinning, leaving residents increasingly vulnerable to violent storms. One house had collapsed, and 18 others had to be moved to higher ground, along with the town's bulk-fuel tanks. Giant waves had washed away the school playground and destroyed $100,000 worth of boats, hunting gear and fish-drying racks. "It's scary," village official Luci Eningowuk told Roosevelt. "Every year we agonize that the next storm will wipe us out."

3   The ice-fishing season in Shishmaref that used to start in October now began in December, since the ocean freezes later each year. Berry picking began in July instead of August. Most distressing for the Inupiaq is that thin ice made it harder to hunt oogruk, the bearded seal that is a staple of their diet and culture.

4   What's going on? Global warming, caused in part by the burning of oil and gas in factories and cars, is traumatizing not only the Gulf of Mexico but also polar regions, where the complex **meteorological** processes associated with snow, permafrost and ice magnify its effects. A study published in *Science* in 2004 found that glaciers in West Antarctica are thinning twice as fast as they did in the 1990s. In Alaska the annual mean air temperature has risen 4°F to 5°F in the past three decades, compared with an average of just under 1°F worldwide.

5   As a result, Alaska's glaciers are melting; insects are devouring vast swaths of forest; and thawing permafrost is sinking roads, pipelines and homes. Arctic Ocean ice has shrunk 5% to 10%, at an accelerating rate. "Shishmaref is the canary in the coal mine—an indicator of what's to come elsewhere," said Gunter Weller, director of the University of Alaska's Co-operative Institute for Arctic Research. "The evidence is overwhelming that humanity has altered the climate."

6   From Miami to Shishmaref, and at many points in between, people say the weather doesn't seem normal anymore. Yet to put matters in perspective, there is no such thing as normal weather. As Midwestern farmers often **opine**, "If you don't like the weather, just wait five minutes." And seasons are rarely normal. Winter snowfall and summer heat waves beat the average some years and fail to reach it in

others. It's tough to pick out overall changes in climate in the face of these natural fluctuations. An unusually warm year, for example, or even three in a row don't necessarily signal a significant general trend.

Yet the earth's climate does change. Ice ages have frosted the planet for tens of 7 thousands of years at a stretch, and periods of warmth have pushed the tropics well into what is now the temperate zone. But given the normal year-to-year variations, the only reliable signal that such changes may be in the works is a long-term shift in worldwide temperature.

And that is precisely what's happening. In 1988, when *Time* named Earth the 8 Planet of the Year, the idea that our world was warming up as a result of human activity was largely **theoretical**. We knew that since the Industrial Revolution began in the 18th century, factories and power plants and automobiles and farms have been loading the atmosphere with heat-trapping gases. But evidence that the climate was actually getting hotter was still **murky**.

Not anymore. Reports, studies and articles from esteemed scientific organiza- 9 tions have now demonstrated that worldwide temperatures climbed more than 1°F over the past century, and that the 1990s were the hottest decade on record. Look around: snow fields, including the legendary snows of Kilimanjaro, are disappearing from mountaintops around the globe. Coral reefs are dying off as the seas get too warm for comfort. Drought is the norm in parts of Asia and Africa. El Niño events, which trigger devastating weather in the eastern Pacific, are more frequent. The Arctic permafrost is starting to melt. Lakes and rivers in colder climates are freezing later and thawing earlier each year. Plants and animals are shifting their ranges poleward and to higher altitudes, and migration patterns for animals as diverse as polar bears, butterflies and beluga whales are being disrupted.

Faced with these hard facts, most scientists no longer doubt that global warm- 10 ing is happening, and almost nobody questions the fact that humans are at least in part responsible. Nor are the changes over. Already, humans have increased the concentration of carbon dioxide, the most abundant heat-trapping gas in the atmosphere, to 30% above preindustrial levels—and each year the percentage increases. The obvious conclusion: temperatures will keep going up.

If the rise is large enough, the results could be disastrous. With seas rising as much 11 as 3 ft., enormous areas of densely populated land—coastal Florida, much of Louisiana, the Nile Delta, the Maldives, Bangladesh—would become uninhabitable. Entire climatic zones might shift dramatically, making central Canada look more like central Illinois, Georgia more like Guatemala. Agriculture would be thrown into turmoil. Hundreds of millions of people would have to migrate from unlivable regions.

Public health would suffer. Rising seas could contaminate water supplies with 12 salt. Higher levels of urban ozone, the result of stronger sunlight and warmer temperatures, could **exacerbate** respiratory illnesses. Warmer temperatures could widen the range of disease-carrying rodents and bugs, such as mosquitoes and ticks, increasing the incidence of dengue fever, malaria, encephalitis, Lyme disease and other afflictions. Humans will have a hard enough time adjusting, especially in poorer countries, but for wildlife the changes could be devastating.

Had enough scary scenarios? Let's get back to cold hard facts—or, more pre- 13 cisely, to warm wet facts. The hurricane season of 2005 was one of the most destructive yet recorded in the North Atlantic, joining 2004 as one of the most violent ever. And these two seasons are part of a trend of increasingly powerful and deadly hurricanes that has been playing out for more than 10 years. Said climatologist Judy Curry, chair of the School of Earth and Atmospheric Sciences at the Georgia Institute of Technology: "The so-called once-in-a-lifetime storm isn't even once in a season anymore."

14   For years, environmentalists have warned that one of the first and most reliable signs of a climatological crash would be an upsurge in Category 5 hurricanes, the kind that thrive in a suddenly warmer world. Scientists are quick to point out that changes in the weather and climate change are two different things. But now even skeptical scientists are starting to wonder whether something serious might be going on.

15   "There is no doubt that climate is changing and humans are partly responsible," Kevin Trenberth, head of the climate-analysis section at the National Center for Atmospheric Research (NCAR) in Boulder, Colo., told Time. "The odds have changed in favor of more intense storms and heavier rainfalls." Says NCAR meteorologist Greg Holland: "These are not small changes. We're talking about a very large change."

16   Some scientists are studying not just climate change but also the even more alarming phenomenon of abrupt climate change. Complex systems like the atmosphere are known to move from one steady state to another with only very brief transitions in between. (Think of water: when put over a flame, it becomes hotter and hotter until suddenly it turns into steam.) Ice cores taken from Greenland in the 1990s by geoscientist Richard Alley of Pennsylvania State University show that the last ice age came to an end not in the slow creep of geological time but in the quick pop of real time, with the entire planet abruptly warming in just three years.

17   "There are thresholds one crosses, and change runs a lot faster," Alley noted. "Most of the time, climate responds as if it's being controlled by a dial, but occasionally it acts as if it's controlled by a switch." Laurence Smith, an associate professor of geography at UCLA who has been studying fast climate change in the Arctic, told *Time*, "We face the possibility of abrupt changes that are economically and socially frightening."

18   To fathom those changes, scientists like geologist Claudia Mora of the University of Tennessee at Knoxville are studying **isotopes** locked in old tree rings to look for clues to past eras of heavy and light rainfall. Pair that information with global-temperature estimates for the same periods, and you can get a pretty good idea of how heat and hurricanes drive each other. "We've taken it back 100 years and didn't miss a storm," said Mora.

19   Studies like these may not be enough to convince the naysayers on global warming. What does seem certain is that the ranks of those skeptics are growing thinner—just like the permafrost in Shishmaref.

Comprehension Check

Purpose and Main Idea

1. What is the topic of this selection?
    a.   climate
    b.   global warming
    c.   extreme weather
    d.   temperature changes

2. Which one of the following is the central idea?
   a. Paragraph 1 "The extraordinary power...."
   b. Paragraph 4 "Global warming, caused...."
   c. Paragraph 5 "The evidence is...."
   d. Paragraph 10 "Faced with these...."
3. What is the *primary* purpose of this selection?
   a. to explain what the term *global warming* means
   b. to inform readers about the effects of global warming
   c. to express an editorial opinion about the causes of extreme weather
   d. to persuade readers that global warming is occurring

Details

4. The thawing of permafrost in Shishmaref is cited as one effect of global warming.
   a. True
   b. False
5. Changes in the weather and climate change are the same thing.
   a. True
   b. False
6. Worldwide temperatures have increased by more than how many degrees over the past century?
   a. 1
   b. 4
   c. 5
   d. 10
7. Who says, "The evidence is overwhelming that humanity has altered the climate"?
   a. Greg Holland
   b. Claudia Mora
   c. Gunter Weller
   d. Kevin Trenberth
8. Paragraph 4 is related to paragraph 5 by
   a. generalization then example.
   b. comparison and contrast.
   c. division and classification.
   d. cause and effect.

Inferences

9. On the topic of global warming, are you a skeptic or a believer, and what is the basis of your choice?
10. Think about the climate in your area over the past few years: Has it been noticeably warmer or cooler than usual, or has it stayed about the same? What conclusion do you draw from this?

Working with Words

Complete sentences 1–8 with these words from Word Alert:

permafrost	skeptic	murky
theoretical	isotopes	opine
meteorological	exacerbate	

1. Rosa believes that global warming is occurring, but her sister remains a _____.
2. Picking at a scab on a wound only serves to _____ the wound's effects.
3. Students complained that the professor's examples were more _____ than proven.
4. The water in which we were wading was so _____ that we could not see our feet.
5. Save your remarks until after the lecture if you wish to _____.
6. If your interests turn to the _____, a career in weather forecasting may be for you.
7. In regions where there is a layer of _____ beneath the topsoil, plants with shallow root systems grow best.
8. Scientists study _____ in nature for clues to the past.

Write your own sentences, using any two of the words from Word Alert.

9. _____
10. _____

Thinking Deeper

Ideas for reflection, discussion, and writing

Make Inferences from Your Reading

1. In paragraph 17, Richard Alley is quoted as saying: "Most of the time, climate responds as if it's being controlled by a dial, but occasionally it acts as if it's controlled by a switch." First, explain the meaning of this comparison. Then give an example of the two ways climate responds.
2. What might be some of the economic and social consequences of global warming? For example, what would happen if our beaches disappeared because of rising water levels? Or what if rising temperatures severely limited the kind and number of crops that could be grown?
3. The authors' views about global warming are based on research that until recently was unquestioned by many in the scientific and academic communities. Yet a growing number of scientists now count themselves among the skeptics, especially regarding the extent to which global warming is the result of human activity. What countries and individuals can or should do about global warming is becoming an increasingly hard question to answer. What do you think?
4. Do a Web search on global warming to find the answers to one or more of these questions: (a) What is the definition of *global warming*? (b) What is the *greenhouse effect*, and what are *greenhouse gases*? (3) What is the *hydrologic*

cycle, and what does it have to do with global warming? (4) Which industries contribute the most carbon dioxide to the atmosphere? (5) What are some alternative energy sources to replace or augment the use of oil? (6) What are some of the controversies surrounding global warming? The following are two sites to try. Remember that URLs and site content change, so ask a librarian to suggest sites if you don't find the information you need:

- www.//cmd.noaa.gov: Global monitoring of the National Oceanic and Atmospheric Administration, scientific data and graphs
- www.epa.gov: U.S. Environmental Protection Agency site on global warming

Write About It

5. Americans are concerned about the economy, a growing deficit, and other problems facing our nation. Write about one of these problems or another problem that is of greatest concern to you.
6. Write about a specific program or initiative at your college or in your community, designed to improve the environment.

FIRST THOUGHTS

To build background for the reading selection, answer the following questions, either on your own or in a group discussion.

1. What kinds of music, TV programs, and movies do you prefer?
2. To what extent do sex and violence in the media have negative effects on behavior?
3. Preview the title, headnote, and first one or two paragraphs. What do you think will follow?

WORD ALERT

Each word below is followed by its paragraph number. Preview the words and definitions before reading. Then review them as necessary during reading. Use context clues and your dictionary to define any additional unfamiliar words.

suffuses (1) spreads throughout or over
degrading (3) disgraceful, dishonorable
venture (4) to risk danger
raunchy (6) obscene, vulgar, grimy
mayhem (7) a state of violent disorder or riotous confusion, havoc
lascivious (11) lustful, lewd

◈ Does a Raunchy Culture Produce Raunchy Kids?

STEPHEN CHAPMAN

Stephen Chapman is a columnist for the *Chicago Tribune* and has contributed articles to national magazines. He writes on national and international affairs.

IF YOU TAKE A LOOK at mass media aimed at teenagers, you start to see a pattern. 1
What topic **suffuses** teenage prime-time dramas? Sex. Movies aimed at high school boys? Violence. Music popular among the SAT-taking crowd? Sex and violence.

You've noticed, and the scholars at the medical journal *Pediatrics* have noticed. 2
They have unveiled two new studies that confirm what we all know: The kids most exposed to sex and violence are the ones most likely to participate in sex and violence.

One study found that teenagers who listen to a lot of music "with **degrading** 3
sexual content" are more likely to have intercourse than those who don't. Another study in the same issue found that high-school students who watch professional wrestling on TV have a habit of getting in fights with their dates.

This may sound like what's known as a blinding flash of the obvious. If you 4
venture into a humid swamp on a hot day, you'll soon be sweating. So if you grow up in a culture drenched in the likes of the Pussycat Dolls and the Samoan Bulldozer, why wouldn't you get soaked?

But what's obvious is not necessarily true. Even these studies don't claim to 5
prove that exposure to unwholesome fare causes unwholesome conduct. The fact that two things are connected doesn't mean one causes the other: Birds fly south and then winter comes, but it's not the birds' exodus that brings on ice and snow.

As the music researchers stipulated, "Our correlational data do not allow us to 6
make causal inferences with certainty." All these articles really prove is that the kids who like **raunchy** music or violent sports are generally the same ones who are prone to troublesome behavior.

The explanation for the connection could be something quite different and 7
spectacularly simple: Kids interested in sex and violence are, well, interested in sex and violence. Those who are inclined to have sex earlier than their peers could be inclined to seek out vulgar rock and rap musicians. Teenagers with a penchant for **mayhem** could be drawn to a sport that glorifies it.

What got overlooked in the research are the grounds for optimism. The music 8
study, which highlighted the possible dangers of "degrading sexual content," actually concluded that "exposure to nondegrading sexual content was negatively associated" with the loss of virginity.

That's right: Kids who listen to a lot of music that merely celebrates sexual 9
pleasure are not more likely to jump in the sack but less likely. Christina Aguilera may be a force for abstinence. How do latter-day Puritans explain that?

The studies got attention because they confirm the notion that today's kids are 10
being poisoned by a culture that glorifies all the wrong things. But parents have been thinking that at least since Beaver Cleaver's era. This time, at least, they're wrong.

11   Despite all the **lascivious** music, sexual activity among teens has been on the decline. A federal survey found that in 1991, 54 percent of high-school students reported they had had sexual intercourse. In 2005, the number was down to 47 percent. Oral sex is allegedly the rage among the pubescent set, but David-Landry, a researcher at the Alan Guttmacher Institute, says its popularity has been stable.

12   Not only are teenagers more cautious about having sex, they are more cautious while having sex: Condom use has risen by more than a third since the early 1990s. From 1990 through 2000 (the latest year for which data are available), the pregnancy rate among adolescents fell every year, for a cumulative decline of 28 percent.

13   The same positive pattern holds for violence. Teens today are considerably less likely to get in fights or carry weapons than they were 15 years ago. Kids under the age of 18 commit only one-third as many crimes as they did in the peak year of 1993. Maybe seeing the wrestlers on TV has convinced a lot of youngsters that pounding on people is something that should be left to professionals.

14   Like adults, who can enjoy murder mysteries without ever feeling the need to commit murder, adolescents apparently can separate the fantasies of mass entertainment from the realities of how they want to live their own lives. Whatever our culture is doing wrong in the way of setting a good example for kids, it must be doing something right.

Comprehension Check

Purpose and Main Idea

1. What is the author's topic?
    a. studies about sex, violence, and teen behavior
    b. teenagers' viewing and listening habits
    c. artistic freedom of expression
    d. pop culture and the mass media
2. Which sentence best states the central idea?
    a. Exposure to sex and violence causes bad behavior.
    b. Sex and violence fill much of today's mass media.
    c. Despite the bad examples around them, a lot of kids are good.
    d. The relationship between culture and behavior is unclear.
3. The author's *primary* purpose is to
    a. inform readers about the studies on violence and sex in media.
    b. persuade readers that there is too much sex and violence in media.
    c. express an opinion that a lewd culture may not necessarily cause bad behavior.
    d. entertain readers with examples of sex and violence in our culture.

Details

4. What the scholars at *Pediatrics* found is that the kids who are most exposed to sex and violence are not necessarily the ones most likely to engage in sexual or violent behavior.
    a. True
    b. False

5. The Pussycat Dolls is an example that supports the idea of "music with degrading sexual content."
    a. True
    b. False
6. Which one of the following was associated with less, not more, sexual activity among teenagers?
    a. sex and violence in the media
    b. professional wrestling on TV
    c. degrading sexual content in music
    d. music that merely celebrates sexual pleasure
7. In a culture saturated with lascivious music and violent images, sexual activity among teens
    a. is on the rise.
    b. has been on the decline.
    c. has stayed the same since 1991.
    d. has decreased after a period of increase.
8. What is the *dominant* organizational pattern in this selection?
    a. cause and effect
    b. sequence
    c. comparison and contrast
    d. classification

Inferences

9. Most people believe that exposure to sex and violence is not good for children. Do you concur with this belief? Why or why not?
10. Do you agree with the author that most teenagers, like most adults, can separate the fantasies of mass entertainment from the realities of life? Why or why not?

Working with Words

Complete sentences 1–6 with these words from Word Alert:

lascivious	suffuses	venture
degrading	raunchy	mayhem

1. Prior to an election, the topic that _____ radio and TV programming is politics.
2. Do not _____ into dangerous areas of the city at night.
3. Some women in business find it _____ when men in the same position expect them to get the coffee.
4. Those who engage in sexual harassment are guilty of lewd and _____ conduct.
5. On a camping trip, you may begin to feel _____ after several days without bathing.

6. Those who lived through the 1960s will never forget the _____ of the campus riots.

Write your own sentences, using any two of the words from Word Alert.

7. _____

8. _____

Thinking Deeper

Ideas for reflection, discussion, and writing

Make Inferences from Your Reading

1. The author says that sex, violence, degrading content in music, and movies aimed at high school boys are typical fare for today's teenagers. Do you agree? Give some examples of media that either do or do not fit this description.
2. In paragraph 14, the author says: "Whatever our culture is doing wrong in the way of setting a good example for kids, it must be doing something right." On what evidence does he base this statement? Give an example from your own experience of something right or wrong in the culture that sets an example for kids.
3. How much sex and violence is too much? Should parents monitor their children's use of the Internet? What music groups or TV programs are inappropriate for children, and where should parents draw the line? These are hard questions for parents. How did your parents answer them? How will you answer them when raising your own children?
4. The U.S. government has done studies on the effects of media sex and violence on young people, as have many groups, some more reliable than others. Search the Internet for a study of the type commented on in this selection. Ask a librarian to help you by suggesting search words and phrases and some URLs to try. When you find a study that interests you, take notes on it and remember to credit the source. Include in your notes who conducted the study, who participated, and what conclusions were reached. Share your findings in a class discussion.

Write About It

5. Do you think that sex and violence in the media is a serious problem, or do you think that this topic is overplayed? Explain your reasons in a paragraph or short essay.
6. Write about some aspect of popular culture (movie, TV show, music) that you think has had either a positive or negative influence on people.

FIRST THOUGHTS

To build background for the reading selection, answer the following questions, either on your own or in a group discussion.

1. How much and how soon should children be taught about the dangers of life?
2. Growing up, did you feel frightened or safe most of the time?
3. Preview the title, headnote, and first one or two paragraphs. What do you think will follow?

WORD ALERT

Each word below is followed by its paragraph number. Preview the words and definitions before reading. Then review them as necessary during reading. Use context clues and your dictionary to define any additional unfamiliar words.

perils (1) dangers
miasma (4) poisonous atmosphere or influence
ubiquitous (6) seeming to be everywhere at the same time
unremitting (7) persistent, never slacking in intensity
deprivation (8) the absence of pleasure, the lack of things one wants
plea (9) an earnest request, an appeal
lure (9) attract or tempt with a promise of pleasure or reward

◈ Frightening—and Fantastic

ANNA QUINDLEN

Anna Quindlen is a Pulitzer Prize–winning author. She has published several fiction and nonfiction books. She is a popular commentator whose columns have run in newspapers and magazines.

1 IN MAY, AS PART OF A PROGRAM TO PREPARE them for college, the seniors at my daughter's high school heard from a nationally recognized expert on date rape. In August, as part of their introduction to life on campus, the students at the liberal-arts college she is now attending heard from a nationally recognized expert on date rape—the same expert, offering the same warnings about the **perils** of sexual assault.

2 Those perils are real. So are the dangers of binge drinking, drug use, unsafe sex, Internet predators, bicycling without a helmet, riding in a car without a seat belt and smoking cigarettes. And perhaps it's also a little dangerous to say of all of the above: enough!

3 I'm the world's biggest fan of education and information. I was happy that my kids learned early how the seed and the egg got together, at school and from their parents. I like the idea of lung-cancer patients' visiting classes to show teenagers just how glamorous smoking can be once you've had chemo. Every time I hear that little snicking sound that means my kids are belted in, I feel a faint sense of well-being, even though they're not really kids anymore. I've always wanted them, and their friends, to have all the information necessary to make smart choices and avoid dangerous situations.

4 But for a long time I've had the uncomfortable feeling that the result has been a generation enveloped by a black **miasma** of imminent disaster. It's not that they hear about the dangers of drugs: they hear about them in school presentations, public-service announcements, print ads, TV movies, "After School Specials," cable documentaries and, of course, from responsible mothers and fathers. They've heard about them in elementary school, middle school, high school and college.

5 The net effect could be that the drumbeat of danger becomes persistent white noise, unremarked, unheard, unheeded. But that wasn't my concern when I realized that my daughter was going to hear the same warning about date rape in summer that she'd just heard in spring. Once, someone asked me what single quality I most wanted to pass on to my children. Without hesitation I replied, "Joie de vivre." Love of life. That sense of waking up in the morning and thinking that there may be good things ready to happen.

6 That fantastic feeling is easily lost in a frightening tide of bad tidings. Once, people drifted into unexamined marriages with illusions about a lifetime of romance, or torrid sex, or two hearts that beat as one. Today people plan weddings dogged by divorce and adultery statistics, hearing **ubiquitous** warnings that marriage is hard work and they might want to try couples counseling even before the ceremony. While once everything was unspoken, now it seems that everything is out there.

7 Or everything but this: that lots of marriages are happy or at least contented, and pulling in harness can be more satisfying than going it alone. That amid the

guys who try to pin you down at a party, it is not so unusual to find one who lights you up and makes you laugh. That sometimes people do stupid things and take stupid chances and get away with it without ruining their lives. A life of **unremitting** caution, without the carefree—or even, occasionally, the careless—may turn out to be half a life, like the Bible with the Ten Commandments but no Song of Solomon or Sermon on the Mount.

A little more than a decade ago, one of my sons told me very sadly that he 8 didn't understand how he was ever going to have children. At first I thought he meant that he didn't know how he would afford them, or have the patience to raise them. It turned out that he couldn't figure out how he could someday impregnate a woman. When I told him that a day would come when it would be safe to have sex without a condom, he looked at me as though I had lost my mind. Clearly he'd gotten the message. But he'd gotten only the **deprivation**, not the joy.

So this is a **plea** for parents to remember to have That Talk with their kids. 9 No, not the one about smoking cigarettes or driving under the influence. That's the one they will certainly get. What they need to hear occasionally is about the pleasures, not just the perils. Even when we talk about September 11, we can tell a tale of human goodness as well as evil, a tale of those who saved strangers as well as those who murdered them. For all the sleazebags who will try to **lure** a kid into a car, there are many Good Samaritans who are just concerned when they see a 12-year-old trudging along the road in the rain. I suppose we live at a time when we can't afford to let them accept the Samaritan's ride. But we also can't afford to have them think that Samaritans no longer exist. All these lectures, lessons and cautionary tales can't be to preserve a lifetime of looking over one shoulder. As Oscar Wilde wrote, "We are all in the gutter, but some of us are looking at the stars."

Comprehension Check

Purpose and Main Idea

1. What is the author's topic?
   a. the dangers children face
   b. one generation's problems
   c. balancing fear and wonder
   d. living life to its fullest
2. Which one of the following sentences *best* states the central idea?
   a. Life is filled with danger but also rewards those who work hard.
   b. We need to tell children about life's pleasures as well as its dangers.
   c. People in this generation are faced with problems their parents never had to face.
   d. The most important thing in life is to enjoy it.
3. The author's *primary* purpose is to
   a. express a point of view.
   b. provide information.
   c. persuade readers to take action.
   d. give an entertaining account.

Details

4. The author does not like the idea of lung cancer patients visiting classrooms to show the effects of smoking.
   a. True
   b. False
5. From this selection, you can tell that the author has more than two children.
   a. True
   b. False
6. The author mentions all of the following as dangers that children face *except* which one?
   a. drug use
   b. binge drinking
   c. unsafe sex
   d. pornography
7. In the past, which one of the following was *not* an illusion of an unexamined marriage?
   a. torrid sex
   b. a lifetime of romance
   c. two hearts beating as one
   d. divorce and adultery statistics
8. What is the organizational pattern in paragraph 6?
   a. sequence
   b. comparison
   c. process
   d. definition

Inferences

9. What else besides marriage have people tended to have illusions about? Give an example of something that was not as good or as bad as you had expected.
10. Do you agree with the author that we may be placing too much emphasis on life's dangers? Explain your answer.

Working with Words

Complete sentences 1–7 with these words from Word Alert:

deprivation	ubiquitous	perils	plea
unremitting	miasma	lure	

1. The Humane Society sent out a _____ for contributions to offset the costs of housing homeless animals.
2. Companies will advertise sales and special offers to _____ customers into their stores.
3. Following the _____ of food and water while it was lost, the returned dog drank and ate eagerly.

4. Certain celebrities are in the news so frequently that their pictures are _____.
5. When rain or snow is _____, there may be nothing to do but sit at home patiently and wait for it to end.
6. Date rape is just one of the _____ today's college students face.
7. The Internet seems littered with a _____ of sites that expose children to sex and violence.

Write your own sentences, using any two of the words from Word Alert.

8. _____
9. _____

Thinking Deeper

Ideas for reflection, discussion, and writing

Make Inferences From Your Reading

1. Who taught you about the "perils" mentioned in this selection? Were your parents, teachers, or others your primary sources of information? Do you feel that you are better or worse off for learning about life's dangers the way you did?
2. In paragraph 9, the author quotes Oscar Wilde: "We are all in the gutter, but some of us are looking at the stars." What meaning can you infer from this statement? What does the quotation have to do with the author's central idea?
3. How and what we should teach students about the dangers of life is one hard question that this selection raises. The author says that she is a "fan of education and information" and is glad that her children learned about sex and other perils in school. What is your opinion about the school's role in teaching our children about the dangers—and also the pleasures—of life?
4. Do a Web search on Anna Quindlen. Find a biography, photograph, and list of her publications. Her official site is with her publisher, Random House. Check with a librarian for the latest URLs and for other suggestions on researching this author.

Write About It

5. In paragraph 5, the author says that *joie de vivre*, love of life, is the single quality that she most wants to pass on to her children. What is one quality that you would like to pass on to your children?
6. Write about a danger you have faced and overcome.

FIRST THOUGHTS

To build background for the reading selection, answer the following questions, either on your own or in a group discussion.

1. What are some of the effects on the children of divorced parents?
2. What problems arise when divorced parents who share custody of a child live far apart?
3. Preview the title, headnote, and first one or two paragraphs. What do you think will follow?

WORD ALERT

Each word below is followed by its paragraph number. Preview the words and definitions before reading. Then review them as necessary during reading. Use context clues and your dictionary to define any additional unfamiliar words.

custody (3) care, supervision, or control

unresolved (3) undecided, unsettled

convert (6) to persuade or induce to adopt a particular religion, faith, or belief

turbulence (6) disturbance, agitation

cameo (9) brief appearance, as of an actor in a film

toll (10) the amount of loss or destruction caused by a disaster

◆ My Long-Distance Life

NICK SHEFF

In this selection, the author explains what it is like to divide his time between two parents living in different towns. Nick Sheff wrote this selection for *Newsweek*'s "My Word" column when he was a junior at Marin Academy High School in San Rafael, California.

I WAS BORN IN Berkeley, where I lived in a small house in the hills surrounded by firs and redwoods. My mom, my dad and me. As early as I can remember, there was arguing. When I was 4, my parents decided that they could no longer live together. 1

That same year, my mom moved to Los Angeles, and a therapist was hired to decide where I would live. My dad called her my worry doctor. Playing with a dollhouse in her office, I showed her the mother's room on one side and the father's room on the other. When she asked me about the little boy's room, I told her he didn't know where he would sleep. 2

Though I was very young, I accepted my parents' separation and divorce and somehow knew it wasn't my fault. Yet I was intensely afraid. Not only was my mom more than 500 miles away, but she had a new husband. My dad had a new girlfriend, and my **custody** was **unresolved**. Everyone said I'd spend time with both parents, but I wanted to know where I would live. 3

The therapist finally decided I'd stay with my dad during the school year and visit my mom on long holidays and for the summers. I began flying between two cities and two different lives. I've probably earned enough miles for a round-trip ticket to Mars. Some people love to fly, but I dreaded the trips. 4

For the first year, one of my parents would accompany me on the flights. At 6, I started traveling on my own. I would pack my toys and clothes in a Hello Kitty backpack and say goodbye to my parent at the gate. The flight attendant would lead me onto the plane. 5

When I was 7, the woman sitting next to me on the plane tried to **convert** me to Christianity. A few years later I was on a flight with such bad **turbulence** that the luggage compartments opened and the man behind me threw up. When I was 12 and on my way to L.A. for Christmas, a lady refused to check her bag and shoved a flight attendant. We couldn't take off for two hours; the police came and dragged her off, to the cheering of other passengers. But flying was just part of what made long-distance joint custody so difficult. 6

I remember the last day of school in the sixth grade. All my friends made plans to go to the beach together—all my friends, but not me. I couldn't join them because I had to fly to L.A. It wasn't that I didn't want to see my mom and stepdad. I just didn't want to leave my friends. As the school year came to a close, I began to shut down. I hated saying goodbye for the summer. It was easier to put up a wall, to pretend I didn't care. My dad drove to school with my packed bags. My friends went off together and I headed to the airport. 7

Arriving in L.A., I was excited to see my mom and stepdad. It had been almost three months since my last visit. But it took a while to adjust. Each set of parents had different rules, values and concerns. 8

9   I am 16 now and I still travel back and forth, but it's mostly up to me to decide when. I've chosen to spend more time with my friends at the expense of visits with my mom. When I do go to L.A., it's like my stepdad put it: I have a **cameo** role in their lives. I say my lines and I'm off. It's painful.

10   What's the **toll** of this arrangement? I'm always missing somebody. When I'm in northern California, I miss my mom and stepdad. But when I'm in L.A., I miss hanging out with my friends, my other set of parents and little brother and sister. After all those back-and-forth flights, I've learned not to get too emotionally attached. I have to protect myself.

11   Many of my friends' parents are divorced. The ones whose mom and dad live near each other get to see both their parents more. These kids can go to school plays and dances on the weekends, and see their friends when they want. But others have custody arrangements like mine. One friend whose dad moved to New Hampshire sees him at Christmas and for one month during the summer. My girlfriend's dad lives in Alaska. They know what I know: it's not fair.

12   No child should be subjected to the hardship of long-distance joint custody. To prevent it, maybe there should be an addition to the marriage vows: Do you promise to have and to hold, for richer and for poorer, in sickness and in health, as long as you both shall live? And if you ever have children and wind up divorced, do you promise to stay within the same geographical area as your kids? Actually, since people often break those vows, maybe it should be a law: if you have children, you must stay near them. Or how about some common sense? If you move away from your children, you have to do the traveling to see them.

13   In two years I'll go to college. I'll be living away from both homes, which will present new problems, such as where I will spend holidays. Whatever happens, I'll continue to build my relationships with both my parents, my siblings and my friends.

14   Before I have children of my own, I'll use my experiences to help make good decisions about whom I choose to marry. However, if I do get a divorce, I will put my children's needs first. I will stay near them no matter what happens.

Comprehension Check

Purpose and Main Idea

1. What is the author's topic?
   a. family therapy following divorce
   b. long-distance joint custody
   c. divorce in the United States
   d. reasons for separation
2. The central idea of this selection is stated in
   a. paragraph 1, last sentence "When I was 4...."
   b. paragraph 3, first sentence "Though I was...."
   c. paragraph 11, last sentence "They know what...."
   d. paragraph 12, first sentence "No child should...."
3. The author's *primary* purpose is to
   a. inform us about the research on children of divorce.
   b. express his views on the reasons that marriages fail.

c. entertain readers with amusing incidents in his long-distance life.

d. persuade readers that divorced parents should live close to their children.

Details

4. Sheff's parents separated when he was four years old.
   a. True
   b. False

5. Sheff's mother lives in
   a. Berkeley.
   b. Alaska.
   c. Los Angeles.
   d. San Francisco.

6. As a young child, what was Sheff's attitude toward his parents' divorce?
   a. He did not accept it.
   b. He knew it was not his fault.
   c. He did not believe in divorce.
   d. He lost respect for both parents.

7. At age 16, Sheff chose to live with his mother.
   a. True
   b. False

8. The author's overall organizational pattern is
   a. definition: He defines the term *joint custody*.
   b. comparison and contrast: He compares children of divorce to children of intact families.
   c. cause and effect: He explains why he thinks long-distance joint custody is unfair.
   d. sequence: He traces his travels between his parents' homes.

Inferences

9. What type of custody arrangement between divorced parents would the author be most likely to support?

10. What alternative to long-distance joint custody does the author propose?

Working with Words

Complete sentences 1–6 with these words from Word Alert:

turbulence   unresolved   convert   custody   cameo   toll

1. If a financial dispute between individuals remains _____, they may have to settle their differences in court.

2. During a presidential election, each candidate tries to _____ as many voters as possible to his or her point of view.

3. The most important decision to be made in a divorce case concerns who will have _____ of the children.

4. Moviegoers enjoy watching a film in which one of their favorite actors has a _____ role, however brief.
5. Because of _____ in the air, several passengers on the flight suffered from motion sickness.
6. During the Middle Ages, the death _____ from plague was high.

Write your own sentences, using any two of the words from Word Alert.

7. _____
8. _____

Thinking Deeper

Ideas for reflection, discussion, and writing

Make Inferences from Your Reading

1. Based on the author's details about his long-distance life, what can you infer about the toll of divorce on children in general?
2. Discuss the various custody arrangements available to divorced parents and the advantages and disadvantages of each.
3. How do children cope with their divorced parents' custody arrangements? Also, criminal activity, drug use, and emotional distress are much higher for children of divorce. How can divorced parents protect their children from these consequences?
4. Do you know how many marriages end in divorce? Do you know which state has the lowest divorce rate? To find the answers to these questions and other questions about divorce in the United States, type the search phrase "divorce statistics" for a list of sites, or try one of these sites. Use the information you find to make inferences about the future of marriage and divorce. Remember to ask a librarian for the latest URLs if you have trouble finding a site.

   - U.S. National Center for Health Statistics
   - U.S. Census Bureau
   - Americans for Divorce Reform
   - Fedstats

Write About It

5. What do you think is the greatest social problem associated with divorce? What is one possible solution?
6. Write about one positive or negative aspect of your own upbringing and how it has shaped your views about marriage and family.

FIRST THOUGHTS

To build background for the reading selection, answer the following questions, either on your own or in a group discussion.

1. What percentage of American marriages would you estimate have ended in divorce?
2. What economic and social pressures face children of divorced parents?
3. Preview the title, headnote, and first one or two paragraphs. What do you think will follow?

WORD ALERT

Each word below is followed by its paragraph number. Preview the words and definitions before reading. Then review them as necessary during reading. Use context clues and your dictionary to define any additional unfamiliar words.

In a textbook chapter, the words to watch may appear in boldface, italics, or a special color.

naturalistic (5) refers to research in which subjects are observed in normal or natural circumstances

externalizing (6) acting out impulses and feelings

authoritative (6) a parenting style that exercises high control with warmth and nurturing

authoritarian (6) a parenting style that exercises high control without warmth

permissive (6) a parenting style that involves either making few demands on children or avoiding child-rearing responsibilities altogether

internalizing (7) holding feelings and impulses inside

joint custody (11) a legal arrangement whereby parents share custody of children

Divorce and Its Effects on Children

KELVIN L. SEIFERT AND ROBERT J. HOFFNUNG

> This textbook reading is excerpted from Chapter 13 of *Childhood and Adolescent Development,* Fifth Edition. The entire chapter is about psychosocial development in middle childhood. The excerpt focuses on parenting and family life. When reading from textbooks, remember that headings may signal topics, main ideas, or important details.

1   MOST PARENTS WHO divorce must make major adjustments in their lives, and these adjustments often affect their children deeply. First, many divorcing parents face sudden economic pressures. Some find themselves financially responsible for two households, that of their former spouse and children and that of the new spouse and children. Many divorced mothers must take on new or additional employment to meet their household responsibilities, but even so their standard of living frequently declines. For many of these women, a reduction of economic resources often is accompanied by dependence on welfare; poorer-quality housing, neighborhoods, schools, and child care; and the need to move to a neighborhood they can afford, which often leads to loss of social support for the child from familiar friends, neighbors, and teachers. In contrast, both noncustodial and custodial fathers are more likely to maintain or improve their standard of living following divorce (Hetherington et al., 1998).

2   Divorce involves many psychological pressures as well. The parent who takes primary custody of the children must learn to manage a household alone, which is a major physical and psychological burden. Some parents may feel deeply isolated from relatives or friends to whom they used to feel close. If relatives do live nearby, divorcing parents often must rely on them for the first time, simply to procure help with child care and household work. Even before actual separation and divorce, many such families go through long periods of distress, tension, and discord. For most, these pressures continue to create stress for two or three years following separation (Corey, 1998; Hetherington et al., 1998).

3   Divorce is especially hard for school-age children. Having outgrown the self-centeredness of the preschool years, school-age children increasingly identify with and rely on their parents as role models to help them establish their own sense of who they are and how they should behave. At a time when children are just learning to be independent from home life, divorce threatens the safe base they have come to rely on to help make increasing independence possible. The loyalty conflicts frequently created by parents who are competing for their children's allegiance can make children fearful that they will lose one of their parents in the process.

4   Judith Wallerstein and Sandra Blakeslee (1996) conducted a long-term follow-up study of middle-SES[1] children who were between six and eight years old at the time of their parents' divorce. She found that even ten years later, these children were burdened by fear of disappointment in love relationships, lowered expectations, and a sense of powerlessness. When compared to children who were older

---

[1] socioeconomic status

FIGURE 13.2 | PERCENTAGE OF U.S. MARRIAGES ENDING IN DIVORCE, 1900–1993

Since the mid-1980s, approximately half of all marriages in the United States have ended in divorce.

or younger at the time of the breakup, school-age children fared far worse in their emotional adjustment and overall competence, including school and social relationships. The profound unhappiness with current relationships and concerns regarding future ones that these children experienced often were masked by their overall conformity to social expectations (see Table 13.2).

Some critics have questioned the degree to which Wallerstein & Blakeslee's findings, which were based on **naturalistic**, case study techniques with a middle-class sample, represent the entire population of parents and children of divorce. Future research using more quantitative approaches and families from a broader range of backgrounds will help determine the validity of their findings (Hetherington et al., 1998).

DIFFERENT EFFECTS ON BOYS AND GIRLS

On the whole, girls and boys tend to respond differently to divorce. Boys often express their distress in **externalizing** ways, becoming more aggressive, willful, and disobedient during the period surrounding separation and divorce. They often lose access to the parent with whom they identify more strongly—their father—because the majority of divorced children live with their mothers and are more frequently victims of parental power struggles and inconsistencies in matters of discipline. In a study of children six years after divorce, Mavris Hetherington (1988, 1991) found that whereas mothers and daughters had reestablished close and positive relationships, problems between mothers and sons persisted. Whereas the most common parenting style for divorced mothers with daughters was **authoritative**, the most common style with sons was **authoritarian** and the next most common **permissive**,

TABLE 13.2 | THE PSYCHOLOGICAL TASKS OF CHILDREN OF DIVORCE

Task 1: Understanding the divorce	Children must first learn to accurately perceive the immediate changes that divorce brings. Later they learn to distinguish between fantasized fears of being abandoned or losing their parents and reality so that they can evaluate their parents' actions and draw useful lessons for their own lives.
Task 2: Strategic withdrawal	Children and adolescents need to get on with their own lives as quickly as possible and get back, physically and emotionally, to the normal tasks of growing up. This poses a dual challenge to children, who must actively remove themselves emotionally from parental distress and conflict to safeguard their individual identities and separate life course.
Task 3: Dealing with loss	Children must overcome two profound losses: the loss of the intact family, together with the symbolic and real protection it provided, and the loss of the presence of one parent, usually the father, from their lives. They must overcome the powerful sense of rejection, humiliation, unlovableness, and powerlessness they feel and feelings of self-blame for causing the divorce.
Task 4: Dealing with anger	The major task for children is to resolve their anger at being hurt by the very people they depend on for protection and love. They must recognize their parents as human beings capable of making mistakes and respect them for their efforts and courage.
Task 5: Working out guilt	Young children often feel responsible for divorce, thinking their misbehavior may have caused one parent to leave. They need to separate from guilty "ties that bind" them too closely to a troubled parent and go on with their own lives.
Task 6: Accepting the permanence of the divorce	At first, children's strong need to deny the divorce can help them cope with the powerful realities they face. Over time, they must accept the divorce as a permanent state of affairs.
Task 7: Taking a chance on love	Achieving realistic hope regarding relationships may be the most important task for both the child and society. Children must create and sustain a realistic vision of their own capacity to love and be loved, knowing that separation and divorce are always possible. Mastering this last task—which depends on successfully negotiating all of the others—leads to psychological freedom from the past and to a second chance.

Source: Adapted from Wallerstein and Blakeslee (1989, 1996).

suggesting that mothers either tried to control their sons' behavior with power assertiveness or gave up trying.

Girls appear to become less aggressive as a result of divorce, tend to worry 7
more about schoolwork, and often take on more household responsibilities. This suggests they are **internalizing**, or holding inside, their distress by trying to act more helpful and responsible than usual (Block et al., 1981). Daughters of divorced parents may also become overly preoccupied with their relationships with males. They are more likely to become involved in dating and sexual activities at an early age, sometimes before the end of elementary school, and more likely to get pregnant and have conflict-ridden relationships with males during their teen years. Girls may also encounter increased risk of sexual abuse from stepparents and parents' dating partners in the period following divorce (Wallerstein & Blakeslee, 1996).

Perhaps the most important effort parents can make to minimize the negative 8
effects of divorce is to try to reduce their own conflicts and to cooperate in providing the best parenting possible for their children. Also important is the appropriate use of professional help to successfully work out postdivorce arrangements, resolve emotional conflicts more effectively, and develop the skills needed to sustain strong and supportive parent-child relationships. Finally, close relationships with mothers who are warm and supportive but still provide firm, consistent control and supervision, particularly in the period immediately following divorce, are associated with positive adjustment for both girls and boys (Armatz et al., 1995; Simons & Johnson, 1996; Stolberg & Walsh, 1988).

CUSTODY ARRANGEMENTS

Relationships between parents and children frequently deteriorate during and im- 9
mediately after a divorce. The parent with physical custody of the children (usually the mother) finds herself dealing not only with her children but also with major new responsibilities for earning a living and making peace—at least in her mind—with the reality of divorce. Parents without physical custody of the children (usually fathers) do not face these daily hassles, but they do report feeling rootless, dissatisfied, and unjustly cut off from their children. Seeing his children every other week or on school vacations may prevent a father from knowing them intimately and being part of their everyday lives, and lead him to become increasingly reliant on special events (such as going to Disney World), when contacts do occur. Noncustodial parents may also believe their financial and emotional support for their children goes unappreciated. Perhaps for these reasons, although fathers often increase the amount of time they spend with their children immediately after divorce, they soon decrease such time well below what it was before the divorce (Hetherington et al., 1998).

For noncustodial fathers and mothers alike, both the quantity and quality of 10
parent-child relationships differ from those of parents who have custody. Noncustodial mothers are, on the average, less competent than custodial mothers in controlling and monitoring their children's behavior, although they are more effective than noncustodial fathers. Noncustodial mothers are also more interested in and better informed about their children's activities; more supportive, sensitive, and responsive to their children's needs; and better able to communicate with their

children than noncustodial fathers are (Hetherington et al., 1998). The postdivorce parenting of fathers is less predictable than that of noncustodial mothers. Some fathers who were previously attached to and involved with their children find their new role too limited and painful, and drift away from their children. Others, however, rise to the occasion and become more involved with their children. The quality of the noncustodial father's relationship with his children and the circumstances in which contacts with them occur are much more important than frequency of visits. When noncustodial fathers remain actively involved in their children's activities and emotional lives, positive developmental outcomes are likely. Even limited contact with noncustodial fathers can enhance children's adjustment when it occurs under supportive, low-conflict conditions (Clarke-Stewart & Hayward, 1996; Simons & Beaman, 1996).

11   Sometimes parents are able to establish **joint custody**, a legal arrangement in which parental rights and responsibilities continue to be shared in a relatively equal manner. The mechanics of the arrangement vary with the child's age and the family's circumstances. The children may live with each parent during alternate weeks, parts of weeks, or even parts of the year. Or, when the children are older, one or more may live with one parent and the rest with the other parent. Joint custody tends to promote greater contact with both parents after divorce, facilitate fathers' involvement, and make mothers' parenting responsibilities less burdensome. Its success, however, depends on parents' willingness and ability to rearrange their lives and maintain the levels of mutual respect and cooperation required to make this arrangement work (Arditti, 1992).

Comprehension Check

Purpose and Main Idea

1. What is the authors' topic?
   a. custody arrangements
   b. effects of divorce
   c. parenting styles
   d. children's behavior
2. Which one of the following best states the authors' central idea?
   a. The law provides different custody arrangements for parents, depending on the circumstances of the divorce.
   b. Children's behavior, to a large extent, depends on the parenting style to which they are exposed.
   c. The adjustments that parents must make following divorce affect their children in several ways.
   d. Boys and girls may react differently when families are recombined following divorce and remarriage.
3. The authors' *primary* purpose in this excerpt is to do which one of the following?
   a. inform readers about the high rate of divorce in the United States
   b. express a preference for the traditional family
   c. persuade parents to work out problems for their children's sake
   d. explain how children react following their parents' divorce

Details

4. The authors cite all but which one of the following as economic pressures that divorced mothers may face?
   a. managing a household alone
   b. the need for additional or new employment
   c. poorer-quality housing
   d. a decline in their standard of living
5. According to the authors, divorce is especially hard on adolescents.
   a. True
   b. False
6. Mavris Hetherington's research showed that divorced mothers fared better at reestablishing positive relationships with daughters than with sons.
   a. True
   b. False
7. According to the authors, what is the most important way in which parents can minimize the negative effects of divorce?
   a. develop good parenting skills
   b. provide firm, consistent control and supervision
   c. seek professional help
   d. cooperate and reduce conflict
8. What is the authors' primary pattern of development in paragraphs 6 and 7?
   a. The authors *compare* boys' and girls' behavior following divorce.
   b. They explain *causes and effects* of divorce on children.
   c. They list stages in the *process* of recovering from divorce.
   d. The authors *classify* children's responses to divorce.

Inferences

9. Based on Figure 13.2, in which two decades did the greatest increase in the percentage of marriages ending in divorce occur?
10. What task in Table 13.2 would cover a child's feelings of heartbreak when bonds with extended family members such as grandparents and cousins are broken?

Working with Words

Complete sentences 1–7 with these words from Word Alert:

internalizing	authoritarian	naturalistic	permissive
externalizing	joint custody	authoritative	

1. Those who allow their children to run and play in restaurants have a _____ parenting style.
2. Students in an education course were asked to conduct a _____ study in which they observed play behavior among kindergarteners.
3. Children who hit and bully others are _____ their anger.

4. Divorced parents who share child-rearing responsibilities equally have a _____ arrangement.
5. _____ parents are loving and caring, while insisting that their children follow rules.
6. A child who is more cooperative than usual may be _____, or holding back, feelings of distress.
7. Parents whose style is _____ may be uncommunicative and lack warmth in dealing with their children.

Write your own sentences, using any two of the words from Word Alert.

8. _____
9. _____

Thinking Deeper

Ideas for reflection, discussion, and writing

Make Inferences from Your Reading

1. In this selection, the authors explain the effects of custody arrangements on the children of divorce. Are their views similar to or different from those expressed by Nick Sheff in "My Long-Distance Life" (Selection 29)? What inference can you make?
2. Seifert and Hoffnung discuss the effects of divorce on children. What problems do they identify, and what are their solutions for minimizing the negative effects of divorce on children? Making inferences from your own experience, give specific examples of divorced parents who have applied solutions similar to those Seifert and Hoffnung advocate.
3. Studies have shown, as in this excerpt, that divorce affects children differently but often negatively. Children of divorce are more likely to do poorly in school, get involved in drugs, become unwed parents, and have other adjustment problems than are children of intact families. Whether to divorce or to stay married is a hard question for some couples, and what we as a society can or should do about the high divorce rate is another hard question. What do you think about divorce and its effects in general, and what alternatives exist for troubled couples?
4. Learning and using the key terms of a discipline will improve your comprehension and retention of concepts. Your computer can help in two ways. First, start an online glossary for each of your courses. Keep a running list of key terms for one or more of your courses. Make two lists for each chapter. The first list should be terms only. In the second list, include the definitions. Use the second list for review. Use the first list as a self-test. Print out the list and write the definitions. Bring up your second list and check your work. Second, build your vocabulary by using online resources such as a dictionary, a thesaurus, and word games. Ask your librarian to suggest some sites for you to browse.

Write About It

5. What are your views about marriage, divorce, child-rearing, or alternative living arrangements? Explain your views on one of these topics.
6. Write about how you or someone you know has had to deal with one of the psychological tasks listed in Table 13.2.

Focus on Work and Career

If you are a young college student, you may view college as an essential step toward landing your first real job. If you are an older student, you may be seeking the opportunity that college provides to rethink, retrain, and restart your life for a better future.

Work not only provides the means to a good life, but also makes up a large part of your identity. Asked to describe themselves, most Americans answer by explaining what they do for a living. Because work takes up such a big part of your life, you will be happiest if you choose a career that enables you to earn money while doing something that you love doing.

The Part 5 selections are about people who have found meaningful work and the skills that ensure career success. As you read and think about the selections, ask yourself these questions: What kind of world do I want to live in? What kind of person do I want to be? What kind of work will I enjoy?

FIRST THOUGHTS

To build background for the reading selection, answer the following questions, either on your own or in a group discussion.

1. Have you spent time in a country whose culture is quite different from your own? What did you learn from the experience?
2. If you had a choice between either remaining in a secure profession or striking out on your own, which would you choose and why?
3. Preview the title, headnote, and first one or two paragraphs. What do you think will follow?

WORD ALERT

Each word below is followed by its paragraph number. Preview the words and definitions before reading. Then review them as necessary during reading. Use context clues and your dictionary to define any additional unfamiliar words.

Esteem (3) favorable regard, respect
debate (4) to consider, discuss, or argue pros and cons
equatorial (6) relating to the equator, or the imaginary line around the earth's middle
complex (7) complicated, intricate
intangible (12) incapable of being perceived through the senses
elite (15) having intellectual, social, or economic status

◈ A Year of African Life Opened My Eyes

JOANN HORNAK

In this essay from *Newsweek's* "My Turn" column, author JoAnn Hornak writes
about her work as a volunteer in a developing country. Hornak's year in Africa
was a time of self-discovery.

ANYONE WHO HAS considered following a dream career is often told by well-meaning   1
family and friends, "Don't quit your day job." I didn't listen.

Three years ago, while I was working as a prosecuting attorney, I took a year's   2
leave of absence to pursue a goal I'd had since college: to volunteer in a developing
country. During the year in Tanzania, I made several discoveries that ultimately led
me to change careers when I returned home.

In Africa I worked on research proposals with several Tanzanian attorneys, in-   3
cluding Julius, a struggling public-interest lawyer at the East Africa Law Society.
One of my first surprises was to find a country where lawyers are held in the highest **esteem**. That may be because with a population of about 30 million, Tanzania
has fewer than 600 lawyers.

One day Julius and I had lunch at a café in Arusha, a tourist town and starting   4
point for safaris to the Serengeti and the Ngorongoro Crater. One of our favorite
pastimes was discussing the many differences between life in the United States and
in Tanzania. Dessert presented another opening for **debate**.

Julius ordered a dish of vanilla and banana ice cream, two of three flavors of-   5
fered on the menu. I told him that in the United States we have at least 50 flavors,
some mixed with chocolate chips, chunks of cookie dough or caramel swirls, sweets
that were difficult to describe because they don't exist in Tanzania. I thought he'd
be interested and ask a lot of questions, so I wasn't prepared for his response.

"That's too many," he said, and then went back to enjoying his two plain   6
scoops melting in the **equatorial** heat. Considering that he longed to visit the United
States someday, I was surprised by his lack of curiosity. But his observation
struck me.

I thought about how **complex** U.S. life can be with our countless lifestyle-   7
and-consumer options. In Tanzania I'd learned to live without luxuries like
constant running water and electricity, a refrigerator, car, television, telephone and
shopping malls. I grew to prefer the lack of choices, the time not spent in making
the perfect selection.

My housemates, Katie from Toronto and Ruth from England, felt the same   8
way. Near the end of our year, we talked about returning to our First World
homes.

"I'm afraid to go back," said Katie.   9

"I'm going to stay in my village and not leave for a month," said Ruth, who   10
grew up in Calne, population 800.

"We don't have villages! What am I going to do?" I worried. I loved the simple,   11
slow pace of African life that had given me time to spend hours each day writing.
I felt I loved it enough to leave the practice of law and make writing my new career.

But when I returned home, reality struck. What if I failed? How would I pay my bills? I was afraid.

12   I went back to the district attorney's office. For months I resisted the decision to take a leap of faith and quit my job that for nearly 10 years had provided a steady paycheck, health insurance, four weeks' paid vacation and the **intangible** benefits of a successful profession. I'm the first and only person in my family to have earned a college degree. To pay for undergrad and law school, I had always had part-time jobs and taken out student loans. I was reluctant to let go of a career I'd worked hard to achieve.

13   But often I'd think back to a conversation I had had at a conference in Nairobi a month before returning to the United States. It was at the Carnivore Restaurant, and I was sitting next to Edwin Mtei, former executive director of the International Monetary Fund. Over dinner of Cape buffalo, crocodile and zebra, Mtei asked if I was going back to my job as a prosecutor. I told him that I was thinking of other possibilities, that I hoped to try something new.

14   "You people have so many choices. You'd never hear a Tanzanian say that. There are so few jobs, we need to take whatever comes along," he said. He wasn't bitter, just pointing out something I hadn't appreciated until I'd spent a year abroad: that I live in a country that gives me the opportunity to reinvent myself.

15   How could I not try to become a writer when, by accident of birth, I had the option and my friends like Julius, the so-called **elite** in Tanzania, didn't? I finally realized that the only things holding me back were fear and the golden handcuffs.

16   I gave notice at the D.A.'s office last August. The past nine months haven't been easy, but I can honestly say my only regret is that I wish I'd done this sooner.

Comprehension Check

Purpose and Main Idea

1.   What is the author's topic?
   a.   working as a volunteer
   b.   changing jobs or careers
   c.   African life and culture
   d.   a year among the Tanzanians
2.   The author's central idea is stated in which one of the following sentences?
   a.   paragraph 2, first sentence "Three years ago...."
   b.   paragraph 2, last sentence "During the year...."
   c.   paragraph 3, first sentence "In Africa I worked...."
   d.   paragraph 16, last sentence "The past nine...."
3.   The author's purpose is to
   a.   persuade readers to volunteer for worthy causes.
   b.   inform readers about life in an African village.
   c.   explain why she changed jobs and started over.
   d.   entertain readers with a story about African life.

Details

4. The author's work in Tanzania involved which one of the following?
   a. legal aid for the poor
   b. social work
   c. planting crops
   d. research proposals
5. When the author told her friend Julius about the many flavors of ice cream available in the United States, she was surprised by his lack of curiosity.
   a. True
   b. False
6. The author says that while in Tanzania, she learned to live without television.
   a. True
   b. False
7. The author resisted changing careers for all but which one of the following reasons?
   a. fear of failure
   b. not knowing what career she wanted to pursue
   c. wondering how she would pay her bills
   d. the intangible benefits of a successful profession
8. The details in paragraph 12 are organized by which one of the following patterns?
   a. classification
   b. comparison and contrast
   c. cause and effect
   d. generalization and example

Inferences

9. What does the author mean when she says that life in the United States is "complex"?
10. In paragraph 15, second sentence, what does "golden handcuffs" mean?

Working with Words

Complete sentences 1–6 with these words from Word Alert:

intangible	debate	complex
equatorial	esteem	elite

1. Many students hope to get into one of the _____ schools, such as Harvard or Yale.
2. Personal satisfaction is one of the _____ benefits of being self-employed.
3. During an election year, voters have an opportunity to hear the candidates _____ issues.
4. The tropical climate in some of the world's _____ regions draws tourists.

5. Some problems are too _____ to be solved with a simple answer.
6. Voters want to elect a president who not only is qualified to do the job but is also worthy of their _____.

Write your own sentences, using any two of the words from Word Alert.

7. _____

8. _____

Thinking Deeper

Ideas for reflection, discussion, and writing

Make Inferences from Your Reading

1. The author says she was reluctant to change jobs for several reasons. Do you think her experience is typical of most people? What would prompt you to change jobs or to keep a job, even if you didn't like it?
2. What purpose does the ice cream example in paragraphs 5 and 6 serve? Based on this example, what can you infer about life in the United States as compared to life in Tanzania?
3. Deciding to change jobs or careers can be one of life's most stressful choices, yet most people change jobs several times during their lives. The process can be a learning experience. What did the author learn about herself, her career, and her outlook for the future? Based on your answer to this question, what inference can you make about your own prospects for the future?
4. Volunteering to work for organizations that help people in need or perform a valued community service is both an educational and a personally rewarding experience. Perhaps service learning is an important part of one of your courses. Find out what volunteer opportunities exist for students at your college or in the community. Your college website is a good place to begin. Based on your search results, what inference can you make about the type of organizations or activities that your college values?

Write About It

5. Reflect on a time when you volunteered for an organization or a time when you were able to help someone solve a problem or achieve a goal. What happened? What did you learn?
6. Write about a job you held and what you learned from it.

FIRST THOUGHTS

To build background for the reading selection, answer the following questions, either on your own or in a group discussion.

1. Do you consider yourself a happy person? Explain your reasons.
2. How much does your happiness depend on the happiness of those around you?
3. Preview the title, headnote, and first one or two paragraphs. What do you think will follow?

WORD ALERT

Each word below is followed by its paragraph number. Preview the words and definitions before reading. Then review them as necessary during reading. Use context clues and your dictionary to define any additional unfamiliar words.

cubicle (1) a small compartment for work

pathogens (2) agents of disease, especially living organisms such as bacteria

contaminated (3) unclean or impure

paradigm (5) an example that serves as a pattern or model

transcends (5) goes beyond

dividend (7) a bonus

delirious (8) filled with uncontrolled excitement or emotion

topography (11) typical features of a region or description thereof

periphery (11) outermost boundary

◈ The Happiness Effect

ALICE PARK

Alice Park heads *Time* magazine's department for science coverage and is a senior reporter. She writes on health and medical issues. In this article, Park suggests that happiness may be catching.

1   THE NEXT TIME you get the flu, there will almost certainly be someone you can blame for your pain. There's the inconsiderate co-worker who decided to drag himself to the office and spent the day sniffling, sneezing and shivering in the **cubicle** next to yours. Or your child's best friend, the one who showed up for a playdate with a runny nose and a short supply of tissues. Then there's the guy at the gym who spent more time sneezing than sweating on the treadmill before you used it.

2   You're right to pass the blame. **Pathogens** like the influenza virus pass like a holiday fruitcake from person to person, but you probably don't think much past the one who gave it directly to you. An infectious-disease expert, on the other hand, would not be satisfied to stop there. What about the person who passed the virus on to your colleague, the one before him and others earlier still? Contagious diseases operate like a giant infectious network, spreading like the latest You Tube clip among friends of friends online. We're social animals; we share.

3   So public health experts are beginning to wonder whether certain health-related behaviors are just as contagious as microbes. If you're struggling with your weight, did you in effect catch a case of fat by learning poor eating and exercise habits from a friend or family member who was similarly infected by someone else? If you smoke, do you light up because you were behaviorally **contaminated** by smokers who convinced you of the coolness of the habit? Even more important, if such unhealthy behaviors are contagious, are healthy ones—like quitting smoking or exercising—equally so? And what if not only behaviors but also moods and mental states work the same way? Can you catch a case of happy?

4   Increasingly, the answer seems to be yes. That's the intriguing conclusion from a body of work by Harvard social scientist Dr. Nicholas Christakis and his political-science colleague James Fowler at the University of California at San Diego. The pair created a sensation with their announcement earlier this month of a 20-year study showing that emotions can pass among a network of people up to three degrees of separation away, so your joy may, to a larger extent than you realize, be determined by how cheerful your friends' friends' friends are, even if some of the people in this chain are total strangers to you.

5   If that's so, it creates a whole new **paradigm** for the way people get sick and, more important, how to get them healthy. It may mean that an individual's well-being is the product not just of his behaviors and emotions but more of the way they feed into a larger social network. Think of it as health, Facebook-style. "We have a collective identity as a population that **transcends** individual identity," says Christakis. "This superorganism has an anatomy, physiology, structure and function that we are trying to understand."

In their most recent paper, published in the *British Medical Journal*, Christakis   6
and Fowler explored the emotional state of nearly 5,000 people and the more than
50,000 social ties they shared. At three points during the long study, all the participants answered a standard questionnaire to determine their happiness level, so that
the scientists could track changes in emotional state. That led to their intriguing
finding of just how contagious happiness can be: if a subject's friend was happy,
that subject was 15% more likely to be happy too; if that friend's friend was happy,
the original subject was 10% more likely to be so. Even if the subject's friend's
friend—entirely unknown to the subject—was happy, the subject still got a
5.6% boost. The happiness chain also worked in the other direction, radiating from
the subject out to her friends.

The happiness **dividend** is more powerful if two people not only know each   7
other but also are equally fond of each other. Happiness is more infectious in mutual
relationships (in which both people name the other as a friend) than in unreciprocated
ones (in which only one is named).

And it's not just in sterile study settings that the contagion of happiness is   8
spreading. Christakis and Fowler noticed that people who are smiling on their Facebook pages tend to cluster together, forming an online social circle like a **delirious**
flock of cyberbirds. And while some of this joy can certainly be traced to the copycat effect—if your friends post smiling pictures, you might feel like a grouch if you
don't too—Christakis and Fowler are analyzing the clusters to see if something
more infectious might be at work.

Skeptics raise other concerns, ones that go beyond the copycat effect. Couldn't   9
happy people simply be exposed to similar lifestyles or social factors that explain
their shared joy, such as favorable weather, low unemployment rates or a winning
baseball team? If that were the case, argue the authors, then happiness would
spread more uniformly among all the relationships; instead, it varied depending on
whether the friendship was mutual or merely one-sided. As the investigators teased
out these factors, they found that environment didn't have nearly the power that
relationships did.

The infectiousness of happiness is only the latest in a series of similar phenom-   10
ena Christakis and Fowler have studied. In 2007 they published a paper showing
that obesity travels across webs in a similar way, with individuals having a 57%
greater risk of being overweight if they have an obese friend. The same holds true
for quitting smoking, with success 30% more common among friends of quitters
than among friends of smokers.

In all these cases, there's a predictable **topography** to how people influence one   11
another, one that can be reduced to a sort of social map. People who are central to
their networks—who in effect are the hub through which most of the other relationships or information flows—may have the most influence on others and in turn are the
most influenced by them. But just because you start off at the center of your web does
not guarantee that you'll stay there. In the 1970s, smokers were more likely to occupy
that focal position in their network of friends and family. Look at a similar social map
today, and you'll see that the smokers have drifted to the **periphery**.

The better this kind of mapping becomes, the more value it has. Officials at the   12
Centers for Disease Control and Prevention (CDC) are exploiting the connectedness
of youngsters in online social networks, for example, to improve flu vaccination

rates, not just among those under age 18 but among all the people to whom these children have ties. "Because of their social and peer networks, children have a higher likelihood of sharing information with the most people," says Jay Bernhardt of the CDC. By targeting youngsters on these sites with information about the importance of annual flu shots, health officials hope to trigger a literal and figurative viral wave of vaccination among the kids' peers, their peers' peers, and even those peers' parents and grandparents.

13   "We are always looking for exciting new areas of research that will help people live healthier," says Richard Suzman, director of the division of behavioral and social research at the National Institute on Aging. "Without a doubt, I see this as a very promising area." And with the health community a web like any other, expect that idea to spread further and further.

Comprehension Check

Purpose and Main Idea

1. What is the author's topic?
   a. emotions
   b. relationships
   c. the happiness effect
   d. emotions and behavior
2. Which one of the following sentences *best* states the author's central idea?
   a. Your friends' emotions and behavior may have an effect on your health.
   b. Researchers are beginning to wonder how behavior affects health and well-being.
   c. Happiness and other emotions can spread like a disease through a social network of friends.
   d. The happiness effect could be the key to understanding how people get sick and how to make them healthy.
3. What is the author's *primary* purpose?
   a. to express an opinion about the happiness effect
   b. to persuade readers that behavior affects health and well-being
   c. to inform readers of new research findings and why they are important
   d. to explain the reasons why we feel happiness or other emotions

Details

4. Christakis and Fowler believe that we have a collective identity that functions as an organism, having an anatomy, physiology, structure, and function.
   a. True
   b. False
5. Researchers found that of the two, environment has more power than relationships when it comes to explaining how happiness spreads.
   a. True
   b. False

6. The researchers found that happiness is more infectious in
   a. extended relationships.
   b. unreciprocated relationships.
   c. networked relationships.
   d. mutual relationships.
7. CDC officials hope to use social network mapping to target children with information on which one of the following?
   a. how to quit smoking
   b. the importance of annual flu shots
   c. ways to improve fitness
   d. proper nutrition
8. Paragraphs 1–3 are developed by which one of the following?
   a. sequence
   b. comparison
   c. process
   d. classification

Inferences

9. In your own words, what is "the happiness effect"?
10. The researchers suggest that your happiness may be determined by how cheerful your friends and their friends are. What evidence have you seen in your own social networking that would support this inference?

Working with Words

Complete sentences 1–9 with these words from Word Alert:

contaminated	topography	delirious	paradigm	cubicle
transcends	pathogens	periphery	dividend	

1. If one apple in a bag is rotten, the others will soon be _____.
2. Be careful what you say at work if you do not want the person sitting in the _____ next to yours to hear.
3. Often the need to help those close to us _____ the need to look after ourselves.
4. When an epidemic is ongoing, it may be difficult to avoid contact with the _____ that cause the disease.
5. Some people prefer to stay on the _____ than to become the center of attention
6. Fans were jumping up and down in the aisles, _____ with anticipation as the band walked onto the stage.
7. Facebook is the _____ of the way people interact in online social networks.
8. Better health is one _____ of getting fit.
9. A map is a visual representation of the _____ of an area, showing lakes and other features.

Write your own sentences, using any two of the words from Word Alert.

10. _____

11. _____

Thinking Deeper

Ideas for reflection, discussion, and writing

Make Inferences from Your Reading

1. If happiness is contagious as the author says, then how does your attitude affect the behavior of other students in a classroom or your coworkers on the job? Similarly, what inference can you make about the effect of any emotion or attitude on those around you?

2. Read again paragraph 8 about the spread of information on Facebook. Based on your experience with online social networks, does this sound familiar? In what ways has your behavior or attitude been influenced by your online friends? What potentially beneficial or harmful effects of online networking have you observed?

3. Since physical and mental health affect an employee's attendance and performance on the job, researchers are constantly looking for ways to improve workers' health and well-being. Explain how the research described in this article could help accomplish this goal.

4. Search the Internet to find information on attitudes and work or emotions and health. Your goal is to find out how changing your attitude or controlling your emotions can improve your performance as a student, your satisfaction at work, or your life in general. A good place to start is a career website, and there are many. Ask your instructor or librarian to help you find appropriate URLs. Share your results in a class discussion.

Write About It

5. In paragraph 3, the author asks "Can you catch a case of happy?" One could just as easily ask "Can you catch a case of sad, or angry?" Write your answer to one of these questions, using examples from your own experience.

6. Any community is a "web" of interactions among people in which information or ideas can spread. Write about one idea or practice that has spread and its positive or negative effects.

FIRST THOUGHTS

To build background for the reading selection, answer the following questions, either on your own or in a group discussion.

1. Have you ever considered cooking for a living? What skills do you think the job of chef requires?
2. Do you know what a research chef is? If not, make an educated guess.
3. Preview the title, headnote, and first one or two paragraphs. What do you think will follow?

WORD ALERT

Each word below is followed by its paragraph number. Preview the words and definitions before reading. Then review them as necessary during reading. Use context clues and your dictionary to define any additional unfamiliar words.

culinary (1) of or relating to cooking

precision (7) exactness, as in performance or amount

collaborative (10) of or relating to working cooperatively with others

accredited (13) having met an applied standard

zest (19) spirited enjoyment, gusto

knack (19) ability or talent

You're a What? Research Chef

OLIVIA CROSBY

Olivia Crosby is a contributing editor of the *Occupational Outlook Quarterly*, from which this selection came. If you like to cook, or if you just enjoy eating, Crosby's review of a fascinating career will provide a fresh insight into the food industry.

1   WHEN ANNE ALBERTINE gets creative in the kitchen, millions taste the results. As a research chef, she mixes good taste with good science, creating recipes for Taco Bell restaurants at its corporate headquarters in Irvine, California. Her tacos, chalupas, and burritos fill the menus of more than 6,500 restaurants. "My team and I make restaurant quality food that can be mass produced," says Anne, "so the **culinary** quality—the freshness, taste, and texture—has to hold up."

2   Research chefs, also called product development or food innovation chefs, create new foods for restaurant chains, coffee shops, and food manufacturing companies. They blend culinary training with a knowledge of food science. "As chefs, we can make food that tastes good and has visual appeal," says Anne. "We can weave flavors together." But research chefs also understand food preservation, mass production, and the technical terms used by scientists. And they use this knowledge in their recipes.

3   Research chefs get ideas for new menu items from many different sources. They often use the results of customer surveys to determine what customers crave. Suggestions are general. They might include requests for a large portion size, a low price, or a certain flavor, such as smoky or sweet. Research chefs give the ideas substance by creating several different recipes to match these characteristics. "My job is to create options," says Anne. For every product that makes it to the public, researchers cook up 30 to 100 alternative recipes that never make it out of the laboratory.

4   Research chefs also find inspiration by following trends in consumer tastes. They sample the menus of fine restaurants, often traveling abroad to stir up their creativity. And chefs read culinary magazines and study cookbooks, searching for recipes to modify.

5   With a set of food qualities in mind, research chefs start experimenting with ingredients. Anne often begins her day with a trip to the grocery store. "I pick up fresh ingredients," she says, "then go play in my test kitchen." She might try different styles of chopping, compare grilling an ingredient with frying it, or contrast vacuum-packed ingredients with frozen ones. In one recipe, Anne was striving for the just right level of spiciness and the best type of cheese to give a toasty flavor. She uses her technical expertise to pick ingredients that will taste good when cooked in bulk, under the real world conditions of a restaurant.

6   Anne's recipes also need to be convenient. To make a burrito that was portable, for example, she decided to grill it. The grilling process seared the burrito so it would stay closed, even when it held more food than the other burritos did.

7   A research chef's test kitchen is similar to the kitchen of any professional chef, with heavy-duty mixers, salamanders—tools for browning the tops of food—and other gadgets. But a research chef's kitchen is designed for **precision**. Graduated

cylinders stand in for measuring cups, and scientific balances that are accurate to the milligram replace the standard countertop scales. Large-batch recipes have to be detailed and accurate so that they can be reproduced in every restaurant. "We strive for quality and consistency," says Anne.

At each stage of development, recipes are tested with customers. In the first testing session, a focus group of customers might choose among 50 or more pictures and written descriptions of possible menu items. "I let the customers tell me what they like," says Anne. "I'm cooking for them, not myself." 8

Eventually, focus groups taste samples of the most appealing of the proposed foods. Responses are taken during experiments conducted in sensory labs by food scientists and marketers. Anne observes and learns from these experiments. "People might say a product is too messy, too spicy, or too expensive, so I tweak it," she says. "With food, small changes in ingredients can make a dramatic impact." 9

When Anne isn't fine-tuning recipes, she meets with other members of the staff. "Development is a **collaborative** process," she says. Financial experts check a recipe's profitability. Market researchers confirm its popularity. Food scientists concentrate on food safety and other considerations. And training and operations managers ensure that the restaurant crews will be able to make the food quickly and well. 10

Meetings like these highlight non-food-related skills that research chefs need in their jobs: good communication skills and the ability to persuade. "You have to prove your hunches," says Anne. She gives evidence that her ideas will be successful, especially when they require a large monetary investment, such as new restaurant equipment. 11

Research chefs who work for food manufacturers instead of restaurant chains perform slightly different tasks. They help food scientists develop flavor additives and prepared and frozen foods. They consult with restaurant chefs to learn what they need and explain flavor possibilities. If the restaurant wants a lemon flavor, for example, should it be acidic, sweet, or peely? Should it be liquid or dry? Research chefs translate the specifications of the restaurant into the technical language of scientists. Research chefs also test food scientists' products, using them in recipes to make sure they taste good. 12

To gain their unique mixture of skills, most research chefs earn a degree in culinary arts from a school **accredited** by the American Culinary Federation. And they take additional classes in food science and chemistry. Anne received a bachelor's degree in general science and worked in consumer product development before following her love of cooking and getting her culinary arts degree. After graduating, she completed several internships with chefs experienced in fine dining, an experience she recommends highly. "Intern with as many different people as you can," she says. "It's important to learn different techniques and to build contacts in the industry." 13

The Research Chefs Association offers certification to research chefs who have culinary education, 3 to 5 years of experience in both research and culinary arts, and a passing score on the certification exam. The Association also offers a culinary scientist certification to those who have a bachelor's degree in food science, at least 8 weeks of accredited culinary education, research experience, and a passing score on a written cooking exam. 14

15 The Research Chefs Association had almost 1,400 members this year, but the number of research chefs may be higher or lower than that number because not every member is a research chef and not every research chef is a member. According to a survey taken at the association conference in 1999, earnings varied widely for research chefs, but many experienced chefs earned between $70,000 and $90,000 per year. This suggests that research chefs often earn more than other chefs do. The Bureau of Labor Statistics does not collect data on research chefs.

16 The benefits of working as a research chef extend beyond earnings. Unlike restaurant and cafeteria chefs, who usually work weekends and evenings to prepare meals and supervise kitchen staff, most research chefs work standard business hours. And although they have deadlines to meet, research chefs usually work at a more relaxed pace than their restaurant counterparts.

17 The chance to be innovative adds spice to the job. "I'm always looking for a new way to achieve something in a recipe," says Anne.

18 And when a recipe succeeds, research chefs share it with a wide audience. "I love seeing a product go national," Anne says. She also enjoys seeing people eating and liking her creations—and if people discover what her job is, they often tell her which of her menu items are their favorites.

19 Knowing that her creations are popular adds **zest** to Anne's work, but the work itself is what she likes best. By mixing a passion for food, a **knack** for science, and a flair for creativity, she wrote a recipe for a career she loves.

Comprehension Check

Purpose and Main Idea

1. What is the author's topic?
   a. cooking
   b. the food industry
   c. being a research chef
   d. how to be a chef
2. Which one of the following best states the author's central idea?
   a. A research chef is different from an ordinary chef.
   b. What it means to be a research chef may surprise you.
   c. Research chefs create recipes for restaurant chains.
   d. Research chefs have skills other than cooking.
3. What is the author's *primary* purpose?
   a. to express interesting facts about the food industry
   b. to inform readers about the qualifications required of a chef
   c. to persuade the reader to consider becoming a research chef
   d. to explain what a research chef is

Details

4. Culinary quality includes freshness, taste, variety, and texture.
   a. True
   b. False

5. You would not find measuring cups in a research chef's kitchen.
   a. True
   b. False
6. The Research Chefs Association is responsible for which one of the following?
   a. awarding degrees
   b. job placement
   c. training
   d. certification
7. According to the author, what ingredient will give food a toasty flavor?
   a. onions
   b. cheese
   c. pepper
   d. bread crumbs
8. Which one of the following is the author's overall organizational pattern?
   a. Process: She explains how to become a research chef.
   b. Comparison: She compares research chefs with restaurant chefs.
   c. Definition: She answers the question, "What is a research chef?"
   d. Cause and effect: She explains why Anne became a research chef.

Inferences

9. In paragraph 9, what does *tweak* mean?
10. The author would probably agree that in addition to cooking skills, what workplace skills are important for a research chef?

Working with Words

Complete sentences 1–6 with these words from Word Alert:

| accredited | precision | knack |
| collaborative | culinary | zest |

1. One of the team members who had a _____ for drawing agreed to make posters to publicize the team's fundraising event.
2. Colleges work hard to maintain their status as _____ institutions.
3. Good interpersonal skills are essential in today's workplace, as so much of the work done is a _____ effort.
4. A student seeking a career as a research chef should major in _____ arts.
5. In an interview, an applicant who shows a certain _____ for the job will be more impressive than one who is indifferent.
6. Race car engines are so highly tuned that they require the use of _____ tools.

Write your own sentences, using any two of the words from Word Alert.

7. _____
8. _____

Thinking Deeper

Ideas for reflection, discussion, and writing

Make Inferences from Your Reading

1. Making inferences from the author's examples, explain in your own words how a research chef differs from an ordinary chef.
2. An author can define a term by using examples, by comparing and contrasting, by stating what something is not in order to show what it is, by examining its parts or functions, or by showing how it works or what it does. Which of these methods does the author of this selection use to define the term *research chef*?
3. The author explains the skills and personal qualities that one needs in order to be a research chef. What are these skills and qualities? Would this job appeal to you as a career goal? Why or why not?
4. If you enjoyed reading this selection, you may also enjoy learning about other unusual jobs and careers. To access another article like this selection, go to the home page of the *Occupational Outlook Quarterly* at http://www.bls.gov/opub/ooq/ooqhome.html and click on "You're a What?" The *Quarterly* is an excellent resource for general career information and for keeping up with trends in the job market. If you have trouble accessing the site, ask a librarian for help. Remember that URLs and site content change frequently.

Write About It

5. What is one personal quality you have that you think most employers would value? Explain your reasons.
6. Would research chef or any job in the culinary arts be a good career choice for you? Why or why not?

FIRST THOUGHTS

To build background for the reading selection, answer the following questions, either on your own or in a group discussion.

1. What do you know about the poet Walt Whitman?
2. Do you think most people are happy in their work?
3. Preview the title, headnote, and first one or two paragraphs. What do you think will follow?

WORD ALERT

Each word below is followed by its line number. Preview the words and definitions before reading. Then review them as necessary during reading. Use context clues and your dictionary to define any additional unfamiliar words.

varied (1) varying, diverse

blithe (2) carefree and lighthearted

mason (4) one who builds or works with stone or brick

hatter (6) one who makes, sells, or repairs hats

robust (10) full of health and strength

melodious (11) pleasant sounding

◆ I Hear America Singing

WALT WHITMAN

Born in New York, Walt Whitman (1819–1892) was a poet, journalist, and essayist. Whitman wrote several books of poetry and prose, but he is best known for his poems. His books of poetry include *Leaves of Grass* and *A Passage to India*.

1 I hear America singing, the varied carols I hear,
2 Those of mechanics, each one singing his as it should be blithe
    and strong,
3 The carpenter singing his, as he measures his plank or beam,
4 The mason singing his, as he makes ready for work, or leaves off
    work,
5 The boatman singing what belongs to him in his boat, the deck-hand
    singing on the steamboat deck,
6 The shoemaker singing as he sits on his bench, the hatter singing
    as he stands,
7 The woodcutter's song, the ploughboy's on his way in the morning,
    or at the noon intermission, or at sundown,
8 The delicious singing of the mother, or of the young wife at work,
    or of the girl sewing or washing,
9 Each singing what belongs to him or her and to none else,
10 The day what belongs to the day—at night the party of young
    fellows, robust, friendly,
11 Singing with open mouths their strong melodious songs.

Comprehension Check

Purpose and Main Idea

1. What is the author's topic?
   a. singing in general
   b. songs about work
   c. America's workers
   d. the meaning of work
2. Which one of the following sentences *best* states the implied central idea of the poem?
   a. The American worker is more likely to be a common laborer than a skilled professional.
   b. Americans are unique individuals, each having a song to sing and a job to do.
   c. Women typically are excluded from the workforce.
   d. After a long day's labor, it is common for workers to enjoy themselves.
3. Which one of the following is the author's *primary* purpose?
   a. to entertain readers with examples of interesting occupations
   b. to express an intense feeling about the American worker

c. to persuade readers to choose work that makes them happy

d. to inform readers about working conditions in the nineteenth century

Details

4. The author's tone (attitude or mood) in this poem can *best* be described as
   a. serious
   b. playful
   c. admiring
   d. solemn

5. The author suggests that the workers of his day had little hope for a better life.
   a. True
   b. False

6. Which one of the following occupations is not mentioned in the poem?
   a. shoemaker
   b. mason
   c. carpenter
   d. tailor

7. The workers are united in one harmonious song
   a. True
   b. False

8. What is the *dominant* organizational pattern of this poem?
   a. process
   b. definition
   c. generalization then example
   d. cause and effect

Inferences

9. What reason can you give for the author's choice of the word "carols" in line 1?

10. Do you think "I hear America singing" is meant to be taken literally or metaphorically? Are the workers really singing, or does "singing" mean something else in this poem?

Working with Words

Complete sentences 1–6 with these words from Word Alert:

melodious	robust	hatter
varied	mason	blithe

1. Working out at a gym can make you feel _____ and fit.

2. A _____ may become famous when one of his creations adorns the head of a celebrity.

3. If the colors of a scarf are _____, you can wear it with many outfits.

4. The sound of a harp is often described as _____.

5. They called her a _____ spirit because she seemed not to have a care in the world.

6. My grandfather was a _____, whose specialty was building brick hearths and chimneys.

Write your own sentences, using any two of the words from Word Alert.

7. _____

8. _____

Thinking Deeper

Ideas for reflection, discussion, and writing

Make Inferences from Your Reading

1. The poem is essentially a list of people engaged in different kinds of work. What is the overall effect of these examples?
2. Why is the singing of the mother, the young wife, and the girl sewing described as "delicious"? Do you think this is a good word choice? Why or why not?
3. Compare today's workforce with the American workforce as described in Whitman's poem. What is different? What is the same? Do people today take the same pride in their work as they did in the past?
4. Search the Internet to find the answers to the following questions. Why has Walt Whitman been called the "Bard of Democracy"? Did Whitman have an interest in music? What impact do the answers to these two questions have on your understanding of the poem? To begin your search, look up Walt Whitman in Wikipedia. Then try a poetry website. To find URLs, Type "Walt Whitman, poet" or "I Hear America Singing" as your search phrase. Or ask a librarian for suggestions.

Write About It

5. Do you hear America singing on campus or at work? Does the singing include the voices of many nationalities and cultures? Write your own list of the "songs" you hear. Model your list after Whitman's poem.
6. Reflect on the line "Each singing what belongs to him or her and to none else." Write about something that belongs to you and its significance.

FIRST THOUGHTS

To build background for the reading selection, answer the following questions, either on your own or in a group discussion.

1. Is obscene language ever appropriate in the workplace? Why or why not?
2. Do you think men or women swear more? Explain your reasons.
3. Preview the title, headnote, and first one or two paragraphs. What do you think will follow?

WORD ALERT

Each word below is followed by its paragraph number. Preview the words and definitions before reading. Then review them as necessary during reading. Use context clues and your dictionary to define any additional unfamiliar words.

conveying (1) communicating, imparting
specious (3) seemingly true, but actually false
intimidates (9) discourages or forces
expletives (11) exclamations or oaths, curse words
pretentious (12) demanding undeserved distinction or merit
defuse (13) make less dangerous or hostile

◆ Foul Language Could Be a Curse on Your Career

JACQUELINE FITZGERALD

What message do your speech habits send? Jacqueline Fitzgerald says that cursing is not the best way to fit in at work. The author is a reporter for the *Chicago Tribune*.

1 AUTHOR JAMES O'CONNOR says there's one area where working women should not catch up with men: When it comes to **conveying** strength, swearing will hurt, not help, your image.

2   "In an effort to advance in the work force and to fit in, women picked up one of men's worst habits," says O'Connor, author of *Cuss Control: The Complete Book on How to Curb Your Cursing* (Three Rivers Press, $12.95).

3   People who swear as a way of sounding strong are using **specious** reasoning, says O'Connor. "It would be like saying, 'If I shout loud enough, I'll win the argument.'"

4   Nicola Summers, a salesperson at the Lynch Auto Group in Chicago, says she frequently encounters women who curse. "It's like they want to outdo the men." she says.

5   And in her male-dominated field, men may have an edge in the swearing stakes. "It's a culture, that's what they do," she says. "They're used to it being all guys, and it's the biggest playground there is."

6   Summers, who doesn't swear, says her co-workers are "very respectful … they calm it down or stop it if I walk in."

7   Another mistake is thinking that in an informal workplace no one would take offense to four-letter words. "A lot of women swear today simply because that's the way the language and the culture have evolved—from a time when ladies didn't swear and gentlemen didn't swear in front of ladies, which was a double standard," O'Connor says. Now "they figure, everybody swears. And people assume nobody minds."

8   Etiquette consultant Ann Marie Sabath says that assumption is risky. "Swearing means different things to different people," she says, "and you never know whom you might offend."

9   If you cuss to communicate displeasure to subordinates, realize that you're creating negative energy. "It **intimidates** rather than motivates," O'Connor says.

10   Sabath and O'Connor agree that relying on curse words to express yourself could hurt your chances for promotion. "It's such an unwritten rule," says Sabath. "We've all done it, but [chronic swearers] are proving that they are allowing their emotions to control them rather than their logic. It just shows you have no class or that you have a very limited vocabulary."

11   Career experts Marjorie Brody and Pamela Holland say hanging out on a lower rung of the career ladder isn't the worst of it. In their book *Help! Was That a Career Limiting Move?* (Career Skills Press, $10.95), they write: "We can only assume that individuals who spew **expletives** and insults would be shocked to realize

that they are committing career suicide.... These words are inappropriate everywhere, but particularly in a work environment."

They also caution against sarcasm, gossip and **pretentious** language as well as 12 jargon, buzzwords and acronyms.

If you want to cut down on cussing, experts advise the following: 13

- Commit to changing, perhaps as a New Year's resolution. If you don't swear in your personal life, it will be second nature for you to avoid it at work.
- When tempted, try counting or pausing for a deep breath before you speak.
- Substitute other words, like stinking, bungled or botched.
- Use humor to **defuse** tempers.

If a colleague swears regularly, tell the person that you've heard enough. Or if 14 you have unfinished business with the person, say; "I'd like to talk to you about this when you're ready to use more professional language."

In the case of a boss who uses foul language, consider banding your depart- 15 ment together to discuss the issue with him or her. If a superior or client swears when you've made a mistake, deal with the problem first, O'Connor says, then explain that you'd prefer to talk without swear words.

Comprehension Check

Purpose and Main Idea

1. What is the author's topic?
    a. habits of conversation
    b. usage of four-letter words
    c. ethical behavior
    d. foul language at work
2. What is the author's central idea?
    a. When it comes to swearing, women are catching up with men.
    b. Foul language can hurt, not help, your career image.
    c. What is acceptable to one person may not be acceptable to another.
    d. Most people today do not take offense at four-letter words.
3. The author's *primary* purpose is to do which one of the following?
    a. express concern that women are swearing as much as men
    b. inform readers that the use of four-letter words is increasing
    c. persuade readers to avoid using foul language at work
    d. explain when swearing may or may not be appropriate

Details

4. O'Connor says about swearing:
    a. Everybody does it.
    b. No one takes offense.
    c. Women picked it up from men.
    d. It's not a bad habit.

5. Ann Marie Sabath says that people who swear are allowing social pressure to control them.
    a.   True
    b.   False
6. Sabath and O'Connor agree that relying on curse words to express yourself could hurt your chances for a promotion.
    a.   True
    b.   False
7. What does O'Connor advise employees to do if they have a boss who swears?
    a.   Ignore it unless it interferes with your work.
    b.   To fit in, adopt your boss's language style.
    c.   Band together to discuss the issue with him or her.
    d.   Learn to accept others' differences.
8. Paragraph 13 is organized by which one of the following patterns?
    a.   definition
    b.   classification
    c.   generalization then example
    d.   process

Inferences

9. Why do you think Brody and Holland caution against the use of sarcasm, gossip, and pretentious language at work? What makes these types of language inappropriate?
10. The title is a pun (play on words) whose understanding depends on the double meaning of which word?

Working with Words

Complete sentences 1–6 with these words from Word Alert:

pretentious   expletives   specious
intimidates   conveying   defuse

1. When the two athletes got into a fight, the coach used humor to _____ the situation.
2. Instead of resorting to _____ when you are angry, try presenting your case calmly and rationally.
3. One way of _____ your thanks is by sending personal notes or giving gifts.
4. Those who try to adopt the habits of another culture may seem more _____ than well traveled.
5. A boss who _____ employees is not likely to get their whole-hearted cooperation.
6. It would be a _____ argument to say that if one glass of wine a day is good for you, then several glasses may be even better.

Write your own sentences, using any two of the words from Word Alert.

7. _____

8. _____

Thinking Deeper

Ideas for reflection, discussion, and writing

Make Inferences from Your Reading

1. The author's sources seem to take it for granted that foul language is common in the workplace. Do you think this is true? What about on campus or in other public places: How common is foul language, and how does it affect you? Are you offended or indifferent, and why?

2. To what extent do you think foul language is a habit? Review Brody and Holland's suggestions for cutting down on swearing in paragraphs 13 and 14. Can these suggestions work? Why or why not? What other suggestions do you have for those who want to clean up their language?

3. The way you speak can send a positive or negative message to employers. On the one hand, job applicants are told, "Be yourself." On the other hand, they are advised to "dress for success" or to create a good impression. What inferences can you make about the success or effectiveness of certain classmates or co-workers based on their dress, attitude, and behavior?

4. Avoiding the use of inappropriate language at work is one example of *office etiquette*, or workplace manners. Poor office etiquette can make or break your career. To learn more about what is appropriate and inappropriate conduct at work, do a Google search using "office etiquette" as your search phrase. This phrase will generate a list of sites from which to choose. Read the summaries and choose one or two sites to browse. Based on the information you find, make a list of "do's and don'ts" to share in a class discussion.

Write About It

5. What is one skill you possess that you think everyone would benefit from having?

6. Write about someone you know whose choice of words got him or her in trouble.

FIRST THOUGHTS

To build background for the reading selection, answer the following questions, either on your own or in a group discussion.

1. If you live with someone, which one of you does most of the housework?
2. Do people seem to do more or less housework today than they did in years past? Why do you think so?
3. Preview the title, headnote, and first one or two paragraphs. What do you think will follow?

WORD ALERT

Each word below is followed by its paragraph number. Preview the words and definitions before reading. Then review them as necessary during reading. Use context clues and your dictionary to define any additional unfamiliar words.

bustled (1) moved energetically and busily
grimy (3) dirty or sooty
slackers (6) those who avoid or neglect work or duty
succession (7) following in order, sequence
fanatic (8) one who is overly enthusiastic, fervent, or zealous
shirking (11) avoiding responsibility

◆ Until Dust Do Us Part

DIRK JOHNSON

Dirk Johnson, writing for the Home section of *Newsweek*, reports on a new study that reveals how the housework burden is shared among today's working couples.

ONCE UPON A time, men were treated like indulged children in the house, as women **bustled** about cleaning, sweeping, cooking. That was 50 years ago, some men say. That was this morning, some women say.

Want to start a fight? Ask about housework and the division of labor. For that matter, ask what housework means. Does gardening count? How about running a snow blower?

To settle the score, a new study from the University of Michigan examines how the housework burden is shared by women and men. The results: women still do much more than men, though men are getting better (actually, men were getting better until about 1985, and then stalled out). But the real news stood out like a streak of clean glass on a **grimy** window: nobody really cares that much about housework at all anymore. In 1965 women did 40 hours of housework a week, men a mere 12. Nowadays women are averaging 27 hours; men, closing the gap, average 16. That means housework has decreased even as average house size has ballooned.

None of this comes as a shock to Gale Zemel's 73-year-old mother, Lita. She simply won't visit her daughter—they go to mom's place or meet at a restaurant. "The clutter drives her nuts," said Gale, a 48-year-old office manager in Oak Park, Ill. "And it's true, the place is a mess."

For millions of Americans, it comes down to math. He works. She works. The kids need to be transported all over creation for soccer and piano lessons. People are too pooped to mop. "Who's got time to clean?" says Hiromi Ono, an author of the report by the Institute for Social Research at Ann Arbor, Mich.

Each of the 6,000 people in the study—from the United States and around the world—kept a daily record of the work they did around the house, from sweeping the kitchen floor to changing the oil. As it turned out, American men were much more helpful than Japanese men (four hours a week), but **slackers** compared to the Swedes (24 hours a week).

When it comes to thankless chores, of course, everyone thinks they're doing too much already and that their other half could be doing just a little bit more. "Every time my husband gets a raise," one suburban Chicago woman bristles, "he starts throwing his clothes all over the floor." Zemel's husband, David Mausner, will tell you he's a pretty helpful mate, a virtue he attributes to "having my consciousness raised in the '70s by a **succession** of girlfriends." Mausner says he's setting tables, clearing them, washing dishes and fixing whatever needs fixing. "When there's something that requires a tool, I'm the guy for the job." His wife sees it somewhat differently. "He does the dishes. Period."

Neither claims to be a **fanatic** about cleaning. Zemel acknowledges: "I don't even know where the iron is." Mausner says simply, "I guess I could do more."

9   People are working hard—just not at hunting dust bunnies. The Michigan researchers credit a strong job market in the 1990s for the phenomenon they term "vanishing housework." Women in their study averaged 24 hours of paid work outside the home, while men averaged 37. (For those keeping score, men total 53 combined hours of job and housework; women 51.)

10   Everybody is simply trying to do too much, says Cheryl Mendelson, the author of the surprise best-seller *Home Comforts: The Art and Science of Keeping House*. With families on the run, she says, the home has been reduced to a changing station, a pit-stop between wind sprints.

11   It's a question of priorities, and some things matter more than others. For all the demands on their time, most parents are not **shirking** when it comes to the kids. Another recent study from the University of Michigan found that most parents—working and stay-at-home—spend more time with the children than parents did 20 years ago. Linda Rufer, a doctor in suburban Milwaukee, said housecleaning ranked a distant second to taking her three children to the Wisconsin Dells last weekend. "Either the house is clean or I see my kids," she said. "And as a pediatrician, it's bad form not to see the kids." For Rufer and plenty of others, the mess will be still there when they get home. The kids, on the other hand, grow up fast. And then they'll be gone.

Comprehension Check

Purpose and Main Idea

1. What is the author's topic?
   a. marriage and family
   b. stay-at-home moms
   c. the truth about housework
   d. house husbands
2. Where is the central idea stated?
   a. paragraph 2, first sentence "Want to start...."
   b. paragraph 3, first sentence "To settle the score...."
   c. paragraph 3, second sentence "The results...."
   d. paragraph 3, third sentence "But the real news...."
3. Which one of the following is the author's *primary* purpose?
   a. to express his own views about the study's results
   b. to inform readers about a University of Michigan study
   c. to persuade readers that the study was not very important
   d. to entertain readers with facts from the study

Details

4. According to the author, what is the real news about housework?
   a. Women do more of it than men.
   b. Men and women share the burden.
   c. Nobody really cares about it.
   d. Housework has decreased since 1965.

5. According to the study, Swedish men were the most helpful around the house.
    a. True
    b. False
6. To what do the Michigan researchers credit "vanishing housework"?
    a. the 1990s job market
    b. too little time
    c. spending more time with kids
    d. increase in average house size
7. The study found that women averaged 24 combined hours of job and housework.
    a. True
    b. False
8. The author's details consist mainly of
    a. opinions.
    b. facts.
    c. reasons.
    d. examples.

Inferences

9. Would Cheryl Mendelson probably agree that most people could benefit from time management? Why?
10. Based on the results of the study, what questions do you think the researchers asked?

Working with Words

Complete sentences 1–6 with these words from Word Alert:

succession	slackers	fanatic
shirking	bustled	grimy

1. Please do not wipe your _____ fingers on the clean white towel.
2. After a _____ of bad grades, my studying finally paid off with a high score on the next test.
3. A housecleaning _____ is someone who will try to take the dishes from in front of you while you are still eating.
4. Unlike the _____, who wait until the last minute to study for an exam, you should avoid procrastination by studying several days in advance.
5. The children _____ around their rooms, cleaning up before their mother came home.
6. Parents who do not make children behave in public places are _____ their disciplinary responsibilities.

Write your own sentences, using any two of the words from Word Alert.

7. _____

8. _____

Thinking Deeper

Ideas for reflection, discussion, and writing

Make Inferences from Your Reading

1. The Michigan study was conducted in the 1990s, during a time of economic prosperity. Would the results be the same today? Who does the housework in today's families? Who takes care of the children, and who makes financial decisions? What effect has the economic recession had on housework and who does it?
2. What is the author's tone in this selection? For example, is it humorous, serious, scholarly? How would you describe it? Find words or examples in the selection to support your inference.
3. The Michigan researchers commented on the fact that two-income families have little time for housework. What are some of the advantages and disadvantages of a two-income family? Use information from the selection and make inferences from your own experience to support your answer.
4. Dirk Johnson is a journalist whose articles have appeared in national newspapers and magazines, and he is the author of several books. Do a Web search on this author to find out more about his life and publications. For a biography, go to http://www.creativewell.com/Johnson.html. Go to Amazon.com to see a list of Johnson's books. A word of caution: There is also a football player named Dirk Johnson, so when you are browsing sites, make sure you get the right person. Remember that URLs and site content change, so ask a librarian for help if you need it.

Write About It

5. Reflect on your childhood. What advantages or disadvantages did you have that you hope your children will or will not have?
6. Write about the one household chore that you dislike, and explain what you do either to avoid doing it or to get it done quickly.

FIRST THOUGHTS

To build background for the reading selection, answer the following questions, either on your own or in a group discussion.

1. Have you ever considered a career in science? Why or why not?
2. Do you think that women are as likely as men to choose a career in one of the sciences? Explain your reasons.
3. Preview the title, headnote, and first one or two paragraphs. What do you think will follow?

WORD ALERT

Each word below is followed by its paragraph number. Preview the words and definitions before reading. Then review them as necessary during reading. Use context clues and your dictionary to define any additional unfamiliar words.

cyclotron (1) a device that accelerates charged subatomic particles
scaling (3) climbing up or over, ascending
innate (4) inborn, possessed at birth
excruciating (5) intensely painful or distressing
systemic (7) affecting an entire system or body
concedes (12) acknowledges as being true

Science and the Gender Gap

BARBARA KANTROWITZ AND JULIE SCELFO

Barbara Kantrowitz is a senior editor at *Newsweek* and Julie Scelfo is a correspondent. Kantrowitz is an award-winning author of articles and books. Both women cover social issues and current trends.

1   To GET A sense of how women have progressed in science, take a quick tour of the physics department at the University of California, Berkeley. This is a storied place, the site of some of the most important discoveries in modern science—starting with Ernest Lawrence's invention of the **cyclotron** in 1931. A generation ago, female faces were rare and, even today, visitors walking through the first floor of LeConte Hall will see a full corridor of exhibits honoring the many distinguished physicists who made history here, virtually all of them white males.

2   But climb up to the third floor and you'll see a different display. There, among the photos of current faculty members and students, are portraits of the current chair of the department, Marjorie Shapiro, and four other women whose research covers everything from the mechanics of the universe to the smallest particles of matter. A sixth woman was hired [recently]. Although they're still only about 10 percent of the physics faculty, women are clearly a presence here. And the real hope may be in the smaller photos to the right: graduate and undergraduate students, about 20 percent of them female. Every year Berkeley sends freshly minted female physics doctorates to the country's top universities. That makes Shapiro optimistic, but also realistic. "I believe things are getting better," she says, "but they're not getting better as fast as I would like."

3   To women in other professions—law, publishing, even politics—academic science can sometimes seem like the world that time forgot. Decades after women began **scaling** the corporate ladder, female physicists, chemists, mathematicians and engineers are still struggling to find their place at the nation's major research universities. Although women now earn about half the graduate degrees in math and chemistry, for example, they hold only about 10 percent of the faculty jobs in those fields. "The U.S. needs as much scientific and technologic brain power as it can get," says Georgia Tech's Sue Rosser, author of *The Science Glass Ceiling*. "It makes no sense to exclude half the population."

4   [In 2005] former Harvard president Lawrence Summers ignited a firestorm by suggesting that a lack of **innate** ability might be the problem. But a report from the National Academy of Sciences details more likely reasons: inadequate child care, a rigid tenure clock that penalizes mothers who take off time after childbirth and a less-than-welcoming attitude among colleagues and administrators. The report urges a national effort to overcome these obstacles.

5   In fact, biology does play a role but not in the way Summers proposed. It generally takes about five years to get a Ph.D.; young scientists are then expected to move on to one or two postdoctoral fellowships. Afterward, if they're among the very best, they'll be hired for a faculty job. That's the start of the tenure clock— generally six years. During that time, they have to show a steady research record

in order to win tenure; any gaps (after giving birth, for example) could mean they get the boot. That rigid schedule forces women scientists in their late 20s and early 30s—prime childbearing years—into an **excruciating** choice between their love of physics or chemistry and their desire to have a family. It's a choice their male peers aren't required to make. Mary Ann Mason, dean of the graduate division at Berkeley, has been studying this issue for years and is codirector of "Do Babies Matter?" a research project on the impact of family on the lives of male and female academics. The tenure system was created by men and is based on a male model that leaves women at a disadvantage, she says. Women worry that any time away from the lab will mean they lose out in the increasingly competitive race for research money. "There is this belief that if you are out of it for more than a year," she says, "you can never come back again."

Until the mid-1990s, most women scientists were on their own as they tried to 6 work around these barriers. "When I was in graduate school," says Alice Agogino, a professor of mechanical engineering at Berkeley, "people would say there was no gender in science, no ethnicity in science. There's just good science. I was intimidated by this, but then I realized it isn't true." Gender, many women scientists say, shows up in everything from whether you work with the professor of your choice to how much lab space you get.

Though individual women may have understood what they were up against, 7 there wasn't much of an organized effort to change things until an August day in 1994, when a group of tenured female faculty members at MIT met with physicist Robert Birgeneau, then the dean of the School of Science, to press their case that there was an institutional bias. "It was really a singular point," says Birgeneau, now the chancellor at Berkeley. Before that day, he says, it was easy to dismiss an individual woman's career problems as the result of a personality conflict or problems in her lab. But after investigating their complaints, he concluded that the problem was **systemic**.

In 1999, MIT issued a groundbreaking report which showed that tenured 8 women professors made less money and received fewer research resources than their male colleagues. The next year MIT's president, Charles Vest, convened a meeting of administrators and scientists from 25 of the most prestigious U.S. universities who issued a unanimous statement agreeing that institutional barriers prevented women from succeeding in science.

Soon after, the National Science Foundation started the ADVANCE grant pro- 9 gram, which gives money annually to institutions or individuals with proposals to encourage women scientists. "The country is spending a lot of money and effort educating women, a substantial brain trust, but they weren't going into faculties, teaching students and doing research," says ADVANCE program director Alice Hogan. ADVANCE program has given out about $100 million in grants to 31 institutions for programs with lasting impact: day-care centers, mentoring and even miniretreats for junior and senior faculty members to get to know each other better.

The beneficiaries of these efforts are women like Lorraine Sadler, a graduate 10 student in physics at Berkeley who studies Bose Einstein condensates (intensely cold quantum state of matter) in her lab in the basement of Birge Hall. "The biggest obstacle I've had is brute force," says Sadler. "Most of the things in this lab are heavy so I started lifting weights." She looks proudly around the sophisticated equipment that records her experiments. "I built this entire lab from an empty room," she says. Sometimes, when visiting male scientists come to the lab, they "don't understand" her position there and treat her as less than an equal. "I give them about two weeks to see the light," she says. Usually, that happens when a problem comes up and Sadler is the only one who can solve it. "The scales fall from their eyes," she says. "It just takes a little bit of patience for them to see that I have the qualifications to be here."

11   Sadler and her colleague Lauren Tompkins, a graduate student in particle physics, say they owe much to Young-Kee Kim, a former Berkeley professor who is now at the University of Chicago. "She made sure everybody knew us," says Tompkins. "She told us, 'You're going to go far'." They needed that confidence boost, especially in physics where, Tompkins says, "physicists have a fear that any kind of change will lead to a degradation" of the field. There was external social pressure as well. Tompkins recalls attending a frat party when she was a freshman. A guy came up and asked the traditional icebreaker: "What are you majoring in?" When Tompkins replied "Physics," he turned on his heels, she says.

12   Shapiro, the physics department chairman, **concedes** that misconceptions about science can make it difficult to keep women in the major. A male student who's in the middle of the class generally thinks he's doing OK, Shapiro says. But a female student in the same position often feels she's not good enough. "I tell them they're doing fine," says Shapiro. "You don't have to be the top student in the class to do physics." But she's also encouraged by the way the current generation of female science students reach out to each other through campus organizations like the Society of Women Engineers or the Society for Women in the Physical Sciences. "When I was a grad student in the late 1970s and early 1980s, we tried to hide the fact that we were female," she says.

13   Beyond the support the female students provide for each other, Berkeley (like other campuses, including Georgia Tech) tries to help by offering new "family friendly" policies like tenure-clock extension after the birth of a child, reduced teaching duties for new parents and a part-time option. "I think we're on the cutting edge," says Agogino. Female students have lots of role models, including Jasmina Vujic, chair of the nuclear engineering department. Not long ago Vujic spoke at career day at her daughter's school. Only four girls showed up for her talk about women in science and engineering, but next door, a room full of girls eagerly awaited a session on women's rights. When that speaker didn't show, Vujic invited the girls to her session. "Half of them came with me," she says, with a smile. And perhaps one of them, inspired by that day, will follow her into the lab.

Comprehension Check

Purpose and Main Idea

1. What is the authors' topic?
   a. women in science
   b. the gender gap in science
   c. careers in science
   d. research opportunities

2. Which one of the following *best* states the central idea?
   a. Women make up a greater percentage of scientists than they did a decade ago.
   b. The University of California, Berkeley, is the site of important scientific discoveries.
   c. The number of women in science still lags behind the number of women in other professions.
   d. It is not unusual today to find women in every field of science.
3. The author's *primary* purpose is to
   a. entertain readers with little-known facts about women in science.
   b. persuade women to choose careers in science.
   c. inform readers that a gender gap in science exists.
   d. express an opinion about the need for women in science.

Details

4. Women earn about half the graduate degrees in math and science but hold only about 10 percent of the faculty jobs in those fields.
   a. True
   b. False
5. Georgia Tech's Sue Rosser is the author of *The Science Glass Ceiling*.
   a. True
   b. False
6. All of the following are barriers to women's advancement in science *except* which one?
   a. a less-than-welcoming attitude among colleagues
   b. mothers being penalized for taking time off
   c. a six-year tenure track
   d. innate ability in science or math
7. There was little in the way of an organized effort to erase the gender gap until
   a. the National Science Foundation started the ADVANCE grant program.
   b. a 1999 report revealed a salary discrepancy between male and female tenured professors.
   c. female faculty at MIT charged the School of Science with having institutional bias.
   d. a meeting of administrators and scientists from 25 universities was convened.
8. What organizational pattern is followed in paragraphs 7 through 9?
   a. process
   b. sequence
   c. definition
   d. comparison

Inferences

9. What is the "glass ceiling" in science or any other profession?
10. Based on your own experience, why do you think fewer women than men choose a career in science?

Working with Words

Complete sentences 1–6 with these words from Word Alert:

excruciating   concedes   scaling
cyclotron   systemic   innate

1. Mountain climbers enjoy the challenge of _____ a rocky cliff.
2. Some believe that intelligence is _____, but others believe that it is developed over time.
3. The invention of the _____ advanced atomic theory and research.
4. An election is not over until one of the contestants _____ to the other.
5. Wearing shoes that are too small can cause _____ pain.
6. Instead of being confined to one site, the infection was _____.

Write your own sentences, using any two of the words from Word Alert.

7. _____
8. _____

Thinking Deeper

Ideas for reflection, discussion, and writing

Make Inferences from Your Reading

1. Read again paragraph 5. How does biology play a role in the gender gap? Do you agree with the authors' conclusions, and why?
2. What evidence have you seen of a "glass ceiling" in science or in another profession or career?
3. The United States lags behind other countries, notably Japan, in science and math. For years, the U.S. government has urged schools to place greater emphasis on science and math, and companies have complained that they must look overseas to find qualified engineers to hire. How would closing the gender gap help alleviate the situation? What can we do to encourage more students to choose majors and careers in science? What can we as parents, teachers, or community members do to foster an interest in science among young children?
4. Many interesting career opportunities exist in the applied sciences as well as the physical sciences. To find out if a career in science is for you, visit your college's career center. Meet with a career counselor to learn about and explore some of the many online resources and interest inventories that are available.

Write About It

5. What would be your ideal job or career, and why?
6. Would a career in one of the sciences interest you? Write about this career and explain what makes it interesting.

FIRST THOUGHTS

To build background for the reading selection, answer the following questions, either on your own or in a group discussion.

1. On the average, how much time do you spend on housework?
2. How do you balance your college obligations with work or family obligations?
3. Preview the title, headnote, and first one or two paragraphs. What do you think will follow?

WORD ALERT

Each word below is followed by its paragraph number. Preview the words and definitions before reading. Then review them as necessary during reading. Use context clues and your dictionary to define any additional unfamiliar words.

maxim (1) a brief, clear statement of a principle or rule of conduct
incentive (2) a punishment or reward that induces action
compensation (2) payment, reimbursement
persist (6) continue
amorphous (9) lacking definite organization or form
dilemma (13) a situation requiring a choice between options

◆ Home-Work Paradox Persists

SHANKAR VEDANTAM

Shankar Vedantam writes for the *Washington Post* on topics of human interest. In this article, the author reminds us that there is no easy solution to the dilemma of family responsibilities versus work obligations.

1   FOR YEARS, ECONOMISTS have taught their students a simple **maxim**: As employers hunt for workers, they want to get the best talent at the lowest price.

2   According to this theory, whether employees want to work long hours or short hours, employers have an **incentive** to accommodate them, because asking people to do something they don't want to do raises the price of labor—workers demand more **compensation**.

3   On this Labor Day, consider a paradox: Millions of Americans say they feel overworked and stressed out. Many say they want to work fewer hours and find a better balance between responsibilities at home and work. Given that people have been saying this for quite a while, employers should have figured out by now that they can save money by being more flexible in workplace arrangements.

4   Emphatically, however, this has not happened. The number of people who work more than 50 hours a week has grown steadily in recent decades—in concert with complaints about long hours.

5   Large surveys have found that while as many as one in six couples would like to have both partners work part time, only one in 50 couples obtains such an arrangement. Technology has made the problem worse: People now can be tied to work around the clock through their BlackBerries—a situation jokingly dubbed "Crackberry addiction."

6   If employees are unhappy and overworked, and employers are having to pay more for unhappy employees, why does the situation **persist** in a rational economic marketplace?

7   Some economists, sociologists and psychologists say the paradox arises because of the changing nature of the workplace. In a growing number of professions managers and owners find it difficult to measure day-to-day performance of employees.

8   When employees make tangible products, it is easy to measure performance based on the quality of the products. But when work is intangible, and involves aesthetics, judgment or social networking, employers do not have easy ways of measuring how important such activity is to the bottom line, Cornell sociologist Marin Clarkberg said.

9   "When you have an undefinable product, there is a temptation to measure output in terms of hours," she said. "In law and a lot of **amorphous** professions, when you are trying to win a case or being a professor, you are doing things like thinking. It's not like little widgets you produce which you can count."

10   At big law firms, the simplest way to track the performance of junior lawyers is to see who bills the most hours above and beyond what is officially required, leading to what Case Western Reserve University economist James Rebitzer calls an "arms race" of hours.

Law associates who work long hours are far more likely to make partner— 11
even if they are no more talented than others, said Renee Landers, who teaches
law at Suffolk University in Boston and has studied the world of big law firms,
where she once worked. In turn, new partners will evaluate their juniors by the
same criteria.

At many companies with a focus on hours most people want to work shorter 12
hours, but no one is willing to ask for them, because the first person to make such a
move will be branded as insufficiently committed to his or her job.

"It's your classic **dilemma**," Landers said. "Everyone knows what the answer 13
is, but no one wants to be the guinea pig."

Clarkberg, Landers and Rebitzer said employees (and their families and 14
communities) are not the only ones to suffer. Customers and the economy also
pay a price, Rebitzer said. The hour that the overworked and sleep-deprived
lawyer bills for work done at 4 a.m. costs the client the same as an hour's work
after a good night's sleep, even though the quality of the lawyer's work is better
at 9 a.m.

Employers pay a price, too, not just in higher wages, but in lost talent—the race 15
systematically filters out talented people whose only flaw is they do not want to
work long hours.

While equal numbers of men and women now graduate from law schools and 16
enter big firms, the proportion of women who make partner remains stuck at
around 17 percent, perhaps because many talented women are not willing to enter
the working-hours arms race, Landers said.

"The rules for work were defined around married men in the first place," 17
Clarkberg said. "These were breadwinner-homemaker families. We have not done
anything to transform the nature of work around the current realities."

Comprehension Check

Purpose and Main Idea

1. What is the author's topic?
   a. overworked, stressed-out Americans
   b. America's changing workplace
   c. the struggle to balance work and family
   d. working at home versus working in an office
2. Which sentence *best* states the central idea?
   a. Employers want to get the best talent at the lowest price.
   b. Employers should provide flexible workplace arrangements.
   c. The problem of managing work and family time persists.
   d. The two-earner family is a fact of modern life.
3. What is the author's *primary* purpose?
   a. to inform readers about a problem that needs a solution
   b. to persuade readers to spend more time with their families
   c. to express a view in favor of better working conditions
   d. to entertain readers with workplace anecdotes

Details

4. According to the author, technology has helped families balance work and home life.
   a. True
   b. False
5. Equal numbers of men and women graduate from law schools and enter large firms.
   a. True
   b. False
6. It is easy to measure performance when it involves
   a. aesthetics.
   b. judgment.
   c. a tangible product.
   d. social networking.
7. What does Renee Landers suggest may be the reason why only 17 percent of women lawyers become partners?
   a. a desire to spend more time with their families
   b. an unwillingness to enter the working-hours arms race
   c. a lack of commitment to the job
   d. not wanting to be the guinea pig
8. What is the relationship between paragraphs 3 and 4?
   a. contrast
   b. sequence
   c. process
   d. example

Inferences

9. Do you agree with the author that most Americans feel overworked and stressed-out? What examples can you provide to support your opinion?
10. Do you agree with the author that workers demand more compensation for doing jobs that they don't want to do? What examples can you provide to support your opinion?

Working with Words

Complete sentences 1–6 with these words from Word Alert:

compensation	incentive	persist
amorphous	dilemma	maxim

1. Here is another _____: If you can't do something well, don't do it at all.
2. Writing a research paper will be difficult until you bring some organization to all your _____ notes and ideas.
3. Many politicians argue that the minimum wage is unfair _____ for labor.

4. The desire for a promotion is one _____ to work hard.
5. Whether to eat what we like or to observe a diet is a _____ for many.
6. According to the weather forecast, rain will _____ throughout the weekend.

Write your own sentences, using any two of the words from Word Alert.

7. _____
8. _____

Thinking Deeper

Ideas for reflection, discussion, and writing

Make Inferences from Your Reading

1. The author quotes Marin Clarkberg as saying, "The rules for work were defined around married men," and "We have not done anything to transform the nature of work around the current realities." What do these comments mean? Do you think the authors of selection 37 would agree or disagree, and why?

2. In paragraph 4, the author says that as the number of work hours per week has grown, so have complaints about long hours. Why does this paradox persist, and what can we do about it?

3. How to balance work and family needs is a question that seems to have no answer, as this author suggests. As a student, what are your time-management issues, and how do you deal with them?

4. Using your library's online catalog, search for a book or article on time management for college students. Skim the book or article for a few practical tips that you can share in class, and be prepared to make a brief report that includes the following: title, author, publication date, and your list or summary of tips for managing time.

Write About It

5. If you had only one piece of advice to give students who were having difficulty managing their time, what would it be and why?

6. What do you value most: time, money, or something else? Write about the one thing in life that is most important to you.

FIRST THOUGHTS

To build background for the reading selection, answer the following questions, either on your own or in a group discussion.

1. How important is it to have good communication skills?
2. What behaviors act as barriers to communication?
3. Preview the title, headnote, and first one or two paragraphs. What do you think will follow?

WORD ALERT

Each word below is followed by its paragraph number. Preview the words and definitions before reading. Then review them as necessary during reading. Use context clues and your dictionary to define any additional unfamiliar words.

In a textbook chapter, the words to watch may appear in boldface, italics, or a special color.

denotation (6) a word's literal, dictionary meaning
connotation (6) a word's subjective, emotional meaning
slang (10) an expression identified with a specific group of people
jargon (10) technical terminology used within specialized groups
euphemisms (10) inoffensive expressions that replace words that may offend
abstract word (12) a word that identifies an idea or a feeling instead of a concrete object
concrete word (12) a word that identifies something that can be seen or touched
noise (24) environmental or competing distractions that hinder effective communication

Barriers to Communication

SCOT OBER

This textbook reading is excerpted from Chapter 1 of *Contemporary Business Communication*, Sixth Edition. The entire chapter is about understanding business communication. The excerpt focuses on communication barriers, a core concern. When reading from textbooks, remember that headings may signal topics, main ideas, or important details.

CONSIDERING THE COMPLEX nature of the communication process, your messages may not always be received exactly as you intended. As a matter of fact, sometimes your messages will not be received at all; at other times, they will be received incompletely or inaccurately. Some of the obstacles to effective and efficient communication are verbal; others are nonverbal. As illustrated in Figure 1.5, these barriers can create an impenetrable "brick wall" that makes effective communication impossible.

VERBAL BARRIERS

Verbal barriers are related to what you write or say. They include inadequate knowledge or vocabulary, differences in interpretation, language differences, inappropriate use of expressions, overabstraction and ambiguity, and polarization.

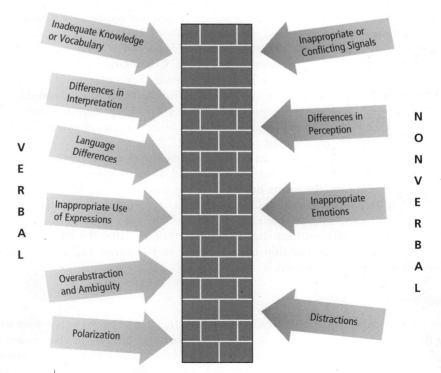

FIGURE 1.5 | VERBAL AND NONVERBAL BARRIERS TO COMMUNICATION

INADEQUATE KNOWLEDGE OR VOCABULARY

3 Before you can even begin to think about how you will communicate an idea, you must, first of all, have the idea; that is, you must have sufficient knowledge about the topic to know what you want to say. Regardless of your level of technical expertise, this may not be as simple as it sounds. Assume, for example, that you are Larry Haas, manager of the finance department at Urban Systems. Dave Kaplan, president of the company, has asked you to evaluate an investment opportunity. You've completed all the necessary research and are now ready to write your report. Or are you?

4   Have you analyzed your audience? Do you know how much the president knows about the investment so that you'll know how much background information to include? Do you know how familiar Dave is with investment terminology? Can you safely use abbreviations like NPV and RRR, or will you have to spell out and perhaps define net present value and required rate of return? Do you know whether the president would prefer to have your conclusions at the beginning of the report, followed by your analysis, or at the end? What tone should the report take? The answers to such questions will be important if you are to achieve your objective in writing the report.

DIFFERENCES IN INTERPRETATION

5 Sometimes senders and receivers attribute different meanings to the same word or attribute the same meaning to different words. When this happens, miscommunication can occur.

6   Every word has both a denotative and a connotative meaning. **Denotation** refers to the literal, dictionary meaning of a word. **Connotation** refers to the subjective, emotional meaning that you attach to a word. For example, the denotative meaning of the word plastic is "a synthetic material that can be easily molded into different forms." For some people, the word also has a negative connotative meaning—"cheap or artificial substitute." For other people, the word means a credit card, as in "He used plastic to pay the bill."

7   Most of the interpretation problems occur because of the personal reactions engendered by the connotative meaning of a word. Do you have a positive, neutral, or negative reaction to the terms broad, bad, aggressive, hard-hitting, workaholic, corporate raider, head-hunter, golden parachute, or wasted? Are your reactions likely to be the same as everyone else's? The problem with some terms is not only that people assign different meanings to the term but also that the term itself might cause such an emotional reaction that the receiver is "turned off" to any further communication with the sender.

LANGUAGE DIFFERENCES

8 In an ideal world, all managers would know the language of each culture with which they deal. International businesspeople often say that you can buy in your native language anywhere in the world, but you can sell only in the language of the local community. Most of the correspondence between U.S. or Canadian firms and foreign firms is in English; in other cases, the services of a qualified interpreter (for oral communication)

or translator (for written communication) may be available. But even with such services, problems can occur. Consider, for example, the following blunders:[10]

- In Brazil, where Portuguese is spoken, a U.S. airline advertised that its Boeing 747s had "rendezvous lounges," without realizing that rendezvous in Portuguese implies prostitution.
- In China, Kentucky Fried Chicken's slogan "Finger-lickin' good" was translated "So good you suck your fingers."
- In Puerto Rico, General Motors had difficulties advertising Chevrolet's Nova model because the name sounds like the Spanish phrase "No va," which means "It doesn't go."

To ensure that the intended meaning is not lost during translation, important documents should first be translated into the second language and then retranslated into English. Be aware, however, that communication difficulties can arise even among native English speakers. For example, a British advertisement for Electrolux vacuum cleaners displayed the headline "Nothing Sucks Like An Electrolux." Copywriters in the United States and Canada would never use this wording! 9

INAPPROPRIATE USE OF EXPRESSIONS

Expressions are groups of words whose intended meanings are different from their literal interpretations. Examples include slang, jargon, and euphemisms. 10

- **Slang** is an expression, often short-lived, that is identified with a specific group of people. Business, of course, has its own slang, such as *24/7, bandwidth, hardball, strategic fit*, and *window of opportunity*. Teenagers, construction workers, immigrants, knowledge professionals, and just about every other subgroup you can imagine all have their own sets of slang. Using appropriate slang in everyday speech presents no problem; it conveys precise information and may indicate group membership. Problems arise, however, when the sender uses slang that the receiver doesn't understand. Using slang when communicating with someone whose native language is not English can cause misunderstandings. Slang that sends a negative nonverbal message about the sender can also be a source of problems.
- **Jargon** is the technical terminology used within specialized groups; it has sometimes been called "the pros' prose." Technology, for example, has spawned a whole new vocabulary. Do you know the meaning of these common computer terms?

applet	FAQ	JPEG	plug 'n' play
blog	Flame	killer app	ROFL
BRB	hacker	locked up	spam
BTW	HTML	patch	worm
CU	IMO	PDA	WYSIWYG
e-commerce			

As with slang, the problem is not in using jargon—jargon provides a very precise and efficient way of communicating with those familiar with it. The problem comes either in using jargon with someone who doesn't understand it or in using jargon in an effort to impress others.

- **Euphemisms** are inoffensive expressions used in place of words that may offend or suggest something unpleasant. Sensitive writers and speakers use euphemisms occasionally, especially to describe bodily functions. How many ways, for example, can you think of to say that someone has died?

11   Slang, jargon, and euphemisms all have important roles to play in business communication—so long as they're used with appropriate people and in appropriate contexts. They can, however, prove to be barriers to effective communication when used to impress, when used too often, or when used in inappropriate settings.

OVERABSTRACTION AND AMBIGUITY

12   An **abstract word** identifies an idea or a feeling instead of a concrete object. For example, *communication* is an abstract word, whereas *memorandum* is a **concrete word,** a word that identifies something that can be seen or touched. Abstract words are necessary in order to communicate about things you cannot see or touch. However, communication problems result when you use too many abstract words or when you use too high a level of abstraction. The higher the level of abstraction, the more difficult it is for the receiver to visualize exactly what the sender has in mind. For example, which sentence communicates more information: "I acquired an asset at the store" or "I bought a laser printer at Best Buy"?

13   Similar communication problems result from the overuse of ambiguous terms such as *a few, some, several,* and *far away,* which have too broad a meaning for use in much business communication.

POLARIZATION

14   At times, some people act as though every situation is divided into two opposite and distinct poles, with no allowance for a middle ground. Of course, there are some true dichotomies. You are either human or nonhuman, and your company either will or will not make a profit this year. But most aspects of life involve more than two alternatives.

15   For example, you might assume that a speaker either is telling the truth or is lying. In fact, what the speaker actually says may be true, but by selectively omitting some important information, he or she may be giving an inaccurate impression. Is the speaker telling the truth or not? Most likely, the answer lies somewhere in between. Likewise, you are not necessarily either tall or short, rich or poor, smart or dumb. Competent communicators avoid inappropriate either/or logic and instead make the effort to search for middle-ground words when such language best describes a situation.

16   Incidentally, remember that what you do not say can also produce barriers to communication. Suppose, for example, that you congratulate only one of the three people who took part in making a company presentation. How would the other two presenters feel—even though you said nothing negative about their performance? Or suppose you tell one of them, "You really did an outstanding job this time." The

presenter's reaction might be, "What was wrong with my performance last time?" (And how about this announcement from the author's seven-year-old son one day after school: "Hey, Dad, guess what? I didn't get my name on the board today." What's the implication?)

NONVERBAL BARRIERS

Not all communication problems are related to what you write or say. Some are related 17 to how you act. Nonverbal barriers to communication include inappropriate or conflicting signals, differences in perception, inappropriate emotions, and distractions.

INAPPROPRIATE OR CONFLICTING SIGNALS

Suppose a well-qualified applicant for an administrative assistant position submits a 18 résumé with a typographical error, or an accountant's personal office is in such disorder that she can't find the papers she needs for a meeting with a client. When verbal and nonverbal signals conflict, the receiver tends to put more faith in the nonverbal signals because nonverbal messages are more difficult to manipulate than verbal messages.

Many nonverbal signals vary from culture to culture. Remember also that the 19 United States itself is a multicultural country: a banker from Boston, an art shop owner from San Francisco, and a farmer from North Dakota are likely to both use and interpret nonverbal signals in quite different ways. What is appropriate in one context might not be appropriate in another.

Communication competence requires that you communicate nonverbal messages 20 that are consistent with your verbal messages and that are appropriate for the context.

DIFFERENCES IN PERCEPTION

Even when they hear the same speech or read the same document, people of different 21 ages, socioeconomic backgrounds, cultures, and so forth often form very different perceptions. We discussed earlier the mental filter by which each communication source is interpreted. Because each person is unique, with unique experiences, knowledge, and viewpoints, each person forms a different opinion about what he or she reads and hears.

Some people tend automatically to believe certain people and to distrust other 22 people. For example, when reading an e-mail from the company president, one employee may be so intimidated by the president that he or she accepts everything the president says, whereas another employee may have such negative feelings about the president that he or she believes nothing the president says.

INAPPROPRIATE EMOTIONS

In most cases, a moderate level of emotional involvement intensifies the communi- 23 cation and makes it more personal. However, too much emotional involvement can be an obstacle to communication. For example, excessive anger can create such an emotionally charged environment that reasonable discussion is not possible.

Likewise, prejudice (automatically rejecting certain people or ideas), stereotyping (placing individuals into categories), and boredom all hinder effective communication. Such emotions tend to create a blocked mind that is closed to new ideas, rejecting or ignoring information that is contrary to one's prevailing belief.

DISTRACTIONS

24 Any environmental or competing element that restricts one's ability to concentrate on the communication task hinders effective communication. Such distractions are called **noise**. Examples of *environmental* noise are poor acoustics, extreme temperature, uncomfortable seating, body odor, poor telephone connections, and illegible photocopies. Examples of *competing* noise are other important business to attend to, too many meetings, and too many reports to read.

25   Competent communicators make the effort to write and speak clearly and consistently and try to avoid or minimize any verbal or nonverbal barriers that might cause misunderstandings.

Comprehension Check

Purpose and Main Idea

1. What is the author's topic?
    a.   improving communication skills
    b.   communication in the business world
    c.   the communication process
    d.   obstacles that hinder communication
2. What is the central idea of this selection?
    a.   Communication is a complex process.
    b.   Effective communication is essential for success in all fields.
    c.   Verbal and nonverbal obstacles prevent good communication.
    d.   Improving communication is easy if you follow several steps.
3. Which one of the following is the author's *primary* purpose?
    a.   to teach readers what the barriers to communication are
    b.   to inform readers about cultural differences in communication
    c.   to persuade readers to improve their communication skills
    d.   to express concern that communication can be misunderstood

Details

4. Verbal barriers to communication include inadequate knowledge and differences in interpretation.
    a.   True
    b.   False
5. The author says that slang is inappropriate in the workplace.
    a.   True
    b.   False

6. According to the author, inappropriate emotions are a communication barrier because they
   a. intensify communication.
   b. make communication more personal.
   c. create a blocked mind.
   d. restrict the ability to concentrate.
7. According to the author, which one of the following is an example of competing noise?
   a. poor acoustics
   b. uncomfortable seating
   c. temperature extremes
   d. too many meetings
8. Which one of the following is the *dominant* organizational pattern in paragraph 12?
   a. process
   b. cause and effect
   c. comparison
   d. definition

Inferences

9. In your own words, explain what a *concrete term* is and give an example.
10. Based on the author's definitions, a student who says, "I can't take good notes in a lecture if I don't like the instructor" is allowing which type of barrier to interfere with effective communication?

Working with Words

Complete sentences 1–8 with these words from Word Alert:

abstract word   connotation   euphemisms   noise
concrete word   denotation   jargon   slang

1. Good writers take time to find the right _____ that will appeal to readers' senses.
2. Although *slender* has a positive meaning, *skinny* has a negative _____.
3. In some circles, "shooting hoops" is _____ for playing basketball.
4. The environmental _____ in the library that interferes with my studying consists of students talking and a lack of comfortable seating.
5. *Sanitation engineer* is one of several _____ for *janitor*.
6. Most politicians will resort to the _____ or idea rather than clearly explaining their views.
7. Look in a dictionary to find the _____ of a word.
8. Using today's business _____, those who tell you to "think outside the box" just want you to be creative.

Write your own sentences, using any two of the words from Word Alert.

9. _____

10. _____

Thinking Deeper

Ideas for reflection, discussion, and writing

Make Inferences from Your Reading

1. When asked to list the skills they value most, employers invariably will include communication skills. What are three major communication skills that you use and observe other people using?
2. The author gives several examples of slang and jargon but no examples of euphemism. Using what you can infer from the author's definition, give an example of a euphemism. Using details from the selection, explain how any euphemism can create barriers to communication.
3. Most jobs or careers require you to interact with others. Discuss the role that communication skills will play in the career you have chosen.
4. A lot of career information is available on the Internet. If you have not explored some of the career sites, you are missing an important resource that can help you with developing a résumé, assessing your career skills, and finding a career that is right for you. As an introduction to career research, visit one of the following sites, or ask for a suggestion from your instructor:

America's CareerInfoNet	http://www.acinet.org
America's Job Bank	http://www.ajb.dni.us
Careerbuilder	http://www.careerbuilder.com
CareersOnLine	http://www.careersonline.com
Hotjobs	http://www.hotjobs.com

Write About It

5. Review Figure 1.5 on page 259 of the excerpt. What do the arrows and bricks stand for? Why do the arrows point the way they do? This type of figure is called a *diagram*. A diagram uses pictures or illustrations to condense and simplify concepts or ideas, making them easier to remember. Read again paragraphs 24 and 25, then make a diagram to illustrate types of distractions. Give your diagram a title and a caption.
6. The author explains several communication barriers. Write about the one that you have seen used most often and explain what you have done, or can do, to overcome the barrier.

FIRST THOUGHTS

To build background for the reading selection, answer the following questions, either on your own or in a group discussion.

1. How do you define *listening*?
2. What are some habits of good listeners?
3. Preview the title, headnote, and first one or two paragraphs. What do you think will follow?

WORD ALERT

Each word below is followed by its paragraph number. Preview the words and definitions before reading. Then review them as necessary during reading. Use context clues and your dictionary to define any additional unfamiliar words.

In a textbook chapter, the words to watch may appear in boldface, italics, or a special color.

listening (1) the ability to understand, analyze, respect, appreciate, and respond appropriately to both nonverbal and spoken messages
comprehensive listening (7) understanding the speaker's meaning
empathic listening (11) understanding and identifying with feelings, thoughts, and motives
analytical listening (14) evaluating the logic and reasonableness of a speaker's message
appreciative listening (17) responding to the way speakers choose and use words
thought speed (21) the words per minute at which people can think compared to the words per minute at which they can speak
golden listening rule (22) listen to others as you would have them listen to you
nonverbal communication (32) unspoken messages from body language and expression
paraphrasing (37) restating what people have said in a way that shows your understanding

◈ What Is Listening?

ISA ENGLEBERG AND JOHN DALY

This textbook reading is excerpted from Chapter 2 of *Presentations in Everyday Life*, Second Edition. The entire chapter is about the relationship between listening and critical thinking. The excerpt focuses on listening behavior.

WHAT IS LISTENING?

1   WE DEFINE EFFECTIVE **listening** as the ability to understand, analyze, respect, appreciate, and appropriately respond to the meaning of another person's spoken and nonverbal message.[1] At first, listening may appear to be as easy and natural as breathing. After all, everyone listens. In fact, just the opposite may be closer to the truth. Although most of us can *hear*, we often fail to *listen* to what others have to say. Hearing and listening are not the same thing. Hearing requires only physical ability; listening requires thinking ability. People who are hearing impaired may be better listeners than those who can hear the faintest sound.

2   Listening is what audiences are supposed to do when speakers talk. In fact, listening is our number one communication activity. Although percentages vary from study to study, Figure 2.1 shows how most of us divide up our daily communication time.

3   One study of college students found that listening occupies more than half of their communicating time.[2] In the corporate world, executives may devote more than 60 percent of their workday listening to others.[3]

4   Yet despite all of the time we spend listening, most of us aren't very good at it. For example, immediately after listening to a short talk, most of us cannot accurately report 50 percent of what was said. Without training, we listen at only 25 percent efficiency.[4] And of that 25 percent, most of what we remember is distorted or inaccurate.[5]

5   As a speaker, you must learn to adjust to and compensate for the poor listening habits of your audience. As an audience member, you will find that your listening ability affects whether you understand and accurately interpret what you hear in a presentation. This dual responsibility on the part of the speaker and audience ensures that presentations achieve their purpose. As we indicated in Chapter 1,

Communication	Percentages
Listening	40–70%
Speaking	20–35%
Reading	10–20%
Writing	5–15%

FIGURE 2.1 | TIME SPENT COMMUNICATING

Source: Isa Engleberg and Dianna Wynn, *Working in Groups*, 3rd Ed., p. 124. © 2003 by Houghton Mifflin Company. Reprinted with permission.

"Presentation Speaking," a successful communication transaction occurs when a speaker's purpose and an audience's response are brought together by a message. Without effective listening, the transaction will fail to produce shared meaning.

TYPES OF LISTENING

Listening is a complex behavior. Researchers have identified several types of listening, each of which employs unique listening skills. 6

TYPES OF LISTENING

Comprehensive listening

Empathic listening

Analytical listening

Appreciative listening

Comprehensive Listening   Comprehensive listening answers this question: What does 7
the speaker mean? **Comprehensive listening** focuses on accurately understanding the meaning of a speaker's spoken and nonverbal messages. Later in this chapter, we discuss how to "listen" to nonverbal communication—the messages speakers send without using words.

Comprehensive listening involves two basic steps. First, make sure you accu- 8
rately hear what is said while simultaneously paying attention to nonverbal cues such as facial expressions, gestures, posture, and vocal quality. Second, make sure that you accurately interpret the speaker's meaning. Can you identify the key points as well as the claims and evidence she uses to support an argument? After all, if you don't comprehend what a person says, you can't be expected to respond in a reasonable way.

Suppose a speaker is trying to persuade you to participate in a voter registra- 9
tion drive. As a comprehensive listener, you may wonder whether "join the voter registration drive" means that you (1) should, in general, support voter registration, (2) should volunteer and help register voters, or (3) should register to vote. The way in which you interpret the meaning of a single comment can determine your response to the whole presentation.

Audience members aren't the only ones who need strong comprehensive listen- 10
ing skills. During a question-and-answer session, speakers need to understand audience questions. In addition, comprehensive listening can be just as important before you speak. It's the type of listening you should use when someone asks you to speak so that you can be sure that you understand the presentation's purpose, audience, logistics, and occasion.

Empathic Listening   Empathic listening answers this question: How does the 11
speaker or audience feel? **Empathic listening** goes beyond understanding what a person means; it focuses on understanding and identifying with a person's situation, feelings, or motives. Can you see the situation through the speaker's eyes? To put the question another way, how would you feel in a similar situation?

12   By not listening for feelings, you may overlook the most important part of a message. Even if you understand every word a person says, you can still miss the anger, enthusiasm, or frustration in a speaker's voice. An empathic listener doesn't have to agree with or feel the same way that a speaker does, but he should try to understand the type and intensity of feelings that the speaker is experiencing. For example, suppose a speaker says that voting is a waste of time. An empathic listener may wonder whether the speaker means that (1) she is stressed and may have more important things to think about, (2) she is frustrated because there aren't any good candidates to vote for, or (3) the line is usually so long at the polling station that standing in it wastes her precious time.

13   Audience members can be empathic listeners in simple ways. For instance, smiling and nodding at someone who is speaking communicates attention and interest. What's more, if you act as though you're listening, you may actually end up listening more effectively and retaining more information!

14 *Analytical Listening*   Analytical listening answers this question: What's my opinion? Of the four types of listening, analytical listening focuses on evaluating whether a message is logical and reasonable. **Analytical listening** asks you to make a judgment based on your evaluation of the speaker's arguments. Is the speaker right or wrong, logical or illogical? Good analytical listeners apply critical thinking skills and understand why they accept or reject a speaker's ideas and suggestions.

15   A speaker makes the following proposal: "Suppose we post signs and offer free rides to the voting polls." An analytical listener might have questions such as these: (1) Will voters misinterpret the ride as pressure to vote for a particular candidate? (2) Wouldn't voters want to check to see that all drivers have adequate car insurance? (3) Is there enough time to design, print, and post the signs before the election?

16   A listener needs analytical listening skills in order to judge the validity of an argument and the factors that separate credible sources from biased ones. To listen analytically, you should evaluate presentations by testing the ways in which they apply the seven basic principles of presentation speaking (as Figure 2.2 shows), to assess the strength and merit of a speaker's ideas and opinions.

17 *Appreciative Listening*   Appreciative listening answers this question: Do I like, value, or enjoy what the speaker is saying? **Appreciative listening** applies to how speakers think and speak—the ways in which they choose and use words and their ability to use humor, tell stories, argue persuasively, or demonstrate understanding. Appreciative listening can reward a speaker who is able to capture and eloquently describe a complex concept or proposal. When a speaker's words, stories, or sense of humor delight us, we listen appreciatively. Appreciative listening skills can help us enjoy and acknowledge good presentations.

18   Suppose that a speaker suggests there is no greater duty in a democracy than that of expressing your opinion at the polling booth on Election Day. An appreciative listener might think that (1) the speaker phrased that idea eloquently; (2) when seen as a patriotic duty rather than as a time-consuming chore, voting seems worthwhile; or (3) the tone of the speaker's voice communicated genuine sincerity.

Purpose Questions:

_____ Is the speaker's purpose clearly stated? If not, what is the speaker trying to achieve?

_____ Could the speaker have a hidden or an ulterior motive?

_____ Did the speaker achieve his or her purpose?

_____ Was achieving the *speaker's* purpose worth the time *you* spent listening?

Audience Questions:

_____ Does the speaker seem to understand the nature and characteristics of the audience?

_____ Does the speaker appear to understand and respect the audience's attitudes and beliefs?

_____ Does it seem as though the speaker is trying to take advantage of the audience in any way?

_____ Could this presentation be delivered to *any* audience, or has the speaker made an effort to adapt it to this audience's interests and needs?

Credibility Questions:

_____ As far as you can determine, is the speaker well informed about the topic?

_____ Does the speaker seem to be sincere and trustworthy?

_____ Does the speaker appear to be genuinely interested in the topic and the audience?

_____ Do you trust and believe this speaker?

_____ Would you invite this speaker to address an audience of colleagues or friends?

Logistics Questions:

_____ Has the speaker stayed within the time limit? If not, what has been the effect of too little or too much speaking?

_____ Has the speaker adapted to the setting of the presentation (considering the size of

the room and the audience, using amplification, using presentation aids)?

_____ If the presentation is taking place on a special occasion, has the speaker adapted to that occasion?

_____ Could this presentation be delivered to any audience in any setting, or has the speaker effectively adapted to this setting and occasion?

Content Questions:

_____ Does the speaker seem well informed?

_____ Is the information relevant to the topic or purpose of the presentation?

_____ Does the speaker identify her or his sources of information?

_____ Does the information seem reasonable and believable? If not, what is the problem?

_____ Does the speaker appear to be misleading the audience?

Organization Questions:

_____ Is the presentation clear and easy to follow?

_____ Are the key points identified and well supported?

_____ Does the speaker go off on tangents that have little to do with the purpose or the key points of the presentation?

Performance Questions:

_____ Was the speaker's delivery effective?

_____ Could you hear and understand what the speaker said?

_____ Did the speaker's gestures, posture, and dress enhance the presentation?

_____ Did the speaker use equipment and presentation aids well?

_____ Did the speaker look directly at the audience?

_____ To what extent did the speaker's delivery affect your opinion of his or her message?

FIGURE 2.2 | QUESTIONS FOR ANALYTICAL LISTENING

LEARNING TO LISTEN

19   You *can* learn specific listening skills, and as we'll soon see, most of them apply two basic principles: (1) use your extra thought speed and (2) apply the "golden listening rule." Once you understand and apply these principles as overriding listening strategies, you can begin to work on specific listening skills.

USE YOUR EXTRA THOUGHT SPEED

20   Most people talk at about 125 to 150 words per minute. According to Ralph Nichols, a respected listening researcher and author, if thoughts were measured in words per minute, most of us could think at three or four times the rate at which we speak.[6] Thus, we have about 400 words' worth of spare thinking time for every minute during which a person talks to us.

21   **Thought speed** is the speed (words per minute) at which most people can think, compared to the speed at which they can speak. So what do we do with all that extra thinking time? Poor listeners use their extra thought speed to daydream, engage in side conversations, take unnecessary notes, or plan how to confront a speaker. Good listeners use their extra thought speed productively when they:

- Identify and summarize key points
- Pay more attention to nonverbal behavior
- Analyze arguments
- Assess the relevance of a speaker's comments

Conscientious audience members don't waste their extra thought speed—they use it to enhance comprehensive and analytical listening.

APPLY THE GOLDEN LISTENING RULE

22   The **golden listening rule** is easy to remember: Listen to others as you would have them listen to you. Unfortunately, this rule can be difficult to follow. It asks you to suspend your own needs in order to attend to someone else's.

23   The golden listening rule applies to the speaker, too. As a speaker, you know your material, but your audience is hearing it for the first time. You may have spent hours crafting your message; your audience may not have given much thought to the issue. You may believe what you're saying; the listener may be skeptical.[7] Conscientious speakers understand and adapt to the ways in which audience members listen to a presentation.

DEVELOP GOOD LISTENING HABITS

24   Although using your extra thought speed and applying the golden listening rule are basic listening principles, ways to practice them may not be obvious. Developing the following six habits can improve your listening ability and help you apply the two basic principles of effective listening. When and how you use these skills depend on whether you are the speaker or an audience member, whether you are

speaking to a large or small group, and whether you have the flexibility to interact with the speaker or audience members during or after a presentation.

THE SIX HABITS OF EFFECTIVE LISTENERS

1. Overcome distractions.
2. Listen for big ideas.
3. "Listen" to nonverbal behavior.
4. Make it personal.
5. Paraphrase.
6. Listen before you leap.

Overcome Distractions Distractions can take many forms.[8] Loud and annoying noises, uncomfortable room temperature and seating, frequent interruptions, distracting decor, and outside activities are environmental distractions. A speaker's delivery can also be distracting. It's hard to listen to a speaker who talks too softly, too rapidly, or too slowly or who speaks in a monotone or with an unfamiliar accent. Even a speaker's mannerisms and appearance can be distracting. Remember the concept of noise in our communication model? Reducing the noise—physical or psychological—that interferes with the communication process can improve your entire audience's ability to listen to your message.

One important form of psychological noise is listener bias. A bias can be either of two things: your own prejudice or an unfair attitude which you hold that stems from prior experience. Bias can also be a preference that inhibits you from making an impartial judgment.[9] If, for example, you "know" you disagree with a viewpoint that is going to be discussed, either you won't listen or you'll spend your time criticizing the speaker. Pro-life audiences may not want to listen to a pro-choice speaker—and vice versa. A gun-control advocate may not have an easy time getting a group of gun owners to listen. Please understand that there's nothing wrong with criticizing a speaker after you've listened comprehensively and analytically to a presentation. The problem results when you let your bias prevent you from listening as a responsible audience member.

When a distraction is environmental, you are well within your rights as a listener or speaker to shut a door, open a window, or turn on more lights. In large groups you may need to ask permission to improve the group's surroundings. If, for example, the room's temperature is too cold or hot, don't hesitate to interrupt your presentation and ask someone to adjust the thermostat—or to do it yourself. Not only will you feel more comfortable, but the audience will also thank you for making it easier to listen. Be a hero. Help your audience by taking action to overcome environmental distractions whenever possible.

Depending on the circumstances and setting of a presentation, you may be able to take direct action to reduce behavioral distractions. If an audience member's behavior is distracting, you may be well within your rights to ask that person to stop talking or moving around. After all, if she is distracting you, the person is probably also distracting others. If a presenter speaks too softly or uses visual aids that are too small, a conscientious audience member may ask him to speak up or to explain what is on a visual.

29 *Listen for Big Ideas*   Good listeners can identify a speaker's purpose, central idea, and key points. Poor listeners tend to listen for and remember isolated facts.

30   Admittedly, sometimes the fault lies with the speaker. When faced with a disorganized speaker who keeps talking long after making a point, listeners may lose track and drift off. In a small group setting, a good listener who senses such problems could interrupt the speaker and ask, "Could you help me out here and summarize your point in a couple of sentences?" Such an interruption is not rude when it is the only way to get the speaker to clarify an important issue. There's also a big difference between asking for a summary and yelling out, "Hey, what's your point?" Although it is tempting for listeners to blame poor speakers when they can't figure out the message, good listeners try to cut through facts and irrelevant comments in order to identify the most important points and main ideas.

31   One way to listen for "big" ideas is to borrow a plan-to-listen tip. Plan to tell someone else what you've heard. We know that when people believe they have to report back on what they've heard, their comprehension increases significantly. Ask yourself the audience's side of the purpose question: What does the speaker want me to know, think, believe, or do after hearing this presentation? Then try to list the key points or ideas the speaker used to achieve that purpose.

32 *"Listen" to Nonverbal Behavior*   Speakers don't always put everything that's important into words. Very often, you can understand a speaker's meaning by noting and interpreting nonverbal communication. **Nonverbal communication** is a general term used to describe the messages that we send without using words. It applies to body language, physical appearance, facial expression, and eye contact as well as to the emotions and emphasis communicated by the tone of a person's voice. Good listeners know that nonverbal behavior can communicate as much as or more meaning than words alone. They pay attention to the "mismatch" between verbal and nonverbal messages, such as when a speaker says, "I'm delighted to see you here today" while cringing and turning toward the door.

33   A change in a speaker's vocal tone or volume may be another way of saying, "Listen up; this is very important." A presenter's sustained eye contact may be a way of saying, "I'm talking to you!" Facial expressions can reveal whether a thought is painful, joyous, exciting, serious, or boring. Even gestures can be used to express a level of excitement that words cannot convey.

34   If, as research indicates, more than half of our meaning is conveyed nonverbally,[10] we are missing a lot of important information if we fail to "listen" to nonverbal behavior! Even Sigmund Freud suggested that "he that has eyes to see and ears to hear may convince himself that no mortal can keep a secret. If his lips are silent, he chatters with his fingertips; betrayal oozes out of him at every pore."[11] No wonder it is difficult to conceal what we mean and feel during a live presentation.

35   Correctly interpreting a speaker's nonverbal responses can tell a listener as much as or more than the spoken words. At the same time, the nonverbal reactions of listeners (head nods, smiles, frowns, eye contact, and sitting posture) can affect the quality, quantity, and content of a speaker's message. Even the setting of a presentation (a nonverbal aspect) can communicate a wealth of meaning about the status, power, and respect given to speakers and listeners.

Make It Personal All of us have had trouble listening and remembering presenta- 36
tions we were not interested in or concerned about. Why expend the energy to listen if you won't be affected? If a politician talks about improving a shopping
district many miles from your neighborhood, why pay attention? If an instructor
lectures on a subject that won't be on the exam, why take notes? If the boss describes his recent fishing trip in agonizing detail, who cares? We hope you've begun
to understand how and why you should listen in such circumstances. First the how:
Find a way in which the speaker's message could affect you. Will the proposal increase your taxes? Will the lecture help you learn or apply other material? Will remembering details of the boss's fishing trip earn you brownie points in the future?
Find a personal reason to listen even when the information seems uninteresting or
irrelevant.

Paraphrase **Paraphrasing** is the ability to restate what people have said in a way 37
that indicates that you understood them. Too often we jump to conclusions and
incorrectly assume that we know what a speaker means and feels. Paraphrasing is
a listening check that asks, "Am I right? Is this what you mean?"

Paraphrasing requires finding new words to describe what you have heard 38
rather than repeating what a person has said. In addition to rephrasing the meaning
of the speaker's message, a paraphrase usually includes a request for confirmation.
Paraphrasing can be used for many purposes:

> *To clarify meaning:* "When you said that you weren't going to the conference,
> did you mean that you want one of us to go instead?"

> *To ensure understanding:* "I know that you said you approve, but I sense
> you're not happy with the outcome. Am I way off?"

> *To summarize:* "What you seem to be saying is that it's not the best time to
> change this policy. Am I right?"

By rephrasing what we have heard and requesting confirmation, we can use
paraphrases to help confirm our perceptions. Effective paraphrasing requires us to
use our extra thought speed to produce a statement that follows the golden listening
rule.

Listen Before You Leap One of the most often-quoted pieces of listening advice to 39
come from Ralph Nichols's writings is that "we must always withhold evaluation
until our comprehension is complete."[12] Good listeners make sure that they understand a speaker before reacting either positively or negatively.

Sometimes when we become angry, friends may tell us to "count to ten" before 40
reacting. Taking the same precaution is also good advice for listening. Counting to
ten, however, implies more than withholding evaluation until you understand
completely. You may comprehend a speaker's words perfectly but be infuriated or
offended by what you hear. If an insensitive speaker refers to the women in the audience as "girls," it may take your counting to twenty to allow you enough time to
collect your thoughts and maintain your ability to listen comprehensively. If a
speaker tells an offensive joke, you may have a double reaction—anger toward the
speaker and disappointment with those who laugh. Try to understand the effects of
offensive comments and emotionally laden words without losing your composure
or concentration.

41   Limit counterarguing. All of us have a tendency to criticize mentally or to refute speakers as we listen to them. Certainly, when you're highly involved with a topic, it's difficult to control this tendency. We recommend maintaining a balance between uncritical acceptance of a speaker's message and flat-out rejection. Effective listeners engage their analytical listening skills to track and assess the validity of a speaker's message; they don't use their listening time to develop harsh or personal attacks.

42   When you listen before you leap, you are not approving of or condoning what someone says. Instead, you are using your extra thought speed to decide how to react to controversial, prejudiced, or offensive comments. Listening before you leap gives you time to adjust your reactions in a way that will help clarify and correct a statement rather than offend, disrupt, or infuriate a speaker or other audience members.

Comprehension Check

Purpose and Main Idea

1. What is the authors' topic?
   a. audience behavior
   b. presenting
   c. communication
   d. listening
2. Which one of the following *best* states the central idea?
   a. Good communication involves effective speaking, writing, and listening.
   b. Listening is a complex activity that anyone can learn to improve.
   c. Speakers must adjust to and compensate for the audience's bad listening habits.
   d. A presentation is successful when it involves both the speaker and the audience.
3. The authors' *primary* purpose is to
   a. persuade students to develop good listening habits.
   b. express a point of view toward listening.
   c. entertain readers with examples of ineffective communication.
   d. inform readers about the types and process of listening.

Details

4. Without training, we listen at only 25 percent efficiency.
   a. True
   b. False
5. Which one of the following answers the question: How does the speaker or audience feel?
   a. comprehensive listening
   b. analytical listening
   c. empathic listening
   d. appreciative listening

6. Which one of the following is an *organization* question for analytical listening?
   a. What is the speaker trying to achieve?
   b. Has the speaker stayed within the time limit?
   c. Did the speaker look directly at the audience?
   d. Are key points identified and well supported?
7. Listener bias is an example of *psychological noise.*
   a. True
   b. False
8. What is the *dominant* organizational pattern followed in the excerpt?
   a. process
   b. comparison
   c. definition
   d. classification

Inferences

9. Based on what you have learned from the excerpt, make an inference about what you can do as a speaker to encourage good listening on the part of your audience.
10. Based on what you have learned from the excerpt, make an inference about what you can do as an audience member to get more out of a speaker's presentation.

Working with Words

Complete sentences 1–9 with these words from Word Alert:

nonverbal communication	appreciative listening	empathic listening
comprehensive listening	analytical listening	paraphrasing
golden listening rule	thought speed	listening

1. Hearing the words is not the same thing as _____ to what is said.
2. According to Ralph Nichols, _____ is the rate at which people can think.
3. Body language, facial expression, and eye contact are forms of _____.
4. Accurate understanding is the focus of _____.
5. _____ applies to how people think and speak.
6. The _____ requires you to suspend your needs in order to attend to someone else's.
7. Identifying with a person's situation or motives calls for _____.
8. _____ depends on your use of logic and reason.
9. I can tell by your _____ of the speaker's words that you understood the lecture.

Write your own sentences, using any two of the words from Word Alert.

10. _____
11. _____

Thinking Deeper

Ideas for reflection, discussion, and writing

Make Inferences from Your Reading

1. The authors explain four types of listening: *comprehensive, appreciative, empathic,* and *analytical.* Based on your understanding of these types, which one do you think may be the easiest for most people? Which one may be the hardest? Explain your reasons.

2. Figure 2.1 shows time spent communicating. Do these figures correspond to what you have observed in your classes or at work? Approximately what percentage of time do you spend on each of the communication activities?

3. Most employers say that good communication skills are what they look for first in an applicant. The personal interview may be your only chance to demonstrate your speaking and listening skills and to create a good first impression. At work, being an effective listener will help you get more out of presentations and meetings. Which tips from this selection can you apply immediately to build better listening skills?

4. Because listening is such an important skill, you will find lots of information on listening on the Internet. Here are two sites to try. Because URLs and site content change frequently, ask your instructor or librarian for additional suggestions. Go to http://www.infoplease.com and type "listening skills" as your search phrase. Look for an article that gives tips on good listening. Share your results in a class discussion.

Write About It

5. Write about a time when a failure to listen led to a misunderstanding or cost you something you wanted.

6. The authors explain several types of listening. Write about the one type of listening that interests you most. Explain what you have learned and how you will use this information to improve the way you communicate.

MORE PERSPECTIVES

An issue *is a matter of public concern. People hold strong opinions about the economy, education, health care, immigration, and other issues that affect their lives and work. If you watch the news or read newspapers regularly, then you know the issues that are of national, state, and local concern. Your college campus also reflects the surrounding society and the issues that matter to it.*

On any issue, there is always more than one perspective. A critical thinker keeps an open mind, considering different perspectives before making a decision or taking sides. A critical thinker also knows that everyone has a right to an opinion, but that some opinions are better informed than others.

The selections in Part 6 examine several issues from different perspectives. As you read each selection, ask yourself these questions: What is the issue? What is the author's viewpoint? Are opposing views acknowledged? What do I think and why?

FIRST THOUGHTS

To build background for the reading selection, answer the following questions, either on your own or in a group discussion.

1. Do you believe that there are circumstances in which suicide may be a valid choice? Explain your reasons.
2. Do you think that physician-assisted suicide should be legal?
3. Preview the title, headnote, and first one or two paragraphs. What do you think will follow?

WORD ALERT

Each word below is followed by its paragraph number. Preview the words and definitions before reading. Then review them as necessary during reading. Use context clues and your dictionary to define any additional unfamiliar words.

neurological (1) having to do with the nervous system

vulnerable (2) at risk of injury or attack

infirm (2) weak in body, feeble

stampede (2) headlong rush or flight

autonomy (3) self-determination, self-regulation

euthanasia (3) the act of ending the life of someone suffering from a terminal or incurable illness

compassionate (4) sympathetic, being deeply aware of others' suffering

fatal (5) causing or capable of causing death

◈ Some Dying Patients Need Help

CHARLES F. McKHANN

Charles F. McKhann, M.D., is professor of surgery at the Yale University School of Medicine and author of *A Time to Die: The Place for Physician Assistance*. In this selection, he argues in favor of legalizing physician-assisted suicide. The selection ran in the *AARP Bulletin,* May 1999, as one of two opposing views written in answer to the question "Should physician-assisted suicide be legalized by the states?"

IN SPITE OF MEDICINE'S best efforts there are people who suffer severely at the end 1 of life, and there always will be. "Bad deaths" include cancer, AIDS and some **neurological** disorders. The aging of our population adds to these an accumulation of frightening disabilities, such as blindness and immobility. Recognition of these problems is transforming us from a society that did not want to think about death at all into one that is increasingly concerned about how life may end. We would like to avoid unnecessary pain and suffering, to retain a reasonable degree of human dignity and self-respect, and many would like to have some control over events at the end of life. Most people hope to live long, healthy lives and also to be assured that they will be spared the worst at the end. The fact is that we have now reached a point where the same medical profession that has added years to our lives can also provide more comfortable deaths for the few who need such help, if it is given the chance to do so legally.

Much is being said about the risks of physician-assisted suicide. The primary 2 focus is on abuse of the individual at the hands of a physician or a family that wants to rid themselves of a burdensome individual. Opponents also feel that assisted suicide would be directed at more **vulnerable** members of society, such as the aged, **infirm,** disabled, poor, minorities and even women. However, health care in the United States finds it easy to neglect these vulnerable people: They will be the last and least likely to benefit from any change in our laws. The new Oregon law addresses potential abuse very specifically, as an article in the October 1998 *Bulletin* pointed out, and there has been no **stampede** to assisted dying in that state.

A second concern is that voluntary shortening of life as an expression of **autonomy** 3 would eventually lead to involuntary **euthanasia,** in which people's lives would be ended against their wills, at the insistence of others, even the state. But if the final step in ending life must be the taking of some medication by the patient himself (i.e., suicide), this possibility is remote indeed.

Physicians have always helped people die, and even now some do so from 4 time to time. Many more say that they would if only it were legal. Until the laws are changed, people who are concerned should ask their doctors while they are still well, or early in a serious illness, if the doctor would provide help in the face of severe suffering. As patients become more insistent, help will become more commonplace. However, it will remain unfair to place all the risk on the shoulders of **compassionate** physicians, because as a society we are unable to pass more humane laws.

5   Eventually new laws must be enacted by state legislatures composed of people who are very sensitive to opposition, primarily from well-organized and well-financed religious groups. Since dying individuals will be unable to complain or vote, the responsibility is really with the healthy 65 percent of the population who say they want to have the laws changed. All of us must think about what we would want if we developed a **fatal** illness with serious suffering, and then push hard for more permissive laws now.

Comprehension Check

Purpose and Main Idea

1. What is the author's topic?
    a. fatal illnesses
    b. medical care
    c. physician-assisted suicide
    d. insurance risks
2. The central idea of the selection is stated in
    a. paragraph 1, first sentence "In spite of...."
    b. paragraph 1, second sentence "'Bad deaths'...."
    c. paragraph 1, fourth sentence "Recognition of...."
    d. paragraph 1, last sentence "The fact is...."
3. The author's *primary* purpose is to
    a. entertain readers with sympathetic stories of the terminally ill.
    b. inform readers that people have always suffered at the end of life.
    c. express his view that physician-assisted suicide should be legal.
    d. persuade healthy readers that it is their responsibility to change the laws regarding physician-assisted suicide.

Details

4. According to the author, "bad deaths" include heart attack, AIDS, and cancer.
    a. True
    b. False
5. Which one of the following is *not* one of the author's stated reasons in support of physician-assisted suicide?
    a. to avoid unnecessary pain and suffering
    b. to retain reasonable dignity and self-respect
    c. to exercise religious freedom
    d. to maintain some control over events at the end of life
6. According to the author, minorities and women are among the groups that would be the least likely to benefit from a change in the laws regarding physician-assisted suicide.
    a. True
    b. False

7. According to the author, which one of the following would prevent involuntary euthanasia?
    a. legalizing physician-assisted suicide
    b. requiring that the patient end his or her own life by taking medication
    c. leaving the decision to end a life in the hands of the state
    d. allowing relatives to decide whether a patient's life should be ended
8. The phrase "a second concern" in paragraph 3 signals the reader that
    a. ideas are being contrasted.
    b. an additional idea follows.
    c. events are related by time.
    d. an effect follows a stated cause.

Inferences

9. Of the reasons the author provides in support of legalizing physician-assisted suicide, which one seems the most common-sense view?
10. At the end of paragraph 5, what is the author asking readers to do?

Working with Words

Complete sentences 1–8 with these words from Word Alert:

neurological	euthanasia	stampede	fatal
vulnerable	autonomy	infirm	compassionate

1. Many gunshot wounds are not _____, and patients are able to recover from them.
2. _____, sometimes called "mercy killing," is a topic of much controversy.
3. Children's inexperience makes them _____ to offers of gifts from people who are out to harm them.
4. When the department store opened its doors, a _____ of consumers rushed to the sales racks.
5. You can make a useful contribution to society by volunteering as a nursing home aide, doing small tasks for the _____.
6. Students who have a high degree of _____ are usually able to manage their time and control their concentration.
7. People who have _____ disorders such as cerebral palsy may need long-term care.
8. Because Jane enjoys working at her local homeless shelter, her friends call her a _____ person.

   Write your own sentences, using any two of the words from Word Alert.

9. _____
10. _____

Thinking Deeper

Ideas for reflection, discussion, and writing

Make Inferences from Your Reading

1. The author takes a position in favor of physician-assisted suicide. Does he state opposing views, and if so, how does he answer them? What other reasons can you think of either for or against physician-assisted suicide?
2. As the population ages, and as treatment for the infirmities of aging improves, what inferences can you make about the possible consequences of people living longer?
3. This author and the author of the next selection were asked the question, "Should physician-assisted suicide be legalized by the states?" Discuss what you know of the controversy surrounding physician-assisted suicide and your own views on the issue.
4. How widespread is legalized euthanasia or physician-assisted suicide? To check your inference, do a Google search using "euthanasia" or "physician-assisted suicide." Your instructor or librarian can help you refine your search or suggest URLs. Share what you learn in a class discussion.

Write About It

5. Would you support legalizing physician-assisted suicide in your home state? Why or why not?
6. Do you think the government should determine how much and what kind of health care people get, based on their age? Explain your reasons.

FIRST THOUGHTS

To build background for the reading selection, answer the following questions, either on your own or in a group discussion.

1. If you have read Selection 41, what additional questions do you have about physician-assisted suicide? If you did not read the selection, then what thoughts do you have about this issue?
2. What other issues are involved in caring for the dying?
3. Preview the title, headnote, and first one or two paragraphs. What do you think will follow?

WORD ALERT

Each word below is followed by its paragraph number. Preview the words and definitions before reading. Then review them as necessary during reading. Use context clues and your dictionary to define any additional unfamiliar words.

abhorrent (1) regarded with horror or loathing
chronic (3) long-lasting, continuing, recurrent
impoverished (4) reduced to poverty
rational (6) reasoned, logical
diminishing (6) decreasing, lessening, making smaller
parlaying (11) betting on a situation in a way that compromises its outcome

◈ Suicide Issue Diverts Us from the Real Problems

JOANNE LYNN

Joanne Lynn, M.D., is director of the Center to Improve Care of the Dying at George Washington University and president of Americans for Better Care of the Dying. In this selection, she argues against legalizing physician-assisted suicide. The selection ran in the *AARP Bulletin,* May 1999, as one of two opposing views written in answer to the question "Should physician-assisted suicide be legalized by the states?"

1   MANY PEOPLE THINK that deciding whether to legalize physician-assisted suicide is a clear-cut issue. They either oppose legalization because they find any killing **abhorrent,** or favor it because they believe people should be allowed to make choices without government interference.

2   Neither of these positions, though, takes into account the very difficult end-of-life issues that confront us. I oppose legalization of physician-assisted suicide because it risks killing people who could and should live their last days comfortably—if only we fixed our health-care system.

3   Until about 50 years ago, most people died suddenly—usually from infections and accidents. Now most of us grow old and then die slowly from a **chronic** illness like cancer or heart disease. Living longer is a good thing, but we need improved health services to live well until the end of life.

4   With better care for people with terminal illnesses, physician-assisted suicide would no longer need to be an option. No patient would have to be overwhelmed by pain, feel alone and afraid or be **impoverished** by medical expenses.

5   Now, however, many people do face those and other problems. One reason is because our medical system badly mismatches spending with actual patient needs. Medicare, for example, was set up to assure that individuals could get surgery when they needed it; the program was not set up to provide continuity of care, pain control or family support, the things dying patients most need. Medicare makes it easier to get a heart transplant than to get pain medicine or home-health aides.

6   Supporters and opponents of legalizing physician-assisted suicide agree we have not learned how to support very sick people and their families. Advocates contend, however, that physician-assisted suicide is still a choice, and that the risks can be contained. They imagine a **rational** person who has painful symptoms but a loving family, predictable illness and adequate finances. In truth, most of us will come to our last months of life with **diminishing** resources, some confusion and uncertainty about the course of our illness—and this occurs in a badly functioning health system that provides few real choices.

7   What is the physician to do when a patient asks for suicide assistance because his care is bankrupting his spouse, his pain is unrelieved, prescription drugs are too costly or the thought of going to a Medicaid nursing home is too threatening?

8   Our first response must be to change the care system—not to make it easier to "choose" to be dead. Assisted suicide is a sideshow that is taking our attention away from urgently needed health-care reform.

What can you do? First, educate yourself. People can ordinarily live well de- 9
spite serious illness. Various books, including our *Hand-book for Mortals* (Oxford
University Press, 1999), can show you how.

Second, you can be an advocate for change in the care system. Americans for 10
Better Care of the Dying posts its "Agitator's Guide" and its legislative agenda
on the Web at www.abcd-caring.com. Or you can request copies by writing to:
Americans for Better Care of the Dying, 2175 K St. N.W., Suite 810, Washington,
D.C. 20037.

Seriously ill people should be able to live comfortably and with dignity to the 11
end. Legalizing physician-assisted suicide is not the answer, as it runs the risk of
parlaying the vulnerability of the elderly and the very sick into a "choice" to die.
Instead we should work toward real, enduring improvement in end-of-life care.

Comprehension Check

Purpose and Main Idea

1. What is the author's topic?
   a. the suicide issue
   b. end-of-life issues
   c. managed health care
   d. Medicare
2. The central idea of the selection is stated in
   a. paragraph 1, first sentence "Many people...."
   b. paragraph 1, second sentence "They either...."
   c. paragraph 2, first sentence "Neither of...."
   d. paragraph 2, last sentence "I oppose...."
3. The author's *primary* purpose is to
   a. express distrust of government involvement in health care.
   b. entertain readers with a true-life account of health care in nursing homes.
   c. persuade readers to work toward improvement in end-of-life care.
   d. inform readers about the health care issues that confront us.

Details

4. The author opposes physician-assisted suicide because she finds all killing
   abhorrent.
   a. True
   b. False
5. According to the author, to live well until the end of life, we need improved
   health services.
   a. True
   b. False
6. Both supporters and opponents of legalizing physician-assisted suicide
   agree that
   a. patients should be free to choose suicide.
   b. physician-assisted suicide has too many risks.

c. we do not know how to support the very sick.

d. our health care system functions adequately.

7. The author offers all but which one of the following as solutions to the problem of inadequate end-of-life care?

a. Reform the healthcare system.

b. Educate yourself.

c. Be an advocate for change.

d. Legalize physician-assisted suicide.

8. Paragraphs 4 and 5 are related by

a. comparison and contrast.

b. generalization then example.

c. cause and effect.

d. steps in a process.

Inferences

9. Do you think the author would agree that prescription drugs at affordable prices would be a real improvement in health care for an elderly patient who is terminally ill? Explain your reasons.

10. Why does the author call assisted suicide a "sideshow"?

Working with Words

Complete sentences 1–6 with these words from Word Alert:

impoverished	parlaying	rational
diminishing	abhorrent	chronic

1. _____ headache sufferers hope for a remedy that not only will stop the pain but will keep the headache from recurring.

2. A crash in the stock market could leave some investors so _____ that it might take them years to regain their wealth.

3. Although the hurricane had been severe, we could tell from the _____ wind and rain that the storm would soon be over.

4. To many parents, the thought of their child getting a tattoo or a pierced navel is _____.

5. Fred made the mistake of _____ his lottery winnings on another bet and lost everything.

6. It is not _____ to have test anxiety when you have studied sufficiently and know the material.

Write your own sentences, using any two of the words from Word Alert.

7. _____

8. _____

Thinking Deeper

Ideas for reflection, discussion, and writing

Make Inferences from Your Reading

1. Where does the author state opposing viewpoints, and how does she counter them? In your opinion, are opposing views fairly represented?
2. In a small group, prepare an argument either for or against physician-assisted suicide. List your points of argument on a sheet of paper, and be prepared to defend your argument in a class discussion.
3. The authors of Selections 41 and 42 deal with the issue of physician-assisted suicide. How do their views differ? Is one argument more convincing than the other? Explain your answer.
4. A related issue is whether life support should be withdrawn from the terminally ill or disabled in the absence of a signed document. In 2005, a Florida case involved Terry Schiavo, a severely disabled woman whose life support was cut off over her parents' protests. The story made the national news. Using "Terry Schiavo" as a search phrase, go to the Internet and find an article on the case. Determine what life-and-death issues were involved and what the courts decided, and be prepared to discuss the case in class.

Write About It

5. In paragraph 9, the author says "People can ordinarily live well despite serious illness." Do you agree or disagree with this statement? What example can you give of someone who has or had a good quality of life while seriously ill?
6. Did reading Selections 41 and 42 or your search results on the Schiavo case either change or reaffirm your views on physician-assisted suicide and related issues? Explain what you think in writing.

FIRST THOUGHTS

To build background for the reading selection, answer the following questions, either on your own or in a group discussion.

1.   Is the death penalty legal in your state?
2.   Are you in favor of or against the death penalty and why?
3.   Preview the title, headnote, and first one or two paragraphs. What do you think will follow?

WORD ALERT

Each word below is followed by its paragraph number. Preview the words and definitions before reading. Then review them as necessary during reading. Use context clues and your dictionary to define any additional unfamiliar words.

exasperation (1) great annoyance or impatience
gurney (3) a metal stretcher with legs on wheels
botched (6) ruined as a result of clumsiness
negotiate (8) to arrange or settle by agreement
inflicting (12) imposing, dealing out something that is a punishment or a burden

◈ In Opposition to the Death Penalty

A. E. P. WALL

A. E. P. Wall is a veteran journalist. He wrote this commentary on the death penalty for the *Orlando Sentinel*.

WHEN O. J. SIMPSON'S souvenirs were auctioned, one bidder said he spent $16,000   1
for items that he planned to burn. This was to show his **exasperation** with the not-guilty verdict in Simpson's trial, which was the trial of the century just before former President Clinton's U.S. Senate trial of the century and just after Paula Jones nominated Clinton as defendant in the sexual-harassment trial of the century. You might think that the laid-back national attitude toward pranks of a capital nature, or those that miss being high crimes by several inches, would bring a sense of hope to the 2,000 people or so now living on death row in U.S. prisons.

Everybody has read about innocent men saved from unjust execution by the   2
state, which is we, you and I. Nobody knows how many innocent men we've killed in the past, legally correct but morally unpardonable.

Has the time come to grant celebrity status to those who await death by artificial   3
lightning in the electric chair or by an artificial drug overdose on a prison **gurney**?

Jesse Joseph Tafero became famous too late. After the state of Florida replaced   4
a natural sponge with a synthetic sponge in the headpiece, flames shot out from Tafero's head. He kept on breathing until three jolts of electricity were applied. Nobody in a position of authority to stop this kind of thing considers it to be cruel and unusual.

Pedro Medina was not the right kind of Florida celebrity either. With the first   5
jolt of electricity, flames sparked from the mask over his face. There was smoke, and there was the stench of burned flesh.

There have been a couple of dozen **botched** executions throughout the country   6
during the past decade and a half.

Most of the folk who await death at the hands of the American public are   7
poor. Some are mentally disabled. Four out of 10 are African-American.

If only they had the Senate Democrats to judge them, they might **negotiate** life   8
without parole—reasonable in capital cases—and reversible if the prisoner is later found to be innocent, leaving fewer scars on the nation's body politic.

In Florida, two influential groups oppose the death penalty outright. It is no   9
longer politically correct to describe them, or anyone, as strange bedfellows, but the Catholic Church in the United States and the American Civil Liberties Union are on the same side. The Catholic Church goes further, also defending the life of the unborn.

Florida has a Catholic population of about 2 million, more than 300,000 of   10
them in the Diocese of Orlando. ACLU members are not that numerous, but they tend to make themselves heard, even without a pulpit.

Among those Catholic millions is the governor, Jeb Bush, a widely respected   11
member of a family that is becoming what the Kennedys were once thought to be.

There's no sign so far that he agrees with the Catholic bishops, who formally declared their opposition to capital punishment in 1974. Pope John Paul II wrote in his encyclical *The Gospel of Life* that cases that might justify executions are rare if not practically nonexistent.

12   The ACLU believes that the death penalty is always unconstitutional under the Eighth Amendment, which forbids **inflicting** "cruel and unusual" punishment, and the Fourteenth Amendment because the discriminatory choice of capital punishment victims violates the equal protection granted to all persons, citizens or not.

13   Whether the jury has six members or a dozen or a hundred, it may define the law in its own language. That may be the language of the streets, the language of race, the language of privilege or the language of politics. A jury gives one person $50 million, sends another to death row, frees one to write a book celebrating the triumph of lawyerly talent.

14   A chap named Thucydides[1] said that in a democracy, the law assures equal justice to all. The massing of more than 2,000 prisoners to await execution in American prisons came about 2,400 years later, most of them equal, at least in poverty.

15   Thomas Jefferson defined it more sharply. In his first Inaugural Address, he saluted "equal and exact justice to all...."

16   There's nothing equal or exact about the death penalty. The theory of vengeance that supports hanging, electrocution, shooting or drugging to death by the state is not applied equally. If it were, convicted rapists would be raped by the official state rapist. A motorist, found guilty of driving while drunk and hitting a pedestrian, would be placed into the middle of the street and run down by the official state drunk.

17   If the ACLU and the Catholic Church and others as disparate can agree on the injustice of rubbing out criminals, whether through frustration or thirst for blood, maybe justice, even exact justice, has a chance.

Comprehension Check

Purpose and Main Idea

1. What is the author's topic?
    a. famous trials
    b. the death penalty
    c. types of executions
    d. unjust execution
2. The central idea of the selection is stated in
    a. paragraph 2 "Nobody knows...."
    b. paragraph 6 "There have been...."
    c. paragraph 12 "The ACLU believes...."
    d. paragraph 16 "There's nothing equal...."
3. The author's *primary* purpose is to
    a. express opposition to the death penalty.
    b. persuade us that the death penalty is unjust.

---

[1] Thucydides was a Greek historian (c. 460–400 B.C.) noted for his account of the Peloponnesian War.

    c.   inform us that a controversy surrounds the death penalty.

    d.   entertain us with accounts of trials of the century.

Details

4. At the time of this writing, according to the author, 2,000 or more people are awaiting execution in U.S. prisons.

    a.   True

    b.   False

5. Most of the prisoners awaiting execution are poor.

    a.   True

    b.   False

6. Two influential groups in Florida that oppose the death penalty are the ACLU (American Civil Liberties Union) and

    a.   the Florida Senate.

    b.   the Catholic Church.

    c.   the American Bar Association.

    d.   Democratic party members.

7. The author's evidence against the death penalty includes all but which one of the following?

    a.   Innocent men have been executed.

    b.   Executions have been botched.

    c.   The death penalty is applied unequally.

    d.   Poll results show widespread opposition.

8. In paragraphs 4 and 5, what purpose do the examples of Tafero and Medina serve?

    a.   They prove that discrimination against minorities exists.

    b.   Both show how Florida deals with capital punishment.

    c.   Both are examples of botched executions.

    d.   They appeal to a reader's sense of humor.

Inferences

9. From which details can you infer a legal basis for the author's argument?

10. Is the author's argument valid or invalid? Explain your reasons.

Working with Words

Complete sentences 1–5 with these words from Word Alert:

exasperation   negotiate   gurney

inflicting   botched

1. Union leaders and management worked together to _____ the terms of their contract.

2. The accident victim was placed on a _____ and rushed to the emergency room.

3. May I borrow a piece of paper? I've _____ this one by writing answers to the wrong questions.
4. Many prisoners are guilty of fighting and _____ wounds on one another when no one is looking.
5. The students reacted with _____ when they saw how many of their test answers were incorrect.

Write your own sentences, using any two of the words from Word Alert.

6. _____
7. _____

Thinking Deeper

Ideas for reflection, discussion, and writing

Make Inferences from Your Reading

1. Working with group members, list and discuss the author's evidence against the death penalty, and rank his reasons from most convincing to least convincing. Share your results with the rest of the class.
2. What evidence can you offer in favor of the death penalty? Working with group members, list, discuss, and rank your evidence from most to least convincing. Share your results with the rest of the class.
3. Whether to retain or to abolish the death penalty has been an issue for some states. How has your state addressed this issue, and do you agree with your lawmakers' decisions? Discuss and explain your answer.
4. Constitutional Amendment 8 is part of the "Bill of Rights." Amendments 8 and 14 spell out our protections under the law. Do a Web search on these amendments. Type "Amendments and U.S. Constitution" as your search phrase. One site to try is http://www.usconstitution.net/constamnotes.html. Click on "quick links" to each amendment. There is also a quiz on the constitution that you can take. Site content and URLs change frequently, so ask for help if you are unable to find appropriate sites. In a class discussion, share what you have learned about Amendments 8 and 14. In addition, make inferences about the meaning of the amendments to come up with one or two examples of how they can be applied in your own life.

Write About It

5. Review the lists of evidence generated for discussion items 1 and 2, then write a paper in which you explain why you are either for or against the death penalty.
6. What do you think is the most important right granted to citizens under the U.S. Constitution?

FIRST THOUGHTS

To build background for the reading selection, answer the following questions, either on your own or in a group discussion.

1. What have you heard or read about prisoners who were wrongly accused?
2. In your opinion, what is the single most important reason to be for or against the death penalty?
3. Preview the title headnote, and first one or two paragraphs. What do you think will follow?

WORD ALERT

Each word below is followed by its paragraph number. Preview the words and definitions before reading. Then review them as necessary during reading. Use context clues and your dictionary to define any additional unfamiliar words.

recede (3) withdraw, retreat, move back or away from

complied (7) acted in accordance with another's command, request, rule, or wishes

flagging (9) declining, weakening

exculpatory (11) acting or tending to clear of guilt or blame

moratorium (11) an authorized period of delay, suspension

tyranny (13) absolute power, especially when exercised unjustly or cruelly

◈ In Defense of the Death Penalty

MARIANNE MEANS

Marianne Means is a journalist for Hearst Newspapers. She wrote this commentary on the death penalty for the *Orlando Sentinel.*

1   WITHIN THE SPAN of a few days, Pope John Paul II pleaded for the life of a convicted killer and college students uncovered evidence that a death-row inmate may have been wrongly sentenced—and the legitimacy of the death penalty was in for another political thumping.

2   Here we go again.

3   The ultimate punishment has become a quietly accepted fact of American life only in the past few years. The Supreme Court ruled back in 1976 that it was constitutionally OK if applied fairly and appropriately. Controversy over the issue was slow to **recede** even though a majority of the public and most national politicians long supported the concept.

4   Opponents have continued to fight capital punishment. They hold candlelight vigils before scheduled executions, help death-row inmates file endless appeals, glamorize killers by selling sympathetic books and raise their voices in moral outrage.

5   But throughout the country, the 38 states that permit the death penalty have executed 500 convicted murderers in the past 23 years with increasingly less public attention. Now, however, fresh ammunition is reviving the old arguments about whether capital punishment can ever be morally justified or administered in a way that does not sometimes mistakenly kill innocent men.

6   During his visit to St. Louis, the Pope tried to revive the issue with strong statements condemning the death penalty. He also asked Missouri Gov. Mel Carnahan to commute the death sentence of Darrell Mease, who was due to die by lethal injection in two weeks.

7   The governor **complied**, although there was no question at trial that Mease was guilty of hiding for three days to ambush a 69-year-old man, his wife and their paraplegic grandson. He shot the three and then walked up to them to shoot each one again in the face in what was described as the most cold-blooded killing ever to take place in the region. His only defense was post-traumatic stress from Vietnam.

8   The incident dramatized the Pope's belief that the state has no right to take any life, even that of someone who has brutally taken the life of another. But his choice for salvation was not a sympathetic one; the victims' families and friends, among others, felt that the killer deserved to die.

9   But to the degree that the Pope's example energizes Catholic officials, we may see the church try to revive its **flagging** efforts to get Catholics to fight the death penalty. (Polls show that lay Catholics support capital punishment by a 2-to-1 margin, roughly equal to that of Protestants.)

10   A more immediate reaction was prompted by the discovery of Northwestern University journalism students that Anthony Porter, who was due to be executed for the 1982 shooting deaths of two teenagers, may be innocent. The students found a Milwaukee man who confessed to the murders for which Porter was convicted.

Death-penalty opponents point out that such mistakes are more common than 11 we realize. In Chicago, alone, 10 death-row inmates have been released since 1977 after the discovery of new **exculpatory** evidence. The cry has gone up for a **moratorium** on executions and drastic revisions in the way the sentence is imposed. Even Chicago Mayor Richard Daley, who calls himself "pro death," now supports a temporary halt to executions.

Yet the possibility of error—still relatively rare—is not, in itself, sufficient to 12 justify abandoning the death penalty.

Obviously an execution, being uniquely irreversible, calls for extra scrutiny. But 13 a great nation cannot tremble before laws to protect the safety of its citizens out of fear that they may be applied imperfectly. That would amount to **tyranny** of the few over the many.

If found guilty, those three white, Texas men who are charged with dragging a 14 black man to his death behind a pickup truck do not deserve a taxpayer subsidy to loaf in a prison cell. Karla Faye Tucker, executed for hacking two people to death with a pickax, didn't deserve it either—despite her belated conversion to Christianity.

Justice requires the ultimate repayment in kind for the ultimate evil of robbing 15 another living, breathing human being of life.

Comprehension Check

Purpose and Main Idea

1. What is the author's topic?
   a. the wrongly accused
   b. criminals' rights
   c. the death penalty
   d. victims' rights
2. The central idea of the selection is stated in
   a. paragraph 3 "The ultimate...."
   b. paragraph 5 "Now, however...."
   c. paragraph 12 "Yet the possibility...."
   d. paragraph 15 "Justice requires...."
3. The author's *primary* purpose is to
   a. inform readers of new arguments against the death penalty.
   b. entertain us with profiles of death-row inmates.
   c. express concern about innocent people who have been executed.
   d. persuade readers that we need the death penalty.

Details

4. According to the author, controversy over the death penalty has had a long history.
   a. True
   b. False

5. According to the author, opponents of capital punishment have done all but which one of the following?
   a. asserted the rights of criminals' victims
   b. held candlelight vigils
   c. helped death-row inmates file appeals
   d. glamorized killers and aroused sympathy for them
6. The possibility of error in sentencing, according to the author, is frequent.
   a. True
   b. False
7. Which one of the following may, in fact, be innocent of the 1982 murder for which he was convicted?
   a. Darrell Mease
   b. Mel Carnahan
   c. Anthony Porter
   d. a white Texas male
8. The organizational pattern in paragraph 11 is
   a. generalization then example.
   b. cause and effect.
   c. sequence.
   d. process.

Inferences

9. Which words in paragraph 14 have emotional overtones? How does the use of these words affect your attitude toward the people and crimes involved?
10. Explain how the statement "Justice requires...." (paragraph 15) is similar in meaning to "an eye for an eye."

Working with Words

Complete sentences 1–6 with these words from Word Alert:

exculpatory	flagging	recede
moratorium	complied	tyranny

1. Rolanda sat on the beach, watching the waves crash on the shore, then _____.
2. The schoolteacher changed activities when he saw that the children's interest was _____.
3. After a shooting at the local high school, the mayor called for a _____ on selling guns until the case was resolved.
4. The students _____ with their instructor's request to work in small groups on their assignments.
5. New _____ evidence proved that the person accused of vandalizing public property was out of town when the crime occurred.
6. Early settlers came to the New World to escape the _____ of their former rulers.

Write your own sentences, using any two of the words from Word Alert.

7. _____

8. _____

Thinking Deeper

Ideas for reflection, discussion, and writing

Make Inferences from Your Reading

1. Where does the author state her position on the death penalty? What evidence does she give to support her position? Does she acknowledge and answer the claims of the opposition? Based on your answers to these questions, would you infer that her argument is balanced or biased, and why?
2. Are you familiar with any of the cases the author mentions? Do you know of other high-profile cases where a death penalty was rendered? Do you think execution was justified in these cases? Why or why not?
3. Selections 43 and 44 address the death penalty from opposing points of view. Discuss each author's evidence and choice of words. Which argument do you think is better supported? Which argument better represents your own views on the issue?
4. Working with a partner or group, find a recent article on the death penalty. Use your library's resources or do your research on the Internet. Read the article and take notes on the author's evidence. How does the author's evidence compare to that of Means and Wall? What new evidence or information does your article contain? Present your findings to the rest of the class.

Write About It

5. What have you learned from reading Selections 43 and 44 and the article you researched for item 4? Explain why your position on the death penalty either has or has not changed.
6. Write about someone you know who was the victim of a crime. Explain what happened and how it was resolved.

FIRST THOUGHTS

To build background for the reading selection, answer the following questions, either on your own or in a group discussion.

1. In your opinion, what is a "real American"?
2. Are you or your ancestors immigrants? If so, from what countries?
3. Preview the title, headnote, and first one or two paragraphs. What do you think will follow?

WORD ALERT

Each word below is followed by its paragraph number. Preview the words and definitions before reading. Then review them as necessary during reading. Use context clues and your dictionary to define any additional unfamiliar words.

immigrants (2) those who leave their native country to settle in another country
contemporary (3) current, of the present time or at the some time as an earlier event
immutable (4) unchanging, not susceptible to change
entrepreneurial (5) willing to assume the risk of a business venture
savvy (5) informed, perceptive, shrewd
inflation (9) a persistent increase in prices, bringing about a decline in purchasing power
descendant (11) one who comes after, someone descended from specified ancestors

◆ An Immigration Policy for "Real Americans"

JACK A. CHAMBLESS

Jack A. Chambless is an economics professor at Valencia Community College in Orlando, Florida. He emigrated from Germany in 1966.

HERE WE GO AGAIN. It seems that every few years someone looks around and starts 1 shouting that too many people are showing up on our shores, in our airports and in our labor markets.

Round 132 in the "Are **Immigrants** Destroying America?" debate is upon us, 2 and politicians from both sides of the aisle are frantically sticking their wet fingers in the political winds to see what Americans want this time.

What is unfortunate in this debate is that we keep ignoring all of the historical 3 and **contemporary** analysis that has been applied to this question, and we keep finding the same facts. We may not like the facts we are finding, but as Aldous Huxley once said, "Facts do not cease to exist because they are ignored."

So, what are the **immutable** truths about the folks who walk, fly and swim to 4 get here?

First, they create jobs, not destroy them. Immigrants from up and down the 5 wealth scale have proved to be incredibly **entrepreneurial**. Many technologically **savvy** immigrants from Western Europe and India helped create thousands of jobs in Silicon Valley. One in six of these companies was started by immigrants.

Many of America's best scientists, economists and engineers are not originally 6 from Kentucky or Florida or Maine. They are from Beijing, Moscow and Bangalore. This reality is because American kids can't do math and science, so Microsoft and Google have had to find these geniuses somewhere else.

Poorer immigrants have created thousands of restaurants, retail shops and 7 other service-based companies. One visit to San Francisco, New York or Chicago will show you how many native-born Americans are earning a paycheck because of the incredible efforts immigrants have put into our quasi-capitalistic market.

Immigrants without money and business plans have filled jobs in meat packing, 8 textiles, lawn care and restaurants that Americans simply won't take. Sadly, it is beneath the dignity of the average American to pick onions or cut fat off a pig 10 hours per day. Who is supposed to fill this gap?

Immigrants have also helped keep our rate of **inflation** down by supplying valu- 9 able labor in areas where shortages would otherwise exist. Imagine what the price of housing or restaurant meals would be if not for immigrant roofers and dishwashers with tremendous work ethics.

We can also thank immigrants for having lower crime rates, higher graduation 10 rates and lower participation in the welfare state than native-born Americans. Routinely, immigrants from the Caribbean show up, look around and find opportunity where many native-born Americans look around and give up on the chance to advance over time.

If I were president of the United States, I would fly to New York and read the 11 plaque on the Statue of Liberty. Then, I would go on television and announce to my fellow Americans that every one of us is a **descendant** of someone who originally was not from here. I might also mention that if we want to help India and China pass us up in the economic superpower game, the surest way of achieving that is to keep immigrants from those nations out.

12   I would also suggest that we are never going to win the war on terror if we do not let liberty-loving people from the Middle East come over here to find out why America is a nice place to live.

13   Finally, I would suggest that if we want to kick out the immigrants, we might want to look at our own history with respect to the first Americans, "real Americans." I seem to recall that when we showed up from Europe—as immigrants—we took away their property, forced them to move to less desirable places and killed many of those who resisted.

14   Perhaps then the best immigration policy of all would be for everyone who is not an American Indian—also known in politically correct terms as a Native American— to leave at once.

Comprehension Check

Purpose and Main Idea

1. What is the author's topic?
    a. immigration
    b. the economy
    c. labor laws
    d. real Americans
2. Which one of the following *best* states the central idea?
    a. Immigrants make up a large segment of the population.
    b. Native Americans are the only "real Americans."
    c. We should welcome immigrants because they are good for America.
    d. Something must be done to curb the number of immigrants coming to America.
3. The author's *primary* purpose is to
    a. entertain readers with anecdotes about immigrants.
    b. convince readers that they ought to support immigration.
    c. inform readers about immigrants' contributions.
    d. express an opinion about immigration.

Details

4. The author believes that immigrants will take jobs that Americans won't do.
    a. True
    b. False
5. According to the author, one in six Silicon Valley companies was started by immigrants.
    a. True
    b. False

6. The author provides which detail to support his view that immigrants have helped keep down the rate of inflation?
   a. taking jobs that Americans refuse to do
   b. being willing to work for low wages and few benefits
   c. creating retail jobs and service-based companies
   d. supplying labor in areas where shortages would exist
7. Which one of the following does the author *not* state as an "immutable truth" about America's immigrants?
   a. They have a lower crime rate.
   b. They are technologically savvy.
   c. Their graduation rates are higher.
   d. They lack an entrepreneurial spirit.
8. The words *first* (paragraph 5) and *also* (paragraph 10) suggest which pattern?
   a. process
   b. order or sequence
   c. listing of examples
   d. steps or stages

Inferences

9. Read the last paragraph. Is the author serious, or is he overstating to make a point? Explain your answer.
10. As an issue, how important is immigration to you? Is it more, less, or of about the same importance compared to other issues?

Working with Words

Complete sentences 1–7 with these words from Word Alert:

entrepreneurial	descendant	inflation	savvy
contemporary	immigrants	immutable	

1. The federal government raises interest rates to slow the economy and curb _____.
2. Many _____ have filled jobs in the textile and restaurant industries.
3. Some view the U.S. Constitution as _____, but others believe that our interpretation of it must change with the times.
4. Many of our _____ issues and concerns have historical roots.
5. As a _____ of Cherokee Indians, John wants to pass on his heritage to his children.
6. Those who are technologically _____ have no trouble learning to use new computers and software.
7. Those who have the _____ spirit build businesses and take economic risks.

   Write your own sentences, using any two of the words from Word Alert.

8. _____
9. _____

Thinking Deeper

Ideas for reflection, discussion, and writing

Make Inferences from Your Reading

1. The author says that Microsoft and Google have had to look overseas for scientists and engineers because "American kids can't do math and science." He also says that immigrants fill jobs that "Americans simply won't take." Are these statements valid inferences and how do you know, or how could you find out?

2. Immigrants have made many contributions to the American culture and economy. The author mentions several contributions. From your own experience, what inferences can you make about immigrants' contributions?

3. An issue under debate is whether to give amnesty to illegals. First of all, are you for or against amnesty for illegal immigrants? Second, suppose illegals were given amnesty. What can you infer would be the result, both economically and socially?

4. The author says in paragraph 10 that we can thank immigrants for having "lower crime rates, higher graduation rates, and lower participation in the welfare state than native-born Americans." As a research tool, the Internet can help you check facts for accuracy. For example, the U.S. government collects statistics on crime, education, and the use of its services. Select one piece of evidence from the article and research it. If you need help finding information, a librarian can point you to appropriate sites and databases and suggest search words and phrases.

Write About It

5. Do you know an immigrant who has overcome hardships to become successful? Do you have an immigrant relative whose story is an inspiration to your family? Write about an immigrant you admire.

6. Write about someone that you think is a "real American."

FIRST THOUGHTS

To build background for the reading selection, answer the following questions, either on your own or in a group discussion.

1. Should we expect immigrants to learn English, assimilate, and become citizens?
2. What do you believe are the rights and privileges of citizenship?
3. Preview the title, headnote, and first one or two paragraphs. What do you think will follow?

WORD ALERT

Each word below is followed by its paragraph number. Preview the words and definitions before reading. Then review them as necessary during reading. Use context clues and your dictionary to define any additional unfamiliar words.

bilingual (2) expressed in or able to speak two languages
republic (3) government whose citizens elect others to govern for them
amnesty (4) a general pardon, especially for political offenders
encroaching (9) taking another's possession or rights gradually or steadily
wanderlust (10) an irresistible desire or impulse to travel
unequivocal (11) without doubt or misunderstanding
indigenous (13) originating and living in an area or environment
assimilation (14) becoming similar, adopting the culture and practices of those around you

English Spoken Here

KATHLEEN PARKER

Kathleen Parker began her career in 1983. Her column is syndicated in 300 newspapers nationwide. She is an award-winning journalist who writes on social issues related to family, children, and gender. Parker is the director of the School of Written Expression at the Buckley School of Public Speaking and Persuasion in Camden, South Carolina.

Para español, oprima el dos.

1   EVEN IF ONE DOES NOT speak Spanish, most Americans are familiar with those words. They hear them nearly any time they make a call to the phone, utility or other company that offers service in two languages. "For Spanish, press two."

2   Even though I speak and love Spanish, I find myself increasingly annoyed by this unsubtle notice that the U.S. is gradually becoming a **bilingual** nation. And therein lies the source of much aggravation American citizens feel as Congress weighs in on illegal immigration.

3   Welcome to the U.S. one and all—within reason and according to the law—but all must become one if we are to remain a strong **republic**. That's the single most compelling truth we seem to know instinctively, even if no one is willing to say it.

4   Whatever one's views in the abstract regarding a guest-worker or modified **amnesty** program, the concrete reality is that many of those seeking to stay in the U.S. are not seeking also to become Americans of the U.S. variety. Indeed, the clear message from some of those protesting—and the content of many e-mails that found their way to my mailbox—is that Mexican immigrants are taking back what they consider to be theirs.

5   At least a segment of those protesting consider themselves to be neither immigrant nor illegal. Signs at one recent rally, for example, read "This is our country, not yours!" and "All Europeans are illegal." Reconquista is the word they choose to define their mission, meaning "reconquest."

6   An e-mailer suggested that I get myself ready for the boat back home because I—being of European descent—don't belong in the U.S. Only American Indians have a rightful claim to the lands my family has occupied since the 1600s, according to the writer's historical yardstick. And only Mexicans have a right to border states that formerly belonged to Mexico.

7   Well. Where to begin? More to the point, where to end?

8   If we're all going back to the nations of our origins, we're going to need a mighty big fleet and some sophisticated splicing equipment. I don't know about my correspondents, but I'm a little bit this and a little bit that, though most of my family names would place me in Ireland. I'm of course happy to reclaim the kingdom, but I'm not sure the present landowners in Connemara would welcome me back as the queen I'm certain I deserve to be.

9   The truth is, I doubt that most illegal immigrants now in the U.S. are interested in reclaiming conquered lands. Most just want a good job and a decent place to raise a family. But the sight of so many who feel entitled to a piece of the U.S.,

combined with a sense of **encroaching** bilingualism, contribute to a spirit of diminishing empathies among even the likeliest of sympathizers.

The idea of "reconquest," meanwhile, is silly. Human populations have been 10 migrating, conquering, surrendering and ceding for 60,000 years or so. We're a rambling sort by nature, apparently, and find national borders annoying obstacles to the **wanderlust** with which we were, for good or bad, endowed.

Rearranging borders and rewriting history to satisfy grudges or to right wrongs 11 would certainly keep us busy, but where would we draw the last line? In the ashes of human history, most likely. The only **unequivocal** ending to unhappy history, unfortunately, has no sequel. Only when everyone is dead is no one offended.

Barring the final solution, we might ask this: Do illegal Mexican immigrants 12 really want Texas or Arizona or California without the U.S. economy, or the U.S. social services, or the inspired government instruments that have made this country so attractive to so many?

That's the pinch, isn't it? The country's riches and benefits are not free for the 13 picking—nor are they all necessarily **indigenous** to the physical territory—but are part of a national package that demands citizenship of its citizenry.

Mexicans are as welcome as any other group of people—and we all came from 14 somewhere else, including the American Indians whose ancestors migrated from elsewhere—but reconquering, alas, requires a military action that could get messy. A simpler, more civilized course involves taking a number, waiting in line, and signing on to the principles of **assimilation**, without which we will not long be a united states of anything or a worthy destination for immigrants.

Para español, meanwhile, Mexico is lovely this time of year. 15

Comprehension Check

Purpose and Main Idea

1. What is the author's topic?
   a. immigration laws
   b. illegal immigration
   c. European immigrants
   d. immigrants' rights
2. Which sentence states the author's central idea?
   a. Paragraph 1 "Even if one does...."
   b. Paragraph 2 "Even though I speak...."
   c. Paragraph 3 "Welcome to the U.S...."
   d. Paragraph 4 "Whatever one's views...."
3. What is the author's purpose?
   a. to argue in favor of legal immigration
   b. to oppose immigration from Mexico
   c. to express a preference for English
   d. to remind us of the facts of history

Details

4. The author expresses annoyance at the prospect of the United States becoming a bilingual nation.
   a. True
   b. False
5. The author's view is that most Mexicans
   a. want to reclaim conquered lands.
   b. feel entitled to a piece of the United States.
   c. seek neither amnesty nor guest worker status.
   d. want a good job and a decent place to raise a family.
6. According to the author, hard work is the price of America's riches and benefits.
   a. True
   b. False
7. The author's details suggest an attitude of _____ toward immigrants.
   a. acceptance with conditions
   b. outright hostility
   c. benign indifference
   d. anger and contempt
8. What is the organizational pattern in paragraph 5?
   a. contrast
   b. process
   c. sequence
   d. definition

Inferences

9. Are the author's statements in paragraph 3 valid or invalid inferences? Why or why not?
10. Do you agree with the author that the country's "riches and benefits" are part of a "national package that demands citizenship"? If so, why, and if not, then who should reap the benefits and under what conditions?

Working with Words

Complete sentences 1–8 with these words from Word Alert:

assimilation   wanderlust   indigenous   republic
unequivocal   encroaching   bilingual   amnesty

1. The child's mother spoke in _____ terms when she said, "Do not stick your finger in the electrical outlet."
2. Those whose _____ is complete speak the language and adopt the customs of their new countries.
3. Plants that are _____ to an area may not grow well in other places.
4. My mother's _____ takes her to a different country every summer.
5. The American government is described as a democracy within a _____.

6. Opinion is divided on whether illegal immigrants should be given _____ or suffer some penalty for breaking the law.
7. The weeds in my garden are _____ at such a rate that they may soon take over.
8. A person who is _____ may have an edge in seeking a job with an international company.

Write your own sentences, using any two of the words from Word Alert.

9. _____
10. _____

Thinking Deeper

Ideas for reflection, discussion, and writing

Make Inferences from Your Reading

1. Immigration is a hot topic that has been under debate in Congress for several years. Strengthening the Mexican/American border, whether illegals should receive services and benefits, and other related matters have sparked controversy. Making inferences from what you have read, either in this article or elsewhere, define the issues as you see them. What should be our greatest concern, and why?
2. Compare and contrast the views on immigration presented in Selections 45 and 46. On what do the authors disagree? Do they have any points of agreement? Which argument is more convincing to you, and why?
3. Selections 45 and 46 offer two perspectives on immigration. What is your perspective? If you could write your own immigration policy, what would it be?
4. Kathleen Parker is a respected and widely syndicated columnist. To access more of her articles or to find out more about her, do a Google search on her name. Based on the topics she writes about and the perspectives she takes, what can you infer are her political views? Remember that sites and URLs change frequently, so seek help if you need it.

Write About It

5. If you could live or work in another country, where would you go and why?
6. What do you expect from anyone who chooses to make his or her home in the United States or in any other country for that matter?

FIRST THOUGHTS

To build background for the reading selection, answer the following questions, either on your own or in a group discussion.

1. Do you enjoy reading poetry? Why or why not?
2. Do you have a favorite poem? If so, what is it and why do you like it?
3. Preview the title, headnote, and first two lines of the poem. What do you think will follow?

WORD ALERT

Each word below is followed by its line number. Preview the words and definitions before reading. Then review them as necessary during reading. Use context clues and your dictionary to define any additional unfamiliar words.

waltzing (4) dancing in triple time with a strong accent on the first beat, moving lightly and easily

romped (5) played or frolicked boisterously

countenance (7) face, facial expression

scraped (12) rubbed with considerable pressure

caked (14) coated, encrusted

◈ My Papa's Waltz

THEODORE ROETHKE

Theodore Roethke (1908–1963) is a critically acclaimed author whose poems explore both the natural and psychological worlds. Before he died, he was poet in residence at the University of Washington.

The whiskey on your breath	1
Could make a small boy dizzy;	2
But I hung on like death:	3
Such waltzing was not easy.	4
We romped until the pans	5
Slid from the kitchen shelf;	6
My mother's countenance.	7
Could not unfrown itself.	8
The hand that held my wrist	9
Was battered on one knuckle;	10
At every step you missed	11
My right ear scraped a buckle.	12
You beat time on my head	13
With a palm caked hard by dirt,	14
Then waltzed me off to bed	15
Still clinging to your shirt.	16

Comprehension Check

Purpose and Main Idea

1. What is the author's topic?
   a. family life
   b. a son's relationship with his father
   c. dancing the waltz
   d. working-class values
2. What is the poem's central idea?
   a. The working class values home life.
   b. Families must cope with many problems.
   c. A man looks back on life with his father.
   d. The waltz is a type of ballroom dancing.
3. The author's *primary* purpose is to
   a. persuade readers that some types of play can be dangerous.
   b. inform readers about the waltz as a type of dance.
   c. entertain readers with the antics of a father and son.
   d. express a feeling about a particular relationship.

Details

4. The mother in this poem seems to enjoy watching her son play with his father.
   a. True
   b. False
5. This poem's setting is a kitchen.
   a. True
   b. False
6. Which one of the following words best describes the poem's tone?
   a. serious
   b. distressed
   c. playful
   d. ironic
7. A "palm caked hard by dirt" suggests that the father
   a. is a farm laborer.
   b. does not keep himself clean.
   c. is unconcerned about his appearance.
   d. works in the soil with his hands.
8. Which one of the following seems the most likely reason that the father misses steps (lines 11 and 12)?
   a. He has been drinking.
   b. He is clumsy.
   c. The boy is heavy.
   d. He is not keeping time.

Inferences

9. Read the poem aloud, paying attention to the end-rhyme and the rhythm, or beat, in the lines. Why do you think Roethke wrote the poem in this form?
10. Why is the mother frowning? What do you think is her attitude toward the father's "waltz"? Explain your reasons.

Working with Words

Complete sentences 1–5 with these words from Word Alert.

countenance   waltzing   romped   scraped   caked

1. When we were children, we _____ and ran around the neighborhood until we were tired.
2. Most people have fallen and ended up with a painful _____ knee or elbow.
3. Children who disobey their mother can tell by her _____ whether she is angry.
4. Jennifer enjoys ballroom dancing, such as _____ or doing the fox trot.
5. Don't tell me you haven't been eating candy because I can see the chocolate _____ around your mouth.

Write your own sentences, using any two of the words from Word Alert.

6. _____

7. _____

Thinking Deeper

Ideas for reflection, discussion, and writing

Make Inferences from Your Reading

1. Why do you think people write about their childhood? Why do readers enjoy reading about family relationships? What makes relationships between men and women, parents and children good topics for literature and other forms of entertainment or self-expression? What inferences can you make to answer these questions?
2. What do you like best about Roethke's poem: the theme, his choice of words, the rhyme, or something else? Explain your reasons.
3. The relationship between a parent and a child is a recurrent theme in all of literature. Whether blessed with a happy childhood or burdened with a painful one, everyone has a story to tell or a memory to relate about a parent. In Roethke's poem, a son remembers playing with his father before bedtime. What is one memory from your childhood, involving your mother, father, or other caretaker that has special significance for you?
4. Using your library's online catalog, find a book of Theodore Roethke's poems. Skim the contents, looking for the titles of several poems that appeal to you. Read the poems and choose one to write about or share in a class discussion.

Write About It

5. Explain why a certain poem or other piece of writing has a special meaning for you.
6. Choose one experience from your childhood that suggests the type of relationship you had with a parent or other family member.

FIRST THOUGHTS

To build background for the reading selection, answer the following questions, either on your own or in a group discussion.

1. What do you know about the poet Robert Hayden?
2. Do you have a favorite poet or other author, and what do you like about his or her work?
3. Preview the title, headnote, and first two lines of the poem. What do you think will follow?

WORD ALERT

Each word below is followed by its line number. Preview the words and definitions before reading. Then review them as necessary during reading. Use context clues and your dictionary to define any additional unfamiliar words.

blueblack (2) very dark blue
banked (5) covered with ashes or fuel for continued low burning
splintering (6) breaking into sharp, slender pieces
indifferently (10) having no particular interest in or concern for
austere (14) strict or severe in discipline
offices (14) duties or functions

◆ Those Winter Sundays

ROBERT HAYDEN

Robert Hayden (1913–1980) was a fellow of the Academy of American Poets. Hayden served two terms as poetry consultant to the Library of Congress and was a professor of English at the University of Michigan.

Sundays too my father got up early	1
and put his clothes on in the blueblack cold,	2
then with cracked hands that ached	3
from labor in the weekday weather made	4
banked fires blaze. No one ever thanked him.	5
I'd wake and hear the cold splintering, breaking.	6
When the rooms were warm, he'd call,	7
and slowly I would rise and dress,	8
fearing the chronic angers of that house,	9
Speaking indifferently to him,	10
who had driven out the cold	11
and polished my good shoes as well.	12
What did I know, what did I know	13
of love's austere and lonely offices?	14

Comprehension Check

Purpose and Main Idea

1. What is the author's topic?
   a. Sunday
   b. a father
   c. family
   d. olden times
2. What is the poem's central idea?
   a. Life was harder in the days before central heating.
   b. Family relationships are complex and hard to explain.
   c. For some people, Sunday is like any other day.
   d. A father's love and sacrifice often goes unappreciated.
3. The author's *primary* purpose is to
   a. inform readers about life at a particular time.
   b. persuade readers to be kinder to their parents.
   c. express an idea or feeling about a father.
   d. entertain us with a story from the past.

Details

4. The situation described in the poem is that of a father warming the house so that the family can dress for church.
   a. True
   b. False
5. Based on the details, the father does physical labor, such as construction or farming.
   a. True
   b. False
6. Which word best describes the tone of the poem's speaker?
   a. angry
   b. sentimental
   c. regretful
   d. cheerful
7. All of the following describe the father *except*
   a. indifferent.
   b. family man.
   c. hard working.
   d. dutiful.
8. In line 9, what does *chronic* mean?
   a. painful
   b. continuing
   c. hopeless
   d. incurable

Inferences

9. What is the child's attitude toward the father? Make inferences from the poem's details to explain your answer.
10. Explain the meaning of the last two lines.

Working with Words

Complete sentences 1–6 with these words from Word Alert:

indifferently	blueblack	offices
splintering	austere	banked

1. Most people perform the _____ of house and yard work dutifully and without thanks.
2. The twinkling stars provided the only light in the _____ midnight sky.
3. Sparsely furnished and lacking any decoration, the room seemed _____ and uninviting.
4. Not caring one way or the other, the student answered the question _____.
5. A fire that has been _____ at bedtime is easy to start in the morning.

6. Watch how you hammer that nail because you want to keep the wood from _____.

Write your own sentences, using any two of the words from Word Alert.

7. _____

8. _____

Thinking Deeper

Ideas for reflection, discussion, and writing

Make Inferences from Your Reading

1. Because a poet has to pack a lot of information into a few lines, every word must count. What word or words in Hayden's poem do you think are especially effective and why?
2. Much of a poem's meaning is related through *images*, words and ideas that create vivid pictures in our minds and help us connect the poet's meaning to our own lives and experience. For example, *cracked hands* (line 3) is an image that suggests hard work. Choose one image from the poem and explain the meaning that you infer from it.
3. Hayden's poem and Roethke's poem (Selection 47) are both about recollections from childhood. What similarities and differences do you see between the ways these poems are written, the themes they explore, and their effect on you?
4. It is easy to find a poem on the Internet if you know its title. Type the title of the poem in quotation marks as your search phrase, which will generate a list of sites to try. One site is http://www.agonia.net. Another good one is Poet's Corner. URLs change, so a librarian may have other suggestions. For another perspective on fathers, find and read "Photograph of My Father in His Twenty-Second Year" by Raymond Carver. Compare this poem to "Those Winter Sundays" and "My Papa's Waltz," and be prepared to discuss all three poems in class. Use the situation described in each poem, the poet's choice of words, and each poem's overall meaning as discussion points.

Write About It

5. What would you like most for your son or daughter to remember about you?
6. Reflect on something your mother or father did for you and for which you never expressed your thanks. Then write about it and express your gratitude.

FIRST THOUGHTS

To build background for the reading selection, answer the following questions, either on your own or in a group discussion.

1. What do you know, or what have you read, about Martin Luther King, Jr.?
2. What do you know, or what have you read, about the civil rights movement of the 1950s and 1960s?
3. Preview the title, headnote, and first one or two paragraphs. What do you think will follow?

WORD ALERT

Each word below is followed by its paragraph number. Preview the words and definitions before reading. Then review them as necessary during reading. Use context clues and your dictionary to define any additional unfamiliar words.

seared (1) scorched, burned

manacles (2) handcuffs

languishing (2) neglected or unattended, existing in miserable conditions

defaulted (4) failed to fulfill an obligation

sweltering (5) oppressively hot

tranquility (5) calmness, serenity

ghetto (7) section of a city occupied by a minority group, often because of economic or social pressure

hew (19) cut, carve out

prodigious (21) great in size or force

◈ I Have a Dream

MARTIN LUTHER KING, JR.

Martin Luther King, Jr., was a minister and leader of the civil rights movement during the 1950s and 1960s. A martyr for his cause, King was assassinated on April 4, 1968, at the age of 39. The following selection is a speech King delivered on the occasion of the march on Washington, D.C., on August 28, 1963. This appeal for racial justice and equality still inspires readers.

FIVE SCORE YEARS AGO, a great American, in whose symbolic shadow we stand, 1 signed the Emancipation Proclamation. This momentous decree came as a great beacon light of hope to millions of Negro slaves who had been **seared** in the flames of withering injustice. It came as a joyous daybreak to end the long night of captivity.

But one hundred years later, we must face the tragic fact that the Negro is still 2 not free. One hundred years later, the life of the Negro is still sadly crippled by the **manacles** of segregation and the chains of discrimination. One hundred years later, the Negro lives on a lonely island of poverty in the midst of a vast ocean of material prosperity. One hundred years later, the Negro is still **languishing** in the corners of American society and finds himself an exile in his own land. So we have come here today to dramatize an appalling condition.

In a sense we have come to our nation's capital to cash a check. When the 3 architects of our republic wrote the magnificent words of the Constitution and the Declaration of Independence, they were signing a promissory note to which every American was to fall heir. This note was a promise that all men—yes, black men as well as white men—would be guaranteed the unalienable rights of life, liberty, and the pursuit of happiness.

It is obvious today that America has **defaulted** on this promissory note insofar 4 as her citizens of color are concerned. Instead of honoring this sacred obligation, America has given the Negro people a bad check, a check which has come back marked "insufficient funds." But we refuse to believe that there are insufficient funds in the great vaults of opportunity of this nation. So we have come to cash this check—a check that will give us upon demand the riches of freedom and the security of justice. We have also come to this hallowed spot to remind America of the fierce urgency of now. This is no time to engage in the luxury of cooling off or to take the tranquilizing drugs of gradualism. Now is the time to make real the promises of Democracy. Now is the time to rise from the dark and desolate valley of segregation to the sunlit path of racial justice. Now is the time to open the doors of opportunity to all of God's children. Now is the time to lift our nation from the quicksands of racial injustice to the solid rock of brotherhood.

It would be fatal for the nation to overlook the urgency of the moment and 5 to underestimate the determination of the Negro. This **sweltering** summer of the Negro's legitimate discontent will not pass until there is an invigorating autumn of freedom and equality; 1963 is not an end, but a beginning. Those who hope that the Negro needed to blow off steam and will now be content will have a rude awakening if the nation returns to business as usual. There will be neither rest nor **tranquility** in America until the Negro is granted his citizenship rights. The whirlwinds of revolt will continue to shake the foundations of our nation until the bright day of justice emerges.

6　　But there is something that I must say to my people who stand on the warm threshold which leads into the palace of justice. In the process of gaining our rightful place we must not be guilty of wrongful deeds. Let us not seek to satisfy our thirst for freedom by drinking from the cup of bitterness and hatred. We must forever conduct our struggle on the high plane of dignity and discipline. We must not allow our creative protest to degenerate into physical violence. Again and again we must rise to the majestic heights of meeting physical force with soul force. The marvelous new militancy which has engulfed the Negro community must not lead us to a distrust of all white people, for many of our white brothers, as evidenced by their presence here today, have come to realize that their destiny is tied up with our destiny and their freedom is inextricably bound to our freedom. We cannot walk alone.

7　　And as we walk, we must make the pledge that we shall march ahead. We cannot turn back. There are those who are asking the devotees of civil rights, "When will you be satisfied?" We can never be satisfied as long as the Negro is the victim of the unspeakable horrors of police brutality. We can never be satisfied as long as our bodies, heavy with the fatigue of travel, cannot gain lodging in the motels of the highways and the hotels of the cities. We cannot be satisfied as long as the Negro's basic mobility is from a smaller **ghetto** to a larger one. We can never be satisfied as long as a Negro in Mississippi cannot vote and a Negro in New York believes he has nothing for which to vote. No, no, we are not satisfied, and we will not be satisfied until justice rolls down like waters and righteousness like a mighty stream.

8　　I am not unmindful that some of you have come here out of great trials and tribulations. Some of you have come fresh from narrow jail cells. Some of you have come from areas where your quest for freedom left you battered by the storms of persecution and staggered by the winds of police brutality. You have been the veterans of creative suffering. Continue to work with the faith that unearned suffering is redemptive.

9　　Go back to Mississippi, go back to Alabama, go back to South Carolina, go back to Georgia, go back to Louisiana, go back to the slums and ghettos of our northern cities, knowing that somehow this situation can and will be changed. Let us not wallow in the valley of despair.

10　　I say to you today, my friends, that in spite of the difficulties and frustrations of the moment I still have a dream. It is a dream deeply rooted in the American dream.

11　　I have a dream that one day this nation will rise up and live out the true meaning of its creed: "We hold these truths to be self-evident, that all men are created equal."

12　　I have a dream that one day on the red hills of Georgia the sons of former slaves and the sons of former slaveowners will be able to sit down together at the table of brotherhood.

13　　I have a dream that one day even the state of Mississippi, a desert state sweltering with the heat of injustice and oppression, will be transformed into an oasis of freedom and justice.

I have a dream that my four little children will one day live in a nation where 14 they will not be judged by the color of their skin but by the content of their character.

I have a dream today. 15

I have a dream that one day the state of Alabama, whose governor's lips are 16 presently dripping with the words of interposition and nullification, will be transformed into a situation where little black boys and black girls will be able to join hands with little white boys and white girls and walk together as sisters and brothers.

I have a dream today. 17

I have a dream that one day every valley shall be exalted, every hill and moun- 18 tain shall be made low, the rough places will be made plain, and the crooked places will be made straight, and the glory of the Lord shall be revealed, and all flesh shall see it together.

This is our hope. This is the faith with which I return to the South. With this 19 faith we will be able to **hew** out of the mountain of despair a stone of hope. With this faith we will be able to transform the jangling discords of our nation into a beautiful symphony of brotherhood. With this faith we will be able to work together, to pray together, to struggle together, to go to jail together, to stand up for freedom together, knowing that we will be free one day.

This will be the day when all of God's children will be able to sing with new 20 meaning

My country, 'tis of thee,
Sweet land of liberty,
  Of thee I sing:
Land where my fathers died,
Land of the pilgrims' pride,
From every mountainside,
  Let freedom ring.

So let freedom ring from the **prodigious** hilltops of New Hampshire. Let free- 21 dom ring from the mighty mountains of New York. Let freedom ring from the heightening Alleghenies of Pennsylvania. Let freedom ring from the snowcapped Rockies of Colorado. Let freedom ring from the curvaceous peaks of California.

But not only that. Let freedom ring from Stone Mountain of Georgia. Let free- 22 dom ring from Lookout Mountain of Tennessee. Let freedom ring from every hill and molehill of Mississippi. From every mountainside, let freedom ring.

When we let freedom ring, when we let it ring from every village and every 23 hamlet, from every state and every city, we will be able to speed up that day when all of God's children, black men and white men, Jews and Gentiles, Protestants and Catholics, will be able to join hands and sing in the words of the old Negro spiritual, "Free at last! Free at last! Thank God almighty, we are free at last!"

Comprehension Check

Purpose and Main Idea

1. The author's topic is
   a. racial justice.
   b. freedom.
   c. democracy.
   d. segregation.
2. The central idea of this selection is stated in
   a. paragraph 1, first sentence "Five score years...."
   b. paragraph 2, first sentence "But one hundred...."
   c. paragraph 4, eighth sentence "Now is the time to rise...."
   d. paragraph 10, first sentence "I say to you...."
3. The author's *primary* purpose is to
   a. inform us that a problem exists.
   b. entertain us with his dreams for the future.
   c. express his anger and indignation.
   d. persuade us to put an end to racial injustice.

Details

4. The "great American" referred to in paragraph 1 is Abraham Lincoln.
   a. True
   b. False
5. According to King, blacks were not free because of
   a. their inalienable rights.
   b. a constitutional amendment.
   c. segregation and discrimination.
   d. the Emancipation Proclamation.
6. In paragraph 6, King cautions his followers to avoid protest.
   a. True
   b. False
7. In paragraph 5, the author's pattern is
   a. comparison and contrast.
   b. cause and effect.
   c. generalization then example.
   d. definition.
8. In paragraphs 10–18, the author's pattern is
   a. comparison and contrast.
   b. cause and effect.
   c. generalization then example.
   d. definition.

Inferences

9. What is King's meaning in paragraph 5, first sentence?
10. What meaning do you infer from this sentence in paragraph 7: "The Negro's basic mobility is from a smaller ghetto to a larger one"?

Working with Words

Complete sentences 1–9 with these words from Word Alert:

tranquility	prodigious	seared
languishing	defaulted	ghetto
sweltering	manacles	hew

1. The prisoner was brought in ——————— to the jail.
2. The student's books lay ——————— in the corner, covered with dust from disuse.
3. Leaders of all races have said that education is the way out of the ——————— and the key to economic and social mobility.
4. Looking out our window, we watched rain clouds form over the ——————— hills beyond.
5. On a ——————— summer day, it is a good idea to stay in the shade.
6. Because of having ——————— on a loan, Chris's credit was ruined.
7. Before putting the roast in the oven, Grandma ——————— it on all sides to seal in the juices.
8. A crater on the moon is called The Sea of ———————, probably because it looks so calm.
9. One who is accomplished at woodworking is able to ——————— out of a block of wood an object of great beauty.

Write your own sentences, using any two of the words from Word Alert.

10. ——————————————————————————————
11. ——————————————————————————————

Thinking Deeper

Ideas for reflection, discussion, and writing

Make Inferences from your Reading

1. King's speech enumerates the "promises of democracy," the cherished freedoms that are the rights of citizenship in the United States. Study the selection to find where these rights and freedoms are stated. Then make inferences about their importance, how they affect your life, and what life would be like without them. Share your views in a class discussion.
2. Discuss paragraphs 10–18. How far have we come since 1963 when King gave this speech? What parts of the dream have been realized? What remains to be accomplished?

3. King's perspective was that more good could be accomplished by nonviolent protest than with violence. Malcolm X and groups like the Black Panthers disagreed. Perhaps history has decided, because of all the prominent African American voices of the 1960s, Martin Luther King's is the one that is most remembered and revered. What do you think?

4. King's 1963 speech was televised, and clips of it have been widely shown since. In February, Black History Month, the speech often plays on TV specials. To access the text and video of the speech, go to http://www.americanrhetoric. com/speeches/ihaveadream.html. Remember that URLs change, so get help from your instructor or librarian if you need it. As you listen to the speech, pay attention to King's delivery, then be prepared to answer these questions in a group discussion: (a) What parts of the speech are especially moving or powerful? (b) What did you notice when listening to the speech that you did not notice when reading it?

Write About It

5. Write about an African American who is a source of inspiration for you.
6. What is one experience that you or someone close to you has had with discrimination?

FIRST THOUGHTS

To build background for the reading selection, answer the following questions, either on your own or in a group discussion.

1. What is the difference between prejudice and stereotypes?
2. What causes some people to discriminate against others?
3. Preview the title, headnote, and first one or two paragraphs. What do you think will follow?

WORD ALERT

Each word below is followed by its paragraph number. Preview the words and definitions before reading. Then review them as necessary during reading. Use context clues and your dictionary to define any additional unfamiliar words.

In a textbook chapter, the words to watch may appear in boldface, in italics, or in a special color.

stereotypes (1) the perceptions, beliefs, and expectations that a person has about members of a certain group

schemas (1) ideas about the world based on past experience and expectations

prejudice (3) a positive or negative attitude toward people in certain groups

discrimination (3) differential treatment of people in different groups

cognitive (7) relating to the mental processes underlying all aspects of human thought

contact hypothesis (10) the idea that stereotypes or prejudice toward a group will decrease as contact with the group increases

Prejudice and Stereotypes

DOUGLAS A. BERNSTEIN AND PEGGY W. NASH

This textbook reading is excerpted from Chapter 14 of *Essentials of Psychology*, Fourth Edition. The entire chapter is about social psychology. The excerpt focuses on two types of social behavior: prejudice and stereotyping. When you read from textbooks, remember that headings may signal topics, main ideas, or important details.

1 ALL OF THE principles behind impression formation, attribution, and attitudes come together in prejudice and stereotypes. **Stereotypes** are the perceptions, beliefs, and expectations a person has about members of some group. They are **schemas** about entire groups of people (Dion, 2003). Usually, they involve the false assumption that all members of a group share the same characteristics. The characteristics that make up the stereotype can be positive, but more often they are negative. The most prevalent and powerful stereotypes focus on observable personal attributes, particularly ethnicity, gender, and age (Operario & Fiske, 2001).

2 The stereotypes people hold can be so ingrained that their effects on behavior can be automatic and unconscious (Banaji, Lemm, & Carpenter, 2001; Blair, Judd, & Fallman, 2004). In one study, for example, European American and African American participants played a video game in which white or black men suddenly appeared on a screen, holding an object that might be a weapon (Correll et al., 2002). The participants had to immediately "shoot" armed men but not unarmed ones. Under this time pressure, participants' errors were not random. If they "shot" an unarmed man, he was more likely to be black than white; when they failed to "shoot" an armed man, he was more likely to be white than black. These differences appeared in both European American and African American participants, but was most pronounced among those who held the strongest cultural stereotypes about blacks.

3 Stereotyping often leads to **prejudice**, which is a positive or negative attitude toward an individual based simply on that individual's membership in some group (Dion, 2003). The word prejudice means "to prejudge." Many theorists believe that prejudice, like other attitudes, has cognitive, affective, and behavioral components. Stereotyped thinking is the cognitive component of prejudicial attitudes. The hatred, admiration, anger, and other feelings people have about stereotyped groups constitute the affective component. The behavioral component of prejudice involves **discrimination**, which is differing treatment of individuals who belong to different groups.

THEORIES OF PREJUDICE AND STEREOTYPING

4 Prejudice and stereotyping may occur for several reasons. Let's consider three explanatory theories, each of which has been supported by research and accounts for many instances of stereotyping and prejudice.

MOTIVATIONAL THEORIES

For some people, prejudice serves to meet certain needs and increases their sense of security. This idea was first proposed by Theodor W. Adorno and his associates more than fifty years ago (Adorno et al., 1950) and was elaborated more recently by Bob Altemeyer (1996, 2004). These researchers suggest that prejudice is especially likely among people who display a personality trait called authoritarianism. According to Altemeyer, authoritarianism is composed of three main elements: (1) acceptance of conventional or traditional values, (2) willingness to unquestioningly follow the orders of authority figures, and (3) an inclination to act aggressively toward individuals or groups identified by authority figures as threats to the person's values or well-being. In fact, people with an authoritarian orientation tend to view the world as a threatening place (Winter, 1996). One way to protect themselves from the threats they perceive all around them is to strongly identify with people like themselves—their in-group—and to reject, dislike, and maybe even punish people from groups that are different from their own (Cottrell & Neuberg, 2005). Looking down on, and discriminating against, members of these out-groups—such as gay men and lesbians, African Americans, or Muslims, for example—may help authoritarian people feel safer and better about themselves (Haddock & Zanna, 1998).

Another motivational explanation of prejudice involves the concept of social identity discussed earlier. Recall that whether or not they display authoritarianism, most people are motivated to identify with their in-group and tend to see it as better than other groups (Brewer & Pierce, 2005). As a result, members of an in-group often see all members of out-groups as less attractive and less socially acceptable than members of the in-group and may thus treat them badly (Jackson, 2002). In other words, prejudice may result when people's motivation to enhance their own self-esteem causes them to disrespect other people.

COGNITIVE THEORIES

Stereotyping and prejudice may also result from the thought processes that people use in dealing with the world. There are so many other people, so many situations in which we meet them, and so many behaviors that others might display that we cannot possibly attend to and remember them all. Therefore, people must use schemas and other **cognitive** shortcuts to organize and make sense of their social world (Moskowitz, 2005). Often these cognitive processes provide accurate and useful summaries of other people, but sometimes they lead to inaccurate stereotypes.

For example, one effective way to deal with social complexity is to group people into social categories. Rather than remembering every detail about everyone we have ever encountered, we tend to put other people into categories such as doctor, senior citizen, Republican, student, Italian, and the like (Dovidio, Kawakami, & Gaertner, 2000). To further simplify perception of these categories, we tend to see group members as being quite similar to one another. This tendency can be seen in the fact that members of one ethnic group may find it harder to distinguish among specific faces in other ethnic groups than in their own (Anthony, Cooper, & Mullen, 1992; Michel et al., 2006). People also tend to assume that all members of a different group hold the same beliefs and values and that those beliefs and values differ from those of their own group (Dion, 2003). Finally, because particularly noticeable stimuli tend to draw a lot of attention, rude behavior by even a few members of an easily identified ethnic group may lead people to see an illusory correlation between rudeness and ethnicity (Hamilton & Sherman, 1994). As a result, they may incorrectly believe that all members of that group are rude.

LEARNING THEORIES

9 Like other attitudes, prejudice can be learned. Some prejudice is learned as a result of personal conflicts with members of different groups, but people also develop negative attitudes toward groups with whom they have had little or no contact. Learning theories suggest that children can pick up prejudices just by watching and listening to parents, peers, and others (Rohan & Zanna, 1996). There may even be a form of biopreparedness (described in the learning chapter) that makes us especially likely to learn to fear people who are strangers or who look different from us (Olson et al., 2001). Movies and television also portray ethnic or other groups in ways that teach stereotypes and prejudice (Brehm et al., 2005). One study revealed that local news coverage often gives the impression that African Americans are responsible for a higher percentage of crimes than is actually the case (Romer, Jamieson, & deCoteau, 1998). No wonder so many young children know about the supposed negative characteristics of other ethnic groups, sometimes long before they ever meet people in those groups (Baron & Banaji, 2006; Quintana, 1998).

REDUCING PREJUDICE

10 One clear implication of the cognitive and learning theories of prejudice and stereotyping is that members of one group are often ignorant or misinformed about the characteristics of people in other groups. Before 1954, for example, most black and white schoolchildren in the United States knew very little about one another because they went to separate schools. Then the Supreme Court declared that segregated public schools should be prohibited. In doing so, the court created a real-life test of the **contact hypothesis,** which states that stereotypes and prejudice toward a group will decrease as contact with that group increases (Pettigrew & Tropp, 2006).

11   Did the desegregation of U.S. schools confirm the contact hypothesis? In a few schools, integration was followed by a decrease in prejudice, but in most places, either no change occurred or prejudice actually increased (Oskamp & Schultz, 1998). However, these results did not necessarily disprove the contact hypothesis. In-depth studies of schools with successful desegregation suggested that contact alone was not enough. Integration reduced prejudice only when certain social conditions were created (Pettigrew & Tropp, 2006). First, members of the two groups had to be of roughly equal social and economic status. Second, school authorities had to promote cooperation and interdependence between ethnic groups by having members of the two groups work together on projects that required reliance on one another to achieve success. Third, the contact between group members had to occur on a one-to-one basis. It was only when individuals got to know each other that the

errors contained in stereotypes became apparent. Finally, the members of each group had to be seen as typical and not unusual in any significant way. When these four conditions were met, the children's attitudes toward one another became more positive.

Elliot Aronson (Aronson & Patnoe, 2000) describes a teaching strategy, called 12 the jigsaw technique, that helps create these conditions. Children from several ethnic groups must work together on a team to complete a task, such as writing a report about a famous person in history. Each child learns a separate piece of information about this person, such as place of birth or greatest achievement, then provides this information to the team (Aronson, 1990). Studies show that children from various ethnic groups who take part in the jigsaw technique and other cooperative learning experiences display substantial reductions in prejudice toward other groups (e.g., Aronson, 1997). The success reported in these studies has greatly increased the popularity of cooperative learning exercises in U.S. classrooms. Such exercises may not eliminate all aspects of ethnic prejudice in children, but they seem to be a step in the right direction.

Can friendly, cooperative, interdependent contact reduce the more entrenched 13 forms of prejudice seen in adults? It may. When equal-status adults from different ethnic groups work jointly toward a common goal, bias and distrust can be reduced, particularly among those in ethnic majority groups (Tropp & Pettigrew, 2005). This is especially true if they come to see themselves as members of the same group rather than as belonging to opposing groups (Dovidio, Kawakami, & Gaertner, 2000; Fiske, 2000). The challenge to be met in creating such cooperative experiences in the real world is that the participants must be of equal status—a challenge made more difficult in many countries by the status differences that still exist between ethnic groups (Dixon, Durrheim, & Tredoux, 2005; Kenworthy et al., 2006).

In the final analysis, contact can provide only part of the solution to the prob- 14 lems of stereotyping, prejudice, and discrimination. To reduce ethnic prejudice, we must develop additional techniques to address the social cognitions and perceptions that lie at the core of bigotry and hatred toward people who are different from ourselves (Monteith, Zuwerink, & Devine, 1994). Altering these mental processes will be difficult because, as we saw earlier, they can operate both consciously and unconsciously, causing even those who do not see themselves as prejudiced to discriminate against individuals who are different (Banaji et al., 2001; Uleman, Blader, & Todorov, 2005). However, recent research suggests that it may be possible to change even unconscious forms of stereotyping and prejudice (Kawakami, Dovidio, & van Kamp, 2005; Plant & Peruche, 2005; Wheeler & Fiske, 2005).

Comprehension Check

Purpose and Main Idea

1. What is the authors' topic?
   a. social psychology
   b. discrimination
   c. prejudice and stereotypes
   d. personality theories

2. What is the authors' central idea?
   a. Prejudice and stereotyping occur in many societies.
   b. Several theories explain prejudice and stereotyping.
   c. Prejudice and stereotypes are common research subjects.
   d. Some people experience prejudice or stereotyping more often than others.
3. The authors' *primary* purpose is to
   a. inform readers about the reasons behind prejudice and stereotypes.
   b. express their opinions on prejudice and stereotyping.
   c. entertain readers with examples of people who have overcome prejudice in their lives.
   d. persuade readers that discrimination is an ingrained behavior that cannot be changed.

Details

4. According to the authors, the most prevalent and powerful stereotypes focus on behavior.
   a. True
   b. False
5. Which theories account for the fact that people can develop negative attitudes toward groups with whom they have had little or no contact?
   a. motivational theories
   b. behavioral theories
   c. cognitive theories
   d. learning theories
6. According to the authors, *authoritarianism* is characterized by all but which one of the following?
   a. aggressiveness toward those seen as threatening
   b. acceptance of traditional or conventional values
   c. identification with all members of society
   d. willingness to follow orders unquestioningly
7. An illusory correlation explains why people tend to attribute the behaviors of a few group members to the group as a whole.
   a. True
   b. False
8. What is the *dominant* pattern by which the ideas in the entire excerpt are organized?
   a. Cause and effect: The authors explain what causes prejudice and stereotyping.
   b. Definition: The authors define prejudice and stereotyping.
   c. Sequence: The authors explain how prejudice develops.
   d. Classification: The authors group common stereotypes into categories.

Inferences

9. In paragraph 13 the authors ask this question: "Can friendly, cooperative, interdependent contact reduce the more entrenched forms of prejudice seen in adults?" How would you answer this question? Give an example from your own experience that supports your answer.
10. Give a real-world example of an *illusory correlation*.

Working with Words

Complete sentences 1–6 with these words from Word Alert:

contact hypothesis	cognitive	stereotypes
discrimination	prejudice	schemas

1. Various groups have been accused of _____ because they did not allow people of a certain sex or ethnic group to be members.
2. Decision making, problem solving, and imagining are only three of the mental activities involved in _____ processing.
3. Children who fear dogs may have formed negative _____ about them based on past encounters.
4. People who think all the members of a certain ethnic group look alike or behave similarly are reacting to _____.
5. According to the _____, prejudice toward a group may decrease as interaction with members of that group increases.
6. A negative attitude toward someone based on his or her race is but one example of _____.

    Write your own sentences, using any two of the words from Word Alert.

7. _____
8. _____

Thinking Deeper

Ideas for reflection, discussion, and writing

Make Inferences from Your Reading

1. In paragraph 11, the authors explain that school integration reduced prejudice among children only when four conditions were met. What were these conditions? What inferences can you make about your own schooling and the values you have formed as a result?
2. The authors also say that stereotypes and prejudice can be reduced through friendly, cooperative, and interdependent contact. What examples can you provide of stereotypes or beliefs that you once held, but that have now changed as a result of your relationships with others?
3. What have you learned from this excerpt that either reinforces or challenges your perspective on prejudice and stereotyping?

4. A computer can be a powerful tool for organizing information and making study guides. Make a comparison chart like the one below which is only partially filled in. Then type the appropriate information from the excerpt into the empty cells. Use the "table" feature in Word, or the corresponding feature in whatever program you have. If you don't know how to make a table, someone in your library, computer, or media center can help you. Share your table in a class discussion.

Type of Theory	Explanation	Text Examples	My Example
Motivational theories	For some people, prejudice may meet certain needs and increase their sense of security	The personality trait of author- itarianism; the concept of social identity	The Boy Scouts' rejection of gay troop leaders
Cognitive theories	Stereotyping and prejudice result from the mental processes people use to deal with the world		
Learning theories			

Write About It

5. Have you ever been the victim of stereotyping, or do you know someone who has? Explain what happened, what you did about it, and what you learned from it.
6. Reflect on your close friendships. Are your friends of the same race or ethnicity as you? Do you have any close friends of different races or ethnicities? To what extent, if any, does prejudice or stereotyping have on your choice of friends?

CREDITS

INDEX